THE CRITICAL PERIOD OF
AMERICAN HISTORY
1783-1789

BY

JOHN FISKE

I am uneasy and apprehensive, more so than during the war.
JAY TO WASHINGTON, *June 27,* 1786.

BOSTON AND NEW YORK
HOUGHTON MIFFLIN COMPANY
The Riverside Press Cambridge

To

MY DEAR CLASSMATES,

FRANCIS LEE HIGGINSON

AND

CHARLES CABOT JACKSON,

I DEDICATE THIS BOOK.

PREFACE.

THIS book contains the substance of the course of lectures given in the Old South Meeting-House in Boston in December, 1884, at the Washington University in St. Louis in May, 1885, and in the theatre of the University Club in New York in March, 1886. In its present shape it may serve as a sketch of the political history of the United States from the end of the Revolutionary War to the adoption of the Federal Constitution. It makes no pretensions to completeness, either as a summary of the events of that period or as a discussion of the political questions involved in them. I have aimed especially at grouping facts in such a way as to bring out and emphasize their causal sequence, and it is accordingly hoped that the book may prove useful to the student of American history.

My title was suggested by the fact of Thomas Paine's stopping the publication of the "Crisis," on hearing the news of the treaty of 1783, with the remark, "The times that tried men's souls are over." Commenting upon this, on page 55 of the present work, I observed that so far from the crisis being over in 1783, the next five years were to be

the most critical time of all. I had not then seen
Mr. Trescot's "Diplomatic History of the Admin-
istrations of Washington and Adams," on page 9
of which he uses almost the same words: "It must
not be supposed that the treaty of peace secured
the national life. Indeed, it would be more correct
to say that the most critical period of the country's
history embraced the time between 1783 and the
adoption of the Constitution in 1788."

That period was preëminently the turning-point
in the development of political society in the western hemisphere. Though small in their mere dimensions, the events here summarized were in a remarkable degree germinal events, fraught with
more tremendous alternatives of future welfare or
misery for mankind than it is easy for the imagination to grasp. As we now stand upon the thresh-
old of that mighty future, in the light of which all
events of the past are clearly destined to seem
dwindled in dimensions and significant only in the
ratio of their potency as causes; as we discern how
large a part of that future must be the outcome of
the creative work, for good or ill, of men of English speech; we are put into the proper mood for
estimating the significance of the causes which determined a century ago that the continent of North
America should be dominated by a single powerful
and pacific federal nation instead of being parcelled out among forty or fifty small communities,
wasting their strength and lowering their moral

tone by perpetual warfare, like the states of ancient Greece, or by perpetual preparation for warfare, like the nations of modern Europe. In my
book entitled "American Political Ideas, viewed
from the Standpoint of Universal History," I have
tried to indicate the pacific influence likely to be
exerted upon the world by the creation and maintenance of such a political structure as our Federal Union. The present narrative may serve as
a commentary upon what I had in mind on page
133 of that book, in speaking of the work of our
Federal Convention as "the finest specimen of
constructive statesmanship that the world has ever
seen." On such a point it is pleasant to find one's
self in accord with a statesman so wise and noble
as Mr. Gladstone, whose opinion is here quoted on
page 223.

To some persons it may seem as if the years
1861–65 were of more cardinal importance than
the years 1783–89. Our civil war was indeed an
event of prodigious magnitude, as measured by any
standard that history affords; and there can be
little doubt as to its decisiveness. The measure of
that decisiveness is to be found in the completeness
of the reconciliation that has already, despite the
feeble wails of unscrupulous place-hunters and un-
teachable bigots, cemented the Federal Union so
powerfully that all likelihood of its disruption
may be said to have disappeared forever. When
we consider this wonderful harmony which so soon

has followed the deadly struggle, we may well believe it to be the index of such a stride toward the
ultimate pacification of mankind as was never
made before. But it was the work done in the
years 1783–89 that created a federal nation capable of enduring the storm and stress of the years
1861–65. It was in the earlier crisis that the pliant
twig was bent; and as it was bent, so has it grown;
until it has become indeed a goodly and a sturdy
tree.

CAMBRIDGE, October 10, 1888.

CONTENTS.

CHAPTER I.

RESULTS OF YORKTOWN.

CHAPTER II.

THE THIRTEEN COMMONWEALTHS.

CHAPTER III.

THE LEAGUE OF FRIENDSHIP.

CHAPTER IV.

DRIFTING TOWARD ANARCHY.

CHAPTER V.

GERMS OF NATIONAL SOVEREIGNTY.

CHAPTER VI.

THE FEDERAL CONVENTION.

CHAPTER VII.

CROWNING THE WORK.

THE CRITICAL PERIOD OF AMERI-
CAN HISTORY.

———◆———

CHAPTER I.

RESULTS OF YORKTOWN.

THE 20th of March, 1782, the day which witnessed the fall of Lord North's ministry, was a
day of good omen for men of English race on both
sides of the Atlantic. Within two years from this
time, the treaty which established the independence
of the United States was successfully negotiated at
Paris ; and at the same time, as part of the series
of events which resulted in the treaty, there went
on in England a rapid dissolution and reorganiza-
tion of parties, which ended in the overwhelming
defeat of the king's attempt to make the forms of
the constitution subservient to his selfish purposes,
and established the liberty of the people upon a
broader and sounder basis than it had ever occupied before. Great indignation was expressed at
the time, and has sometimes been echoed by British historians, over the conduct of those Whigs
who never lost an opportunity of expressing their
approval of the American revolt. The Duke of
Richmond, at the beginning of the contest, ex-

pressed a hope that the Americans might succeed,

Sympathy be-
tween British
Whigs and the
revolutionary
party in Amer-
ica.
because they were in the right.   Charles
Fox spoke of General Howe's first victory as " the terrible news from Long
Island."   Wraxall says that the celebrated buff and blue colours of the Whig party
were adopted by Fox in imitation of the Continental uniform ; but his unsupported statement is
open to question.   It is certain, however, that in
the House of Commons the Whigs habitually al-
luded to Washington's army as " our army," and
to the American cause as " the cause of liberty ; "
and Burke, with characteristic vehemence, declared
that he would rather be a prisoner in the Tower
with Mr. Laurens than enjoy the blessings of freedom in company with the men who were seeking
to enslave America.   Still more, the Whigs did all
in their power to discourage enlistments, and in
various ways so thwarted and vexed the government that the success of the Americans was by
many people ascribed to their assistance.   A few
days before Lord North's resignation, George On-
slow, in an able defence of the prime minister, exclaimed, " Why have we failed so miserably in this
war against America, if not from the support and
countenance given to rebellion in this very House ? "

Now the violence of party leaders like Burke
and Fox owed much of its strength, no doubt, to
mere rancorousness of party spirit.   But, after
making due allowance for this, we must admit that
it was essentially based upon the intensity of their
conviction that the cause of English liberty was
inseparably bound up with the defeat of the king's

attempt upon the liberties of America. Looking beyond the quarrels of the moment, they preferred to have freedom guaranteed, even at the cost of temporary defeat and partial loss of empire. Time has shown that they were right in this, but the majority of the people could hardly be expected to comprehend their attitude. It seemed to many that the great Whig leaders were forgetting their true character as English statesmen, and there is no doubt that for many years this was the chief source of the weakness of the Whig party. Sir Gilbert Elliot said, with truth, that if the Whigs had not thus to a considerable extent arrayed the national feeling against themselves, Lord North's ministry would have fallen some years sooner than it did. The king thoroughly understood the advantage which accrued to him from this state of things; and with that shortsighted shrewdness of the mere political wire-puller, in which few modern politicians have excelled him, he had from the outset preferred to fight his battle on constitutional questions in America rather than in England, in order that the national feeling of Englishmen might be arrayed on his side. He was at length thoroughly beaten on his own ground, and as the fatal day approached he raved and stormed as he had not stormed since the spring of 1778, when he had been asked to entrust the government to Lord Chatham. Like the child who refuses to play when he sees the game going against him, George threatened to abdicate the throne and go over to Hanover, leaving his son to get along with the Whig statesmen. But presently

It weakened the Whigs in England.

he took heart again, and began to resort to the same kind of political management which had served him so well in the earlier years of his reign. Among the Whig statesmen, the Marquis of Rockingham had the largest political following. He represented the old Whig aristocracy, his section of the party had been first to urge the recognition of American independence, and his principal followers were Fox and Burke. For all these reasons he was especially obnoxious to the king. On the other hand, the Earl of Shelburne was, in a certain sense, the political heir of Lord Chatham, and represented principles far more liberal than those of the Old Whigs. Shelburne was one of the most enlightened statesmen of his time. He was an earnest advocate of parliamentary reform and of free trade. He had paid especial attention to political economy, and looked with disgust upon the whole barbaric system of discriminative duties and commercial monopolies which had been so largely instrumental in bringing about the American Revolution. But being in these respects in advance of his age, Lord Shelburne had but few followers. Moreover, although a man of undoubted integrity, quite exempt from sordid or selfish ambition, there was a cynical harshness about him which made him generally disliked and distrusted. He was so suspicious of other men that other men were suspicious of him; so that, in spite of many admirable qualities, he was extremely ill adapted for the work of a party manager.

It was doubtless for these reasons that the king,

Character of Lord Shelburne.

when it became clear that a new government must be formed, made up his mind that Lord Shelburne would be the safest man to conduct it. In his hands the Whig power would not be likely to grow too strong, and dissensions would be sure to arise, from which the king might hope to profit. The first place in the treasury was accordingly offered to Shelburne ; and when he refused it, and the king found himself forced to appeal to Lord Rockingham, the manner in which the bitter pill was taken was quite characteristic of George III. He refused to meet Rockingham in person, but sent all his communications to him through Shelburne, who, thus conspicuously singled out as the object of royal preference, was certain to incur the distrust of his fellow ministers.

The structure of the new cabinet was unstable enough, however, to have satisfied even such an enemy as the king. Beside Rockingham himself, Lord John Cavendish, Charles Fox, Lord Keppel, and the Duke of Richmond were all Old Whigs. To offset these five there were five New Whigs, the Duke of Grafton, Lords Shelburne, Camden, and Ashburton, and General Conway; while the eleventh member was none other than the Tory chancellor, Lord Thurlow, who was kept over from Lord North's ministry. Burke was made paymaster of the forces, but had no seat in the cabinet. In this curiously constructed cabinet, the prime minister, Lord Rockingham, counted for little. Though a good party leader, he was below mediocrity as a statesman, *Political instability of the Rockingham ministry.* and his health was failing, so that he could not at tend to business. The master spirits were the two secretaries of state, Fox and Shelburne, and they wrangled perpetually, while Thurlow carried the news of all their quarrels to the king, and in cabinet meetings usually voted with Shelburne. The ministry had not lasted five weeks when Fox began to predict its downfall. On the great question of parliamentary reform, which was brought up in May by the young William Pitt, the government was hopelessly divided. Shelburne's party was in favour of reform, and this time Fox was found upon the same side, as well as the Duke of Richmond, who went so far as to advocate universal suffrage. On the other hand, the Whig aristocracy, led by Rockingham, were as bitterly opposed as the king himself to any change in the method of electing parliaments ; and, incredible as it may seem, even such a man as Burke maintained that the old system, rotten boroughs and all, was a sacred part of the British Constitution, which none could handle rudely without endangering the country! But in this moment of reaction against the evil influences which had brought about the loss of the American colonies, there was a strong feeling in favour of reform, and Pitt's motion was only lost by a minority of twenty in a total vote of three hundred. Half a century was to elapse before the reformers were again to come so near to victory.

But Lord Rockingham's weak and short-lived ministry was nevertheless remarkable for the amount of good work it did in spite of the king's dogged opposition. It contained great administrative talent, which made itself felt in the most

adverse circumstances. To add to the difficulty,
the ministry came into office at the critical moment
of a great agitation in Ireland. In less than three
months, not only was the trouble successfully removed, but the important bills for disfranchising
revenue officers and excluding contractors from
the House of Commons were carried, and a tremendous blow was thus struck at the corrupt influence of the crown upon elections. Burke's great
scheme of economical reform was also put into operation, cutting down the pension list and dimin-
ishing the secret service fund, and thus destroying
many sources of corruption. At no time, perhaps,
since the expulsion of the Stuarts, had so much
been done toward purifying English political life
as during the spring of 1782. But during the progress of these important measures, the jealousies
and bickerings in the cabinet became more and
more painfully apparent, and as the question of
peace with America came into the foreground, these
difficulties hastened to a crisis.

From the policy which George III. pursued with
regard to Lord Shelburne at this time, one would
suppose that in his secret heart the king wished,
by foul means since all others had failed, to defeat
the negotiations for peace and to prolong the war.
Seldom has there been a more oddly Obstacles in
complicated situation. Peace was to be the way of a
treaty of
made with America, France, Spain, and peace.
Holland. Of these powers, America and France
were leagued together by one treaty of alliance,
and France and Spain by another, and these treaties in some respects conflicted with one another in

the duties which they entailed upon the combat-
ants. Spain, though at war with England for purposes of her own, was bitterly hostile to the United
States; and France, thus leagued with two allies
which pulled in opposite directions, felt bound to
satisfy both, while pursuing her own ends against
England. To deal with such a chaotic state of
things, an orderly and harmonious government in
England should have seemed indispensably necessary. Yet on the part of England the negotiation
of a treaty of peace was to be the work of two
secretaries of state who were both politically and
personally hostile to each other. Fox, as secretary
of state for foreign affairs, had to superintend the
negotiations with France, Spain, and Holland.
Shelburne was secretary of state for home and
colonial affairs; and as the United States were
still officially regarded as colonies, the American
negotiations belonged to his department. With
such a complication of conflicting interests, George
III. might well hope that no treaty could be made.

The views of Fox and Shelburne as to the best
method of conceding American independence were
very different. Fox understood that France was
really in need of peace, and he believed that she
would not make further demands upon England if
American independence should once be recognized.
Accordingly, Fox would have made this concession
at once as a preliminary to the negotiation. On
the other hand, Shelburne felt sure that France
would insist upon further concessions, and he
thought it best to hold in reserve the recognition
of independence as a consideration to be bargained

for. Informal negotiations began between Shelburne and Franklin, who for many years had been
warm friends. In view of the impending change
of government, Franklin had in March sent a letter to Shelburne, expressing a hope that peace
might soon be restored. When the letter reached
London the new ministry had already been formed,
and Shelburne, with the consent of the cabinet,
answered it by sending over to Paris an agent, to
talk with Franklin informally, and ascertain the
terms upon which the Americans would make
peace. The person chosen for this purpose was
Richard Oswald, a Scotch merchant, who owned
large estates in America, — a man of very frank
disposition and liberal views, and a friend of Adam
Smith. In April, Oswald had several conversa-
tions with Franklin. In one of these Oswald talks
with Franklin.
conversations Franklin suggested that,
in order to make a durable peace, it was desirable
to remove all occasion for future quarrel; that the
line of frontier between New York and Canada
was inhabited by a lawless set of men, who in time
of peace would be likely to breed trouble between
their respective governments; and that therefore
it would be well for England to cede Canada to
the United States. A similar reasoning would
apply to Nova Scotia. By ceding these countries
to the United States it would be possible, from
the sale of unappropriated lands, to indemnify the
Americans for all losses of private property during
the war, and also to make reparation to the Tories,
whose estates had been confiscated. By pursuing
such a policy, England, which had made war on

America unjustly, and had wantonly done it great
injuries, would achieve not merely peace, but reconciliation, with America; and reconciliation, said
Franklin, is "a sweet word." No doubt this was
a bold tone for Franklin to take, and perhaps it
was rather cool in him to ask for Canada and Nova
Scotia; but he knew that almost every member
of the Whig ministry had publicly expressed the
opinion that the war against America was an unjust and wanton war; and being, moreover, a
shrewd hand at a bargain, he began by setting his
terms high. Oswald doubtless looked at the matter very much from Franklin's point of view, for
on the suggestion of the cession of Canada he expressed neither surprise nor reluctance. Franklin
had written on a sheet of paper the main points
of his conversation, and, at Oswald's request, he
allowed him to take the paper to London to show
to Lord Shelburne, first writing upon it a note expressly declaring its informal character. Franklin
also sent a letter to Shelburne, describing Oswald
as a gentleman with whom he found it very pleasant to deal. On Oswald's arrival in London, Shelburne did not show the notes of the conversation to
any of his colleagues, except Lord Ashburton. He
kept the paper over one night, and then returned
it to Franklin without any formal answer. But
the letter he showed to the cabinet, and on the 23d
of April it was decided to send Oswald back to
Paris, to represent to Franklin that, on being restored to the same situation in which she was left
by the treaty of 1763, Great Britain would be willing to recognize the independence of the United

States. Fox was authorized to make a similar
representation to the French government, and the
person whom he sent to Paris for this purpose was
Thomas Grenville, son of the author of the Stamp
Act.

As all British subjects were prohibited from entering into negotiations with the revolted colonies,
it was impossible for Oswald to take any decisive
step until an enabling act should be carried through
Parliament. But while waiting for this he might
still talk informally with Franklin. Fox thought
that Oswald's presence in Paris indicated a desire
on Shelburne's part to interfere with the negotiations with the French government; and indeed,
the king, out of his hatred of Fox and his inborn
love of intrigue, suggested to Shelburne that Oswald " might be a useful check on that part of the
negotiation which was in other hands." But Shelburne paid no heed to this crooked advice, and
there is nothing to show that he had the least desire to intrigue against Fox. If he had, he would
certainly have selected some other agent than Oswald, who was the most straightforward of men,
and scarcely close-mouthed enough for a diploma-
tist. He told Oswald to impress it upon Franklin
that if America was to be independent at all she
must be independent of the whole world, and must
not enter into any secret arrangement with France
which might limit her entire freedom of action in
the future. To the private memorandum which
desired the cession of Canada for three reasons,
his answers were as follows : " 1. *By way of rep-
araiion.* — Answer. No reparation can be heard

of. 2. *To prevent future wars.* — Answer. It is
to be hoped that some more friendly method will
be found. 3. *As a fund of indemnification to
loyalists.* — Answer. No independence to be acknowledged without their being taken care of."
Besides, added Shelburne, the Americans would be
expected to make some compensation for the surrender of Charleston, Savannah, and the city of
New York, still held by British troops. From this
it appears that Shelburne, as well as Franklin,
knew how to begin by asking more than he was
likely to get.

While Oswald submitted these answers to Franklin, Grenville had his interview with Vergennes,
Grenville has an interview with Ver- gennes. and told him that, if England recognized
the independence of the United States,
she should expect France to restore the
islands of the West Indies which she had taken
from England. Why not, since the independence of the United States was the sole avowed
object for which France had gone to war? Now
this was on the 8th of May, and the news of
the destruction of the French fleet in the West
Indies, nearly four weeks ago, had not yet reached
Europe. Flushed with the victories of Grasse, and
exulting in the prowess of the most formidable
naval force that France had ever sent out, Vergennes not only expected to keep the islands which
he had got, but was waiting eagerly for the news
that he had acquired Jamaica into the bargain. In
this mood he returned a haughty answer to Grenville. He reminded him that nations often went to
war for a specified object, and yet seized twice **as**

much if favoured by fortune ; and, recurring to the instance which rankled most deeply in the memories of Frenchmen, he cited the events of the last war. In 1756 England went to war with France over the disputed right to some lands on the Ohio River and the Maine frontier. After seven years of fighting she not only kept these lands, but all of Canada, Louisiana, and Florida, and ousted the French from India into the bargain. No, said Vergennes, he would not rest content with the independence of America. He would not even regard such an offer as a concession to France in any way, or as a price in return for which France was to make a treaty favourable to England. As regards the recognition of independence, England must treat directly with America.

Grenville was disappointed and chagrined by this answer, and the ministry made up their minds that there would be no use in trying to get an honourable peace with France for the present. Accordingly, it seemed better to take Vergennes at his word, though not in the sense in which he meant it, and, by granting all that the Americans could reasonably desire, to detach them from the French alliance as soon as possible. On the 18th of May there came the news of the stupendous victory of Rodney over Grasse, and all England rang with jubilee. Again it had been shown that " Britannia rules the wave ; " and it seemed that, if America could be separately pacified, the House of Bourbon might be successfully defied. Accordingly, on the 23d, five days after the news of victory, the ministry decided " to

Effects of Rodney's victory.

propose the independence of America in the first
instance, instead of making it the condition of a
general treaty." Upon this Fox rather hastily
maintained that the United States were put at once
into the position of an independent and foreign
power, so that the business of negotiating with
them passed from Shelburne's department into his
own. Shelburne, on the other hand, argued that,
as the recognition of independence could not take
effect until a treaty of peace should be concluded,
the negotiation with America still belonged to him,
as secretary for the colonies. Following Fox's instructions, Grenville now claimed the right of negotiating with Franklin as well as with Vergennes;
but as his written credentials only authorized him
to treat with France, the French minister suspected
foul play, and turned a cold shoulder to Grenville.
For the same reason, Grenville found Franklin
very reserved and indisposed to talk on the subject
of the treaty. While Grenville was thus rebuffed
and irritated he had a talk with Oswald, in the
course of which he got from that simple and high-
minded gentleman the story of the private paper
relating to the cession of Canada, which Franklin
had permitted Lord Shelburne to see. Grenville
immediately took offence; he made up his mind
that something underhanded was going on, and that
this was the reason for the coldness of Franklin
and Vergennes; and he wrote an indignant letter
about it to Fox. From the wording of this letter,
Fox got the impression that Franklin's proposal
was much more serious than it really was. It
naturally puzzled him and made him angry, for the

attitude of America implied in the request for a cession of Canada was far different from the attitude presumed by the theory that the mere offer of independence would be enough to detach her from her alliance with France. The plan of the ministry seemed imperilled. Fox showed Grenville's letter to Rockingham, Richmond, and Cavendish; and they all inferred that Shelburne was playing a secret part, for purposes of his own. This was doubtless unjust to Shelburne. Perhaps his keeping the matter to himself was simply one more illustration of his want of confidence in Fox; or, perhaps he did not think it worth while to stir up the cabinet over a question which seemed too preposterous ever to come to anything. Fox, however, cried out against Shelburne's alleged duplicity, and made up his mind at all events to get the American negotiations transferred to his own department. To this end he moved in the cabinet, on the last day of June, that the independence of the United States should be unconditionally acknowledged, so that England might treat as with a foreign power. The motion was lost, and Fox announced that he should resign his office. His resignation would probably of itself have broken up the ministry, but, by a curious co- *Fall of the Rockingham ministry, July 1, 1782.* incidence, on the next day Lord Rockingham died; and so the first British government begotten of Washington's victory at Yorktown came prematurely to an end.

The Old Whigs now found some difficulty in choosing a leader. Burke was the greatest statesman in the party, but he had not the qualities of

a party leader, and his connections were not sufficiently aristocratic. Fox was distrusted by many
people for his gross vices, and because of his way-
wardness in politics. In the dissipated gambler,
who cast in his lot first with one party and then
with the other, and who had shamefully used his
matchless eloquence in defending some of the worst
abuses of the time, there seemed as yet but little
promise of the great reformer of later years, the
Charles Fox who came to be loved and idolized by
all enlightened Englishmen. Next to Fox, the
ablest leader in the party was the Duke of Richmond, but his advanced views on parliamentary reform put him out of sympathy with the majority of
the party. In this embarrassment, the choice fell
upon the Duke of Portland, a man of great wealth
and small talent, concerning whom Horace Walpole observed, " It is very entertaining that two or
three great families should persuade themselves
that they have a hereditary and exclusive right of
giving us a head without a tongue ! " The choice
was a weak one, and played directly into the hands
of the king. When urged to make the Duke of
Portland his prime minister, the king replied that
he had already offered that position to Lord Shelburne. Hereupon Fox and Cavendish
resigned, but Richmond remained in
office, thus virtually breaking his connection with the Old Whigs. Lord Keppel also
remained. Many members of the party followed
Richmond and went over to Shelburne. William
Pitt, now twenty-three years old, succeeded Cavendish as chancellor of the exchequer ; Thomas

*Shelburne
prime minis-
ter.*

Townshend became secretary of state for home and colonies, and Lord Grantham became foreign secretary. The closing days of Parliament were marked by altercations which showed how wide the breach had grown between the two sections of the Whig party. Fox and Burke believed that Shelburne was not only playing a false part, but was really as subservient to the king as Lord North had been. In a speech ridiculous for its furious invective, Burke compared the new prime minister with Borgia and Catiline. And so Parliament was adjourned on the 11th of July, and did not meet again until December.

The task of making a treaty of peace was simplified both by this change of ministry and by the total defeat of the Spaniards and French at Gibraltar in September. Six months before, England had seemed worsted in every quarter. Now England, though defeated in America, was victorious as regarded France and Spain. The avowed object for which France had entered into alliance with the Americans was to secure the independence of the United States, and this point was now substantially gained. The chief object for which Spain had entered into alliance with France was to drive the English from Gibraltar, and this point was now decidedly lost. France had bound herself not to desist from the war until Spain should recover Gibraltar; but now there was little hope of accomplishing this, except by some fortunate bargain in the treaty, and Vergennes tried to persuade England to cede the great stronghold in exchange for West Florida, which Spain had lately conquered, or for Oran or Guadaloupe. Failing in this, he adopted a plan for satisfying Spain at the expense of the United States; and he did this the more willingly as he had no love for the Ameri-

French policy opposed to American interests.

cans, and did not wish to see them become too powerful. France had strictly kept her pledges; she had given us valuable and timely aid in gaining our independence; and the sympathies of the French people were entirely with the American cause. But the object of the French government had been simply to humiliate England, and this end was sufficiently accomplished by depriving her of her thirteen colonies.

The immense territory extending from the Alleghany Mountains to the Mississippi River, and from the border of West Florida to the Great Lakes, had passed from the hands of France into those of England at the peace of 1763; and by the Quebec Act of 1774 England had declared the southern boundary of Canada to be the Ohio River. At present the whole territory, from Lake Superior down to the southern boundary of what is now Kentucky, belonged to the state of Virginia, whose backwoodsmen had conquered it from England in 1779. In December, 1780, Virginia had provisionally ceded the portion north of the Ohio to the United States, but the cession was not yet completed. The region which is now Tennessee belonged to North Carolina, which had begun to make settlements there as long ago as 1758. The trackless forests included between Tennessee and West Florida were still in the hands of wild tribes of Cherokees and Choctaws, Chickasaws and

Creeks. Several thousand pioneers from North
Carolina and Virginia had already set- The valley of
tled beyond the mountains, and the the Mississippi ; Aran-
white population was rapidly increasing. da's prophecy.
This territory the French government was very unwilling to leave in American hands. The possibility of enormous expansion which it would afford to
the new nation was distinctly foreseen by sagacious
men. Count Aranda, the representative of Spain
in these negotiations, wrote a letter to his king just
after the treaty was concluded, in which he uttered
this notable prophecy : " This federal republic is
born a pygmy. A day will come when it will be a
giant, even a colossus, formidable in these countries. Liberty of conscience, the facility for establishing a new population on immense lands, as
well as the advantages of the new government,
will draw thither farmers and artisans from all the
nations. In a few years we shall watch with grief
the tyrannical existence of this same colossus."
The letter went on to predict that the Americans
would presently get possession of Florida and attack Mexico. Similar arguments were doubtless
used by Aranda in his interviews with Vergennes,
and France, as well as Spain, sought to prevent
the growth of the dreaded colossus. To this end
Vergennes maintained that the Americans ought
to recognize the Quebec Act, and give up to England all the territory north of the Ohio River.
The region south of this limit should, he thought,
be made an Indian territory, and placed under the
protection of Spain and the United States. A
line was to be drawn from the mouth of the Cum-

berland River, following that stream about as far
as the site of Nashville, thence running southward
to the Tennessee, thence curving eastward nearly
to the Alleghanies, and descending through what
is now eastern Alabama to the Florida line. The
territory to the east of this irregular line was to be
under the protection of the United States; the territory to the west of it was to be under the protection of Spain. In this division, the settlers beyond
the mountains would retain their connection with
the United States, which would not touch the Mississippi River at any point. Vergennes held that
this was all the Americans could reasonably demand, and he agreed with Aranda that they had
as yet gained no foothold upon the eastern bank
of the great river, unmindful of the fact that at
that very moment the fortresses at Cahokia and
Kaskaskia were occupied by American garrisons.

Upon another important point the views of the
French government were directly opposed to American interests. The right to catch fish
on the banks of Newfoundland had been
shared by treaty between France and England;
and the New England fishermen, as subjects of the
king of Great Britain, had participated in this
privilege. The matter was of very great importance, not only to New England, but to the United
States in general. Not only were the fisheries a
source of lucrative trade to the New England people, but they were the training-school of a splendid
race of seamen, the nursery of naval heroes whose
exploits were by and by to astonish the world.
To deprive the Americans of their share in these

The New-
foundland
fisheries.

fisheries was to strike a serious blow at the strength
and resources of the new nation. The British government was not inclined to grant the privilege,
and on this point Vergennes took sides with England, in order to establish a claim upon her for
concessions advantageous to France in some other
quarter. With these views, Vergennes secretly
aimed at delaying the negotiations ; for as long as
hostilities were kept up, he might hope to extort
from his American allies a recognition of the
Spanish claims and a renouncement of the fisheries, simply by threatening to send them no further
assistance in men or money. In order to retard
the proceedings, he refused to take any steps whatever until the independence of the United States
should first be irrevocably acknowledged by Great
Britain, without reference to the final settlement
of the rest of the treaty. In this Vergennes was
supported by Franklin, as well as by Jay, who had
lately arrived in Paris to take part in the negotiations. But the reasons of the American commissioners were very different from those of Vergennes. They feared that, if they began to treat
before independence was acknowledged, they would
be unfairly dealt with by France and Spain, and
unable to gain from England the concessions upon
which they were determined.

Jay soon began to suspect the designs of the
French minister. He found that he was sending
M. de Rayneval as a secret emissary to Lord Shelburne under an assumed name ; he ascertained
that the right of the United States to the Mississippi valley was to be denied ; and he got hold of

a dispatch from Marbois, the French secretary of
legation at Philadelphia, to Vergennes,
opposing the American claim to the
Newfoundland fisheries. As soon as
Jay learned these facts, he sent his friend Dr.
Benjamin Vaughan to Lord Shelburne to put him
on his guard, and while reminding him that it was
greatly for the interest of England to dissolve the
alliance between America and France, he declared
himself ready to begin the negotiations without
waiting for the recognition of independence, provided that Oswald's commission should speak of
the thirteen United States of America, instead of
calling them colonies and naming them separately.
This decisive step was taken by Jay on his own responsibility, and without the knowledge of Franklin, who had been averse to anything like a separate negotiation with England. It served to set
the ball rolling at once. After meeting the mes-
sengers from Jay and Vergennes, Lord Shelburne
at once perceived the antagonism that had arisen
between the allies, and promptly took advantage of
it. A new commission was made out for Oswald,
in which the British government first described
our country as the United States; and early in
October negotiations were begun and proceeded
rapidly. On the part of England, the affair
was conducted by Oswald, assisted by Strachey
and Fitzherbert, who had succeeded Grenville.
In the course of the month John Adams arrived
in Paris, and a few weeks later Henry Laurens,
who had been exchanged for Lord Cornwallis and
released from the Tower, was added to the com-

Jay detects the schemes of Vergennes.

pany. Adams had a holy horror of Frenchmen
in general, and of Count Vergennes in particular.
He shared that common but mistaken view of
Frenchmen which regards them as shallow, frivo-
lous, and insincere ; and he was indignant at the
position taken by Vergennes on the question of the
fisheries. In this, John Adams felt as all New
Englanders felt, and he realized the importance of
the question from a national point of view, as became the man who in later years was to earn lasting renown as one of the chief founders of the
American navy. His behaviour on reaching Paris
was characteristic. It is said that he left Count
Vergennes to learn of his arrival through the
newspapers. It was certainly some time before
he called upon him, and he took occasion, besides,
to express his opinions about republics and monarchies in terms which courtly Frenchmen thought
very rude.

The arrival of Adams fully decided the matter
as to a separate negotiation with England. He
agreed with Jay that Vergennes should be kept as
far as possible in the dark until everything was
cut and dried, and Franklin was reluctantly
obliged to yield. The treaty of alliance between
France and the United States had expressly stipulated that neither power should ever
make peace without the consent of the Franklin over-
ruled by Jay
and Adams.
other, and in view of this Franklin was
loth to do anything which might seem like aban-
doning the ally whose timely interposition had
alone enabled Washington to achieve the crowning triumph of Yorktown. In justice to Ver-

gennes, it should be borne in mind that he had
kept strict faith with us in regard to every point
that had been expressly stipulated; and Franklin, who felt that he understood Frenchmen better than his colleagues, was naturally unwilling to
seem behindhand in this respect. At the same
time, in regard to matters not expressly stipulated,
Vergennes was clearly playing a sharp game
against us; and it is undeniable that, without de-
parting technically from the obligations of the alliance, Jay and Adams — two men as honourable as
ever lived — played a very sharp defensive game
against him. The traditional French subtlety was
no match for Yankee shrewdness. The treaty with
England was not concluded until the consent of
France had been obtained, and thus the express
stipulation was respected; but a thorough and de-
tailed agreement was reached as to what the purport of the treaty should be, while our not too
friendly ally was kept in the dark. The annals of
modern diplomacy have afforded few stranger
spectacles. With the indispensable aid of France
we had just got the better of England in fight, and
now we proceeded amicably to divide territory and
commercial privileges with the enemy, and to make
arrangements in which the ally was virtually ig-
nored. It ceases to be a paradox, however, when
we remember that with the change of government
in England some essential conditions of the case
were changed. The England against which we
had fought was the hostile England of Lord North;
the England with which we were now dealing was
the friendly England of Shelburne and Pitt. For

the moment, the English race, on both sides of the Atlantic, was united in its main purpose and divided only by questions of detail, while the rival colonizing power, which sought to work in a direction contrary to the general interests of English-speaking people, was in great measure disregarded.

As soon as the problem was thus virtually reduced to a negotiation between the American commissioners and Lord Shelburne's ministry, the air was cleared in a moment. The principal questions had already been discussed between Franklin and Oswald. Independence being first acknowledged, the question of boundaries came up for settlement. England had little interest in regaining the territory between the Alleghanies and the Mississippi, the forts in which were already held by American soldiers, and she relinquished all claim upon it. The Mississippi River thus became the dividing line between the United States and the Spanish possessions, and its navigation was made free alike to British and American ships. Franklin's suggestion of a cession of Canada and Nova Scotia was abandoned without discussion. It was agreed that the boundary line should start at the mouth of the river St. Croix, and, running to a point near Lake Madawaska in the highlands separating the Atlantic watershed from that of the St. Lawrence, should follow these highlands to the head of the Connecticut River, and then descend the middle of the river to the forty-fifth parallel, thence running westward and through the centre of the water communications of the Great Lakes to the Lake of the

The separate American treaty, as agreed upon: 1. Boundaries;

Woods, thence to the source of the Mississippi, which was supposed to be west of this lake. This line was marked in red ink by Oswald on one of Mitchell's maps of North America, to serve as a memorandum establishing the precise meaning of the words used in the description. It ought to have been accurately fixed in its details by surveys made upon the spot; but no commissioners were appointed for this purpose. The language relating to the northeastern portion of the boundary contained some inaccuracies which were revealed by later surveys, and the map used by Oswald was lost. Hence a further question arose between Great Britain and the United States, which was finally settled by the Ashburton treaty in 1842.

The Americans retained the right of catching fish on the banks of Newfoundland and in the Gulf of St. Lawrence, but lost the right of drying their fish on the Newfoundland coast. On the other hand, no permission was given to British subjects to fish on the coasts of the United States. As regarded commercial intercourse, Jay sought to establish complete reciprocal freedom between the two countries, and a clause was proposed to the effect that " all British merchants and merchant ships, on the one hand, shall enjoy in the United States, and in all places belonging to them, the same protection and commercial privileges, and be liable only to the same charges and duties as their own merchants and merchant ships; and, on the other hand, the merchants and merchant ships of the United States shall enjoy in all places belonging to his Britannic Majesty the

2. Fisheries; commercial intercourse;

same protection and commercial privileges, and be liable only to the same charges and duties as British merchants and merchant ships, saving always to the chartered trading companies of Great Britain such exclusive use and trade, and the respective ports and establishments, as neither the other subjects of Great Britain nor any the most favoured nation participate in." Unfortunately for both countries, this liberal provision was rejected on the ground that the ministry had no authority to interfere with the Navigation Act.

Only two questions were now left to be disposed of, — the question of paying private debts, and that of compensating the American loyalists for the loss of property and general rough treatment which they had suffered. There were many old debts outstanding from American to 3. Private British merchants. These had been for debts; the most part incurred before 1775, and while many honest debtors, impoverished during the war, felt unable to pay, there were doubtless many others who were ready to take advantage of circumstances and refuse the payment which they were perfectly able to make. It was scarcely creditable to us that any such question should have arisen. Franklin, indeed, argued that these debts were more than fully offset by damages done to private property by British soldiers : as, for example, in the wanton raids on the coasts of Connecticut and Virginia in 1779, or in Prevost's buccaneering march against Charleston. To cite these atrocities, however, as a reason for the non-payment of debts legitimately owed to innocent merchants in London and Glas-

gow was to argue as if two wrongs could make a
right. The strong sense of John Adams struck at
once to the root of the matter. He declared " he
had no notion of cheating anybody. The questions of paying debts and compensating Tories
were two." This terse statement carried the day,
and it was finally decided that all private debts on
either side, whether incurred before or after 1775,
remained still binding, and must be discharged at
their full value in sterling money.

The last question of all was the one most difficult
to settle. There were many loyalists in the United
States who had sacrificed everything in the support
of the British cause, and it was unquestionably the
duty of the British government to make every possible effort to insure them against further injury,
and, if practicable, to make good their losses already incurred. From Virginia and the New England states, where they were few in number, they
had mostly fled, and their estates had been confiscated. In New York and South Carolina, where
they remained in great numbers, they were still
waging a desultory war with the patriots, which
far exceeded in cruelty and bitterness the struggle
between the regular armies. In many cases they
had, at the solicitation of the British government,
joined the invading army, and been organized into
companies and regiments. The regular troops defeated at King's Mountain, and those whom Arnold
took with him to Virginia, were nearly
all American loyalists. Lord Shelburne
felt that it would be wrong to abandon
these unfortunate men to the vengeance of their

4. Compensa-
tion of
loyalists.

fellow countrymen, and he insisted that the treaty
should contain an amnesty clause providing for the
restoration of the Tories to their civil rights, with
compensation for their confiscated property. However disagreeable such a course might seem to the
victorious Americans, there were many precedents
for it in European history. It had indeed come to
be customary at the close of civil wars, and the
effect of such a policy had invariably been good.
Cromwell, in his hour of triumph, inflicted no
disabilities upon his political enemies; and when
Charles II. was restored to the throne the healing
effect of the amnesty act then passed was so great
that historians sometimes ask what in the world
had become of that Puritan party which a moment
before had seemed supreme in the land. At the
close of the war of the Spanish Succession, the
rebellious people of Catalonia were indemnified for
their losses, at the request of England, and with a
similar good effect. In view of such European
precedents, Vergennes agreed with Shelburne as
to the propriety of securing compensation and further immunity for the Tories in America. John
Adams insinuated that the French minister took
this course because he foresaw that the presence
of the Tories in the United States would keep the
people perpetually divided into a French party
and an English party; but such a suspicion was
quite uncalled for. There is no reason to suppose
that in this instance Vergennes had anything at
heart but the interests of humanity and justice.

On the other hand, the Americans brought forward very strong reasons why the Tories should

not be indemnified by Congress. First, as Franklin urged, many of them had, by their misrepre-
sentations to the British government, helped to stir
up the disputes which led to the war; and as they
had made their bed, so they must lie in it. Secondly, such of them as had been concerned in burning and plundering defenceless villages, and wield-
ing the tomahawk in concert with bloodthirsty
Indians, deserved no compassion. It was rather
for them to make compensation for the misery they
had wrought. Thirdly, the confiscated Tory property had passed into the hands of purchasers who
had bought it in good faith and could not now be
dispossessed, and in many cases it had been distributed here and there and lost sight of. An
estimate of the gross amount might be made, and
a corresponding sum appropriated for indemnification. But, fourthly, the country was so impoverished by the war that its own soldiers, the brave
men whose heroic exertions had won the independence of the United States, were at this moment
in sore distress for the want of the pay which Congress could not give them, but to which its honour
was sacredly pledged. The American government
was clearly bound to pay its just debts to the friends
who had suffered so much in its behalf before it
should proceed to entertain a chimerical scheme
for satisfying its enemies. For, fifthly, any such
scheme was in the present instance clearly chimerical. The acts under which Tory property had
been confiscated were acts of state legislatures, and
Congress had no jurisdiction over such a matter.
If restitution was to be made, it must be made by

the separate states. The question could not for a moment be entertained by the general government or its agents.

Upon these points the American commissioners were united and inexorable. Various suggestions were offered in vain by the British. Their troops still held the city of New York, and it was doubtful whether the Americans could hope to capture it in another campaign. It was urged that England might fairly claim in exchange for New York a round sum of money wherewith the Tories might be indemnified. It was further urged that certain unappropriated lands in the Mississippi valley might be sold for the same purpose. But the Americans would not hear of buying one of their own cities, whose independence was already acknowledged by the first article of the treaty which recognized the independence of the United States: and as for the western lands, they were wanted as a means of paying our own war debts and providing for our veteran soldiers. Several times Shelburne sent word to Paris that he would break off the negotiation unless the loyalist claims were in some way recognized. But the Americans were obdurate. They had one advantage, and knew it. Parliament was soon to meet, and it was doubtful whether Lord Shelburne could command a sufficient majority to remain long in office. He was, accordingly, very anxious to complete the treaty of peace or at least to detach America from the French alliance, as soon as possible. The American commissioners were also eager to conclude the treaty. They had secured very favourable terms, and were loth to run any risk of spoiling what had been done. Accordingly, they made a proposal in the form of a compromise, which nevertheless settled the point in their favour. The matter, they said, was beyond the jurisdiction of Congress, but they agreed that Congress should *recommend* to the several states to desist from further proceedings against the Tories, and to reconsider their laws on this subject; it should further recommend that persons with claims upon confiscated lands might be authorized to use legal means of recovering them, and to this end might be allowed to pass to and fro without personal risk for the term of one year. The British commissioners accepted this compromise, unsatisfactory as it was, because it was really impossible to obtain anything better without throwing the whole negotiation overboard. The constitutional difficulty was a real one indeed. As Adams told Oswald, if the point were further insisted upon, Congress would be obliged to refer it to the several states, and no one could tell how long it might be before any decisive result could be reached in this way. Meanwhile, the state of war would continue, and it would be cheaper for England to indemnify the loyalists herself than to pay the war bills for a single month. Franklin added that, if the loyalists were to be indemnified, it would be necessary also to reckon up the damage they had done in burning houses and kidnapping slaves, and then strike a balance between the two accounts; and he gravely suggested that a special commission might be appointed for this purpose. At the prospect of endless discussion which this suggestion involved, the British commissioners gave way and accepted the American terms, although they were frankly told that too much must not be expected from the recommendation of Congress. The articles were signed on the 30th of November, six days before the meeting of Parliament. Hostilities in America were to cease at once, and upon the completion of the treaty the British fleets and armies were to be immediately withdrawn from every place which they held within the limits of the United States. A supplementary and secret article provided that if England, on making peace with Spain, should recover West Florida, the northern boundary of that province should be a line running due east from the mouth of the Yazoo River to the Chattahoochee.

Thus by skilful diplomacy the Americans had gained all that could reasonably be asked, while the work of making a general peace was greatly simplified. It was declared in the preamble that the articles here signed were provisional, and that the treaty was not to take effect until terms of peace should be agreed on between England and France. Without delay, Franklin laid the whole matter, except the secret article, before Vergennes, who forthwith accused the Americans of ingratitude and bad faith. Franklin's reply, that at the worst they could only be charged with want of diplomatic courtesy, has sometimes been condemned as *Vergennes does not like the way in which it has been done.* insincere, but on inadequate grounds. He had consented with reluctance to the separate negotiation, because he did not wish to give France any

possible ground for complaint, whether real or ostensible. There does not seem, however, to have
been sufficient justification for so grave a charge
as was made by Vergennes. If the French negotiations had failed until after the overthrow of the
Shelburne ministry ; if Fox, on coming into power,
had taken advantage of the American treaty to
continue the war against France ; and if under
such circumstances the Americans had abandoned
their ally, then undoubtedly they would have become guilty of ingratitude and treachery. There
is no reason for supposing that they would ever
have done so, had the circumstances arisen. Their
preamble made it impossible for them honourably
to abandon France until a full peace should be
made, and more than this France could not reasonably demand. The Americans had kept to the strict
letter of their contract, as Vergennes had kept to
the strict letter of his, and beyond this they meted
out exactly the same measure of frankness which
they received. To say that our debt of gratitude
to France was such as to require us to acquiesce in
her scheme for enriching our enemy Spain at our
expense is simply childish. Franklin was undoubtedly right. The commissioners may have been
guilty of a breach of diplomatic courtesy, but nothing more. Vergennes might be sarcastic about it
for the moment, but the cordial relations between
France and America remained undisturbed.

On the part of the Americans the treaty of Paris
was one of the most brilliant triumphs
in the whole history of modern diplomacy. Had the affair been managed by men of

A great diplo-
matic victory.

ordinary ability, some of the greatest results of the Revolutionary War would probably have been lost; the new republic would have been cooped up between the Atlantic Ocean and the Alleghany Mountains; our westward expansion would have been impossible without further warfare in which European powers would have been involved; and the formation of our Federal Union would doubtless have been effectively hindered, if not, indeed, altogether prevented. To the grand triumph the varied talents of Franklin, Adams, and Jay alike contributed. To the latter is due the credit of detecting and baffling the sinister designs of France; but without the tact of Franklin this probably could not have been accomplished without offend ing France in such wise as to spoil everything. It is, however, to the rare discernment and boldness of Jay, admirably seconded by the sturdy Adams, that the chief praise is due. The turning-point of the whole affair was the visit of Dr. Vaughan to Lord Shelburne. The foundation of success was the separate negotiation with England, and here there had stood in the way a more formidable obstacle than the mere reluctance of Franklin. The chevalier Luzerne and his secretary Marbois had been busy with Congress, and that body had sent well-meant but silly and pusillanimous instructions to its commissioners at Paris to be guided in all things by the wishes of the French court. To disregard such instructions required all the lofty courage for which Jay and Adams were noted, and for the moment it brought upon them something like a rebuke from Congress, conveyed in a letter from Robert Livingston. As Adams said, in his vehement way, "Congress surrendered their own sovereignty into the hands of a French minister. Blush! blush! ye guilty records! blush and perish! It is glory to have broken such infamous orders." True enough; the commissioners knew that in diplomacy, as in warfare, to the agent at a distance from his principal some discretionary power must be allowed. They assumed great responsibility, and won a victory of incalculable grandeur.

The course of the Americans produced no effect upon the terms obtained by France, but it seriously modified the case with Spain. Unable to obtain Gibraltar by arms, that power hoped to get it by The Spanish diplomacy; and with the support of treaty. France she seemed disposed to make the cession of the great fortress an ultimatum, without which the war must go on. Shelburne, on his part, was willing to exchange Gibraltar for an island in the West Indies; but it was difficult to get the cabinet to agree on the matter, and the scheme was violently opposed by the people, for the heroic defence of the stronghold had invested it with a halo of romance and endeared it to every one. Nevertheless, so persistent was Spain, and so great the desire for peace on the part of the ministry, that they had resolved to exchange Gibraltar for Guadaloupe, when the news arrived of the treaty with America. The ministers now took a bold stand, and refused to hear another word about giving up Gibraltar. Spain scolded, and threatened a renewal of hostilities, but France was unwilling to give further assistance, and the matter was settled by England's surrendering East Florida, and allowing the Spaniards to keep West Florida and Minorca, which were already in their hands.

By the treaty with France, the West India islands of Grenada, St. Vincent, St. Christopher, Dominica, Nevis, and Montserrat were restored to England, which in turn restored St. The French treaty. Lucia and ceded Tobago to France. The French were allowed to fortify Dunkirk, and received some slight concessions in India and Africa; they retained their share in the Newfoundland fisheries, and recovered the little neighbouring islands of St. Pierre and Miquelon. For the fourteen hundred million francs which France had expended in the war, she had the satisfaction of detaching the American colonies from England, thus inflicting a blow which it was confidently hoped would prove fatal to the maritime power of her ancient rival; but beyond this short-lived satisfaction, the fallaciousness of which events were soon to show, she obtained very little. On the 20th of January, 1783, the preliminaries of peace were signed between England, on the one hand, and France and Spain, on the other. A truce was at the same time concluded with Holland, which was soon followed by a peace, in which most of the conquests on either side were restored.

A second English ministry was now about to be wrecked on the rock of this group of treaties. Lord Shelburne's government had at no time been a strong one. He had made many enemies by his liberal and reforming measures, and he had alienated most of his colleagues by his reserved de-

meanour and seeming want of confidence in them.
In December several of the ministers resigned.
The strength of parties in the House of Commons
was thus quaintly reckoned by Gibbon : " Minister 140 ; Reynard 90 ; Boreas 120 ; the rest unknown or uncertain." But " Reynard " and " Boreas " were now about to join forces in one of the
strangest coalitions ever known in the history of

politics. No statesman ever attacked
Coalition of
Fox with   another more ferociously than Fox had
North.
attacked North during the past ten
years.   He had showered abuse upon him ; accused
him of " treachery and falsehood," of " public per-
fidy," and " breach of a solemn specific promise ; "
and had even gone so far as to declare to his face
a hope that he would be called upon to expiate his
abominable crimes upon the scaffold.   Within a
twelvemonth he had thus spoken of Lord North
and his colleagues : " From the moment when I
shall make any terms with one of them, I will rest
satisfied to be called the most infamous of mankind.   I would not for an instant think of a coalition with men who, in every public and private
transaction as ministers, have shown themselves
void of every principle of honour and honesty.   In
the hands of such men I would not trust my honour
even for a moment."   Still more recently, when at
a loss for words strong enough to express his belief
in the wickedness of Shelburne, he declared that
he had no better opinion of that man than to deem
him capable of forming an alliance with North.
We may judge, then, of the general amazement
when, in the middle of February, it turned out

that Fox had himself done this very thing. An
" ill-omened marriage," William Pitt called it in
the House of Commons. " If this ill-omened mar‹
riage is not already solemnized, I know a just and
lawful impediment, and in the name of the public
safety I here forbid the banns." Throughout the
country the indignation was great. Many people
had blamed Fox for not following up his charges
by actually bringing articles of impeachment
against Lord North. That the two enemies should
thus suddenly become leagued in friendship seemed
utterly monstrous. It injured Fox extremely in
the opinion of the country, and it injured North
still more, for it seemed like a betrayal of the king
on his part, and his forgiveness of so many insults
looked mean-spirited. It does not appear, however, that there was really any strong personal ani-
mosity between North and Fox. They were both
men of very amiable character, and almost inca-
pable of cherishing resentment. The language of
parliamentary orators was habitually violent, and
the huge quantities of wine which gentlemen in
those days used to drink may have helped to make
it extravagant. The excessive vehemence of political invective often deprived it of half its effect.
One day, after Fox had exhausted his vocabulary
of abuse upon Lord George Germaine, Lord North
said to him, " You were in very high feather to-day,
Charles, and I am glad you did not fall upon me."
On another occasion, it is said that while Fox was
thundering against North's unexampled turpitude,
the object of his furious tirade cosily dropped off
to sleep. Gibbon, who was the friend of both

statesmen, expressly declares that they bore each other no ill will. But while thus alike indisposed to harbour bitter thoughts, there was one man for whom both Fox and North felt an abiding distrust and dislike; and that man was Lord Shelburne, the prime minister.

As a political pupil of Burke, Fox shared that statesman's distrust of the whole school of Lord Chatham, to which Shelburne belonged. In many respects these statesmen were far more advanced than Burke, but they did not sufficiently realize the importance of checking the crown by means of a united and powerful ministry. Fox thoroughly understood that much of the mischief of the past twenty years, including the loss of America, had come from the system of weak and divided ministries, which gave the king such great opportunity for wreaking his evil will. He had himself been a member of such a ministry, which had fallen seven months ago. When the king singled out Shelburne for his confidence, Fox naturally concluded that Shelburne was to be made to play the royal game, as North had been made to play it for so many years. This was very unjust to Shelburne, but there is no doubt that Fox was perfectly honest in his belief. It seemed to him that the present state of things must be brought to an end, at whatever cost. A ministry strong enough to curb the king could be formed only by a coalescence of two out of the three existing parties. A coalescence of Old and New Whigs had been tried last spring, and failed. It only remained now to try the effect of a coalescence of Old Whigs and Tories.

Such was doubtless the chief motive of Fox in this extraordinary move. The conduct of North seems harder to explain, but it was probably due to a reaction of feeling on his part. He had done violence to his own convictions out of weak compassion for George III., and had carried on the American war for four years after he had been thoroughly convinced that peace ought to be made. Remorse for this is said to have haunted him to the end of his life. When in his old age he became blind, he bore this misfortune with his customary lightness of heart; and one day, meeting the veteran Barré, who had also lost his eyesight, he exclaimed, with his unfailing wit, " Well, colonel, in spite of all our differences, I suppose there are no two men in England who would be gladder to *see* each other than you and I." But while Lord North could jest about his blindness, the memory of his ill-judged subservience to the king was something that he could not laugh away, and among his nearest friends he was sometimes heard to reproach himself bitterly. When, therefore, in 1783, he told Fox that he fully agreed with him in thinking that the royal power ought to be curbed, he was doubtless speaking the truth. No man had a better right to such an opinion than he had gained through sore experience. In his own ministry, as he said to Fox, he took the system as he found it, and had not vigour and resolution enough to put an end to it; but he was now quite convinced that in such a country as England, while the king should be treated with all outward show of respect, he ought on no account to be allowed to exercise any real power.

Now this was in 1783 the paramount political question in England, just as much as the question of secession was paramount in the United States in 1861. Other questions could be postponed; the question of curbing the king could not. Upon this all-important point North had come to agree with Fox; and as the principal motive of their coalition may be thus explained, the historian is not called upon to lay too much stress upon the lower motives assigned in profusion by their political enemies. This explanation, however, does not quite cover the case. The mass of the Tories would never follow North in an avowed attempt to curb the king, but they agreed with the followers of Fox, though not with Fox himself, in holy horror of parliamentary reform, and were alarmed by a recent declaration of Shelburne that the suffrage must be extended so as to admit a hundred new county members. Thus while the two leaders were urged to coalescence by one motive, their followers were largely swayed by another, and this added much to the mystery and general unintelligibleness of the movement. In taking this step Fox made the mistake which was characteristic of the Old Whig party. He gave too little heed to the great public outside the walls of the House of Commons. The coalition, once made, was very strong in Parliament, but it mystified and scandalized the people, and this popular disapproval by and by made it easy for the king to overthrow it.

It was agreed to choose the treaty as the occasion for the combined attack upon the Shelburne ministry. North, as the minister who had conducted the unsuccessful war, was bound to oppose the treaty, in any case. It would not do for him to admit that better terms could not have been made. The treaty was also very unpopular with Fox's party, and with the nation at large. It was thought that too much territory had been conceded to the Americans, and fault was found with the article on the fisheries. But the point which excited most indignation was the virtual abandonment of the loyalists, for here the honour of England was felt to be at stake. On this ground the treaty was emphatically condemned by Burke, Sheridan, and Wilberforce, no less than by North. It was ably defended in the Commons by Pitt, and in the Lords by Shelburne himself, who argued that he had but the alternative of accepting the terms as they stood, or continuing the war; and since it had come to this, he said, without spilling a drop of blood, or incurring one fifth of the expense of a year's campaign, the comfort and happiness of the American loyalists could be easily secured. By this he meant that, should America fail to make good their losses, it was far better for England to indemnify them herself than to prolong indefinitely a bloody and ruinous struggle. As we shall hereafter see, this liberal and enlightened policy was the one which England really pursued, so far as practicable, and her honour was completely saved. That Shelburne and Pitt were quite right there can now be little doubt. But argument was of no avail against the resistless power of the coalition. On the 17th of February Lord John Cavendish moved an amendment to the

Fall of Shelburne's ministry.

ministerial address on the treaty, refusing to approve it.   On the 21st he moved a further amendment condemning the treaty.   Both motions were
carried, and on the 24th Lord Shelburne resigned.
He did not dissolve Parliament and appeal to the
country, partly because he was aware of his personal unpopularity, and partly because, in spite of
the general disgust at the coalition, there was little
doubt that on the particular question of the treaty
the public opinion agreed with the majority in Parliament, and not with the ministry.   For this reason, Pitt, though personally popular, saw that it
was no time for him to take the first place in the
government, and when the king proceeded to offer
it to him he declined.

For more than five weeks, while the treasury
was nearly empty, and the question of peace or war
still hung in the balance, England was without a
regular government, while the angry king went
hunting for some one who would consent to be his
prime minister.   He was determined not to submit
to the coalition.   He was naturally enraged at Lord North for turning against
him.   Meeting one day North's father, Lord Guilford, he went up to him, tragically wringing his
hands, and exclaimed in accents of woe, "Did I
ever think, my Lord Guilford, that your son would
thus have betrayed me into the hands of Mr.
Fox?"   He appealed in vain to Lord Gower, and
then to Lord Temple, to form a ministry.   Lord
Gower suggested that perhaps Thomas Pitt, cousin
of William, might be willing to serve.   "I desired
him," said the king, "to apply to Mr. Thomas Pitt,

*The king's
wrath.*

or Mr. Thomas anybody." It was of no use. By
the 2d of April Parliament had become furious at
the delay, and George was obliged to yield. The
Duke of Portland was brought in as nominal prime
minister, with Fox as foreign secretary, North as
secretary for home and colonies, Cavendish as
chancellor of the exchequer, and Keppel as first
lord of the admiralty. The only Tory in the cabinet, excepting North, was Lord Stormont, who
became president of the council. The commissioners, Fitzherbert and Oswald, were recalled from
Paris, and the Duke of Manchester and David
Hartley, son of the great philosopher, were appointed in their stead. Negotiations continued
through the spring and summer. Attempts were
made to change some of the articles, especially the
obnoxious article concerning the loyalists, but all
to no purpose. Hartley's attempt to negotiate
a mutually advantageous commercial treaty with
America also came to nothing. The
definitive treaty which was finally signed
on the 3d of September, 1783, was an
exact transcript of the treaty which
Shelburne had made, and for making which the
present ministers had succeeded in turning him out
of office. No more emphatic justification of Shelburne's conduct of this business could possibly have
been obtained.

The treaty is adopted, after all, by the co-alition minis-try, which presently falls.

The coalition ministry did not long survive the
final signing of the treaty. The events of the next
few months are curiously instructive as showing
the quiet and stealthy way in which a political
revolution may be consummated in a thoroughly

conservative and constitutional country. Early in
the winter session of Parliament Fox brought in
his famous bill for organizing the government of
the great empire which Clive and Hastings had
built up in India. Popular indignation at the
ministry had been strengthened by its adopting
the same treaty of peace for the making of which
it had assaulted Shelburne ; and now, on the passage of the India Bill by the House of Commons,
there was a great outcry. Many provisions of the
bill were exceedingly unpopular, and its chief object
was alleged to be the concentration of the immense
patronage of India into the hands of the old Whig
families. With the popular feeling thus warmly
enlisted against the ministry, George III. was now
emboldened to make war on it by violent means ;
and, accordingly, when the bill came up in the
House of Lords, he caused it to be announced, by
Lord Temple, that any peer who should vote in its
favour would be regarded as an enemy by the king.
Four days later the House of Commons, by a vote
of 153 to 80, resolved that " to report any opinion,
or pretended opinion, of his majesty upon any bill
or other proceeding depending in either house of
Parliament, with a view to influence the votes of
the members, is a high crime and misdemeanour,
derogatory to the honour of the crown, a breach of
the fundamental privileges of Parliament, and sub-
versive of the constitution of this country." A
more explicit or emphatic defiance to the king
would have been hard to frame. Two days afterward the Lords rejected the India Bill, and on the
next day, the 18th of December, George turned
the ministers out of office.

In this grave constitutional crisis the king invited William Pitt to form a government, and this
young statesman, who had consistently opposed the
coalition, now saw that his hour was
come. He was more than any one else
the favourite of the people. Fox's political reputation was eclipsed, and North's
was destroyed, by their unseemly alliance. People were sick of the whole state of things which
had accompanied the American war. Pitt, who
had only come into Parliament in 1780, was free
from these unpleasant associations. The unblem-
ished purity of his life, his incorruptible integrity,
his rare disinterestedness, and his transcendent
ability in debate were known to every one. As the
worthy son of Lord Chatham, whose name was
associated with the most glorious moment of English history, he was peculiarly dear to the people.
His position, however, on taking supreme office at
the instance of a king who had just committed
an outrageous breach of the constitution, was extremely critical, and only the most consummate
skill could have won from the chaos such a victory
as he was about to win. When he became first
lord of the treasury and chancellor of the exchequer, in December, 1783, he had barely completed his twenty-fifth year. All his colleagues in
the new cabinet were peers, so that he had to fight
single-handed in the Commons against the united
talents of Burke and Sheridan, Fox and North;
and there was a heavy majority against him, besides. In view of this adverse majority, it was
Pitt's constitutional duty to dissolve Parliament

*Constitutional
crisis, ending
in the over-
whelming vi'
tory of Pitt,
May, 1784.*

and appeal to the country. But Fox, unwilling to imperil his great majority by a new election, now made the fatal mistake of opposing a dissolution; thus showing his distrust of the people and his dread of their verdict. With consummate tact, Pitt allowed the debates to go on till March, and then, when the popular feeling in his favour had grown into wild enthusiasm, he dissolved Parliament. In the general election which followed, 160 members of the coalition lost their seats, and Pitt obtained the greatest majority that has ever been given to an English minister.

Thus was completed the political revolution in England which was set on foot by the American victory at Yorktown. Its full significance was only gradually realized. For the moment it might seem that it was the king who had triumphed. He had shattered the alliance which had been formed for the purpose of curbing him, and the result of the election had virtually condoned his breach of the constitution. This apparent victory, however, had been won only by a direct appeal to the people, and all its advantages accrued to the people, and not to George III. His ingenious system of weak and divided ministries, with himself for balance-wheel, was destroyed. For the next seventeen years the real ruler of England was not George III., but William Pitt, who, with his great popular following, wielded such a power as no English sovereign had possessed since the days of Elizabeth. The political atmosphere was cleared of intrigue; and Fox, in the legitimate attitude of

Overthrow of George III.'s system of personal government.

leader of the new opposition, entered upon the glorious part of his career. There was now set in motion that great work of reform which, hindered for a while by the reaction against the French revolutionists, won its decisive victory in 1832. Down to the very moment at which American and British history begin to flow in distinct and separate channels, it is interesting to observe how closely they are implicated with each other. The victory of the Americans not only set on foot the British revolution here described, but it figured most prominently in each of the political changes that we have witnessed, down to the very eve of the overthrow of the coalition. The system which George III. had sought to fasten upon America, in order that he might fasten it upon England, was shaken off and shattered by the good people of both countries at almost the same moment of time.

CHAPTER II.

"THE times that tried men's souls are over,"
said Thomas Paine in the last number of the
"Crisis," which he published after hearing that the
negotiations for a treaty of peace had been concluded. The preliminary articles had been signed
at Paris on the 20th of January, 1783. The news
arrived in America on the 23d of March, in a letter to the president of Congress from Lafayette,
who had returned to France soon after the victory
at Yorktown. A few days later Sir Guy Carleton
received his orders from the ministry to proclaim a
cessation of hostilities by land and sea. A similar
proclamation made by Congress was formally communicated to the army by Washington on the 19th
of April, the eighth anniversary of the first bloodshed on Lexington green. Since Wayne had
driven the British from Georgia, early in the preceding year, there had been no military operations
between the regular armies. Guerrilla warfare
between Whig and Tory had been kept up in
parts of South Carolina and on the frontier of
New York, where Thayendanegea was still alert
and defiant; while beyond the mountains the tomahawk and scalping-knife had been busy, and
Washington's old friend and comrade, Colonel

Crawford, had been scorched to death by the fire-brands of the red demons ; but the armies had sat still, awaiting the peace which every one felt sure must speedily come. After Cornwallis's surrender, Washington marched his army back to the Hudson, and established his headquarters at Newburgh. Rochambeau followed somewhat later, and in September joined the Americans on the Hudson ; but in December the French army marched to Boston, and there embarked for France. After the formal cessation of hostilities on the 19th of April, 1783, Washington granted furloughs to most of his soldiers ; and these weather-beaten veterans trudged homeward in all directions, in little groups of four or five, depending largely for their subsistence on the hospitality of the farm-houses along the road. Arrived at home, their muskets were hung over the chimney-piece as trophies for grandchildren to be proud of, the stories of their exploits and their sufferings became household legends, and they turned the furrows and drove the cattle to pasture just as in the " old colony times." Their furloughs were equivalent to a full discharge, for on the 3d of September the definitive treaty was signed, and the country was at peace. On the 3d of November the army was formally disbanded, and on the 25th of that month Sir Guy Carleton's army embarked from New York. Small British garrisons still remained in the frontier posts of Ogdensburg, Oswego, Niagara, Erie, Sandusky, Detroit, and Mackinaw, but by the terms of the treaty these places were to be promptly surrendered to the United States. On

Departure of the British troops, Nov. 25, 1783.

the 4th of December a barge waited at the South
Ferry in New York to carry General Washington
across the river to Paulus Hook. He was going to
Annapolis, where Congress was in session, in order
to resign his command. At Fraunces's Tavern,
near the ferry, he took leave of the officers who so
long had shared his labours. One after another
they embraced their beloved commander, while
there were few dry eyes in the company. They
followed him to the ferry, and watched the depart-
ing boat with hearts too full for words, and then
in solemn silence returned up the street. At Philadelphia he handed to the comptroller of the treasury a neatly written manuscript, containing an
accurate statement of his expenses in the public
service since the day when he took command of
the army. The sums which Washington had thus
spent out of his private fortune amounted to
$64,315. For his personal services he declined to
take any pay. At noon of the 23d, in the presence of Congress and of a throng of ladies and

Washington
resigns his
command,
Dec. 23.

gentlemen at Annapolis, the great general gave up his command, and requested
as an "indulgence" to be allowed to
retire into private life. General Mifflin, who during the winter of Valley Forge had conspired with
Gates to undermine the confidence of the people
in Washington, was now president of Congress,
and it was for him to make the reply. "You retire," said Mifflin, "from the theatre of action
with the blessings of your fellow-citizens, but the
glory of your virtues will not terminate with your
military command; it will continue to animate

remotest ages." The next morning Washington hurried away to spend Christmas at his pleasant home at Mount Vernon, which, save for a few hours in the autumn of 1781, he had not set eyes on for more than eight years. His estate had suffered from his long absence, and his highest ambition was to devote himself to its simple interests. To his friends he offered unpretentious hospitality. "My manner of living is plain," he said, "and I do not mean to be put out of it. A glass of wine and a bit of mutton are always ready, and such as will be content to partake of them are always welcome. Those who expect more will be disappointed." To Lafayette he wrote that he was now about to solace himself with those tranquil enjoyments of which the anxious soldier and the weary statesman know but little. "I have not only retired from all public employments, but I am retiring within myself, and shall be able to view the solitary walk and tread the paths of private life with heartfelt satisfaction. Envious of none, I am determined to be pleased with all ; and this, my dear friend, being the order of my march, I will move gently down the stream of life until I sleep with my fathers."

In these hopes Washington was to be disappointed. "All the world is touched by his republican virtues," wrote Luzerne to Vergennes, "but it will be useless for him to try to hide himself and live the life of a private man : he will always be the first citizen of the United States." It indeed required no prophet to foretell that the American people could not long dispense with the services of this greatest of citizens. Washington had already put himself most explicitly on record as the leader of the men who were urging the people of the United States toward the formation of a more perfect union. The great lesson of the war had not been lost on him. Bitter experience of the evils attendant upon the weak government of the Continental Congress had impressed upon his mind the urgent necessity of an immediate and thorough reform. On the 8th of June, in view of the approaching disbandment of the army, he had addressed to the governors and presidents of the several states a circular letter, which he wished to have regarded as his legacy to the American people. In this letter he insisted upon four things as essential to the very existence of the United States as an independent power. First, His "legacy" to the American people, June 8, 1783. there must be an indissoluble union of all the states under a single federal government, which must possess the power of enforcing its decrees; for without such authority it would be a government only in name. Secondly, the debts incurred by Congress for the purpose of carrying on the war and securing independence must be paid to the uttermost farthing. Thirdly, the militia system must be organized throughout the thirteen states on uniform principles. Fourthly, the people must be willing to sacrifice, if need be, some of their local interests to the common weal; they must discard their local prejudices, and regard one another as fellow-citizens of a common country, with interests in the deepest and truest sense identical.

The unparalleled grandeur of Washington's character, his heroic services, and his utter disinterestedness had given him such a hold upon the people
as scarcely any other statesman known to history,
save perhaps William the Silent, has ever possessed. The noble and sensible words of his circular letter were treasured up in the minds of all
the best people in the country, and when the time
for reforming the weak and disorderly government
had come it was again to Washington that men
looked as their leader and guide. But that time
had not yet come. Only through the discipline
of perplexity and tribulation could the people be
brought to realize the indispensable necessity of
that indissoluble union of which Washington had
spoken. Thomas Paine was sadly mistaken when,
in the moment of exultation over the peace, he declared that the trying time was ended. The most
trying time of all was just beginning. It is not
too much to say that the period of five years following the peace of 1783 was the most critical
moment in all the history of the American people.
The dangers from which we were saved in 1788
were even greater than the dangers from which we
were saved in 1865. In the War of Secession
the love of union had come to be so strong that
thousands of men gave up their lives for it as cheerfully and triumphantly as the martyrs of older
times, who sang their hymns of praise   Absence of a
even while their flesh was withering in   sentiment of
                                         union, and
the relentless flames. In 1783 the love   consequent
                                         danger of
of union, as a sentiment for which men   anarchy.
would fight, had scarcely come into   existence

among the people of these states. The souls of
the men of that day had not been thrilled by the
immortal eloquence of Webster, nor had they
gained the historic experience which gave to Webster's words their meaning and their charm. They
had not gained control of all the fairest part of the
continent, with domains stretching more than three
thousand miles from ocean to ocean, and so situated
in geographical configuration and commercial relations as to make the very idea of disunion absurd,
save for men in whose minds fanaticism for the
moment usurped the place of sound judgment.
The men of 1783 dwelt in a long, straggling series
of republics, fringing the Atlantic coast, bordered
on the north and south and west by two European
powers whose hostility they had some reason to
dread. But nine years had elapsed since, in the
first Continental Congress, they had begun to act
consistently and independently in common, under
the severe pressure of a common fear and an immediate necessity of action. Even under such circumstances the war had languished and come nigh
to failure simply through the difficulty of insuring
concerted action. Had there been such a government that the whole power of the thirteen states
could have been swiftly and vigorously wielded as a
unit, the British, fighting at such disadvantage as
they did, might have been driven to their ships in less
than a year. The length of the war and its worst
hardships had been chiefly due to want of organization. Congress had steadily declined in power and
in respectability; it was much weaker at the end
of the war than at the beginning; and there was

reason to fear that as soon as the common pressure was removed the need for concerted action would quite cease to be felt, and the scarcely formed Union would break into pieces. There was the greater reason for such a fear in that, while no strong sentiment had as yet grown up in favour of union, there was an intensely powerful sentiment in favour of local self-government. This feeling was scarcely less strong as between states like Connecticut and Rhode Island, or Maryland and Virginia, than it was between Athens and Megara, Argos and Sparta, in the great days of Grecian history. A most wholesome feeling it was, and one which needed not so much to be curbed as to be guided in the right direction. It was a feeling which was shared by some of the foremost Revolutionary leaders, such as Samuel Adams and Richard Henry Lee. But unless the most profound and delicate statesmanship should be forthcoming, to take this sentiment under its guidance, there was much reason to fear that the release from the common adhesion to Great Britain would end in setting up thirteen little republics, ripe for endless squabbling, like the republics of ancient Greece and mediæval Italy, and ready to become the prey of England and Spain, even as Greece became the prey of Macedonia.

As such a lamentable result was dreaded by Washington, so by statesmen in Europe it was generally expected, and by our enemies it was eagerly hoped for. Josiah Tucker, Dean of Gloucester, was a far-sighted man in many things; but he said, "As to the future grandeur of America, and its being a rising empire under one head, whether republican or monarchical, it is one of the idlest and most visionary notions that ever was conceived even by writers of romance. The mutual antipathies and clashing interests of the Americans, their difference of governments, habitudes, and manners, indicate that they will have no centre of union and no common interest. They never can be united into one compact empire under any species of government whatever; a disunited people till the end of time, suspicious and distrustful of each other, they will be divided and subdivided into little commonwealths or principalities, according to natural boundaries, by great bays of the sea, and by vast rivers, lakes, and ridges of mountains." Such were the views of a liberal-minded philosopher who bore us no ill-will. George III. said officially that he hoped the Americans would not suffer from the evils which in history had always followed the throwing off of monarchical government: which meant, of course, that he hoped they *would* suffer from such evils. He believed we should get into such a snarl that the several states, one after another, would repent and beg on their knees to be taken back into the British empire. Frederick of Prussia, though friendly to the Americans, argued that the mere extent of country from Maine to Georgia would suffice either to break up the Union, or to make a monarchy necessary. No republic, he said, had ever long existed on so great a scale. The Roman republic had been transformed into a despotism mainly by the excessive enlargement of its area. It was only

False historic analogies.

little states, like Venice, Switzerland, and Holland, that could maintain a republican government. Such arguments were common enough a century ago, but they overlooked three essential differences between the Roman republic and the United States. The Roman republic in Cæsar's time comprised peoples differing widely in blood, in speech, and in degree of civilization; it was perpetually threatened on all its frontiers by powerful enemies; and representative assemblies were unknown to it. The only free government of which the Roman knew anything was that of the primary assembly or town meeting. On the other hand, the people of the United States were all English in speech, and mainly English in blood. The differences in degree of civilization between such states as Massachusetts and North Carolina were considerable, but in comparison with such differences as those between Attika and Lusitania they might well be called slight. The attacks of savages on the frontier were cruel and annoying, but never since the time of King Philip had they seemed to threaten the existence of the white man. A very small military establishment was quite enough to deal with the Indians. And to crown all, the American people were thoroughly familiar with the principle of representation, having practised it on a grand scale for four centuries in England, and for more than a century in America. The governments of the thirteen states were all similar, and the political ideas of one were perfectly intelligible to all the others. It was essentially fallacious, therefore, to liken the case of the United States to that of ancient Rome.

But there was another feature of the case which was quite hidden from the men of 1783. Just before the assembling of the first Continental Congress James Watt had completed his steam-engine; in the summer of 1787, while the Federal Convention was sitting at Philadelphia, John Fitch launched his first steamboat on the Delaware River; and Stephenson's invention of the locomotive was to follow in less than half a century. Even with all other conditions favourable, it is doubtful if the American Union could have been preserved to the present time without the railroad. But for the military aid of railroads our government would hardly have succeeded in putting down the rebellion of the southern states. In the debates on the Oregon Bill in the United States Senate in 1843, the idea that we could ever have an interest in so remote a country as Oregon was loudly ridiculed by some of the members. It would take ten months — said George McDuffie, the very able senator from South Carolina — for representatives to get from that territory to the District of Columbia and back again. Yet since the building of railroads to the Pacific coast, we can go from Boston to the capital of Oregon in much less time than it took John Hancock to make the journey from Boston to Philadelphia. Railroads and telegraphs have made our vast country, both for political and for social purposes, more snug and compact than little Switzerland was in the Middle Ages or New England a century ago.

At the time of our Revolution the difficulties of

travelling formed an important social obstacle to the union of the states. In our time the persons who pass in a single day between New York and Boston by six or seven distinct lines of railroad and steamboat are numbered by thousands. In 1783 two stage-coaches were enough for all the travellers, and nearly all the freight besides, that went between these two cities, except such large freight as went by sea around Cape Cod. The journey began at three o'clock in the morning. Horses were changed every twenty miles, and if the roads were in good condition some forty miles would be made by ten o'clock in the evening. In bad weather, when the passengers had to get down and lift the clumsy wheels out of deep ruts, the progress was much slower. The loss of life from accidents, in proportion to the number of travellers, was much greater than it has ever been on the railway. Broad rivers like the Connecticut and Housatonic had no bridges. To drive across them in winter, when they were solidly frozen over, was easy; and in pleasant summer weather to cross in a row-boat was not a dangerous undertaking. But squalls at some seasons and floating ice at others were things to be feared. More than one instance is recorded where boats were crushed and passengers drowned, or saved only by scrambling upon ice-floes. After a week or ten days of discomfort and danger the jolted and jaded traveller reached New York. Such was a journey in the most highly civilized part of the United States. The case was still worse in the South, and it was not so very much

Difficulty of travelling a hundred years ago.

better in England and France. In one respect the traveller in the United States fared better than the traveller in Europe: the danger from highwaymen was but slight.

Such being the difficulty of travelling, people never made long journeys save for very important reasons. Except in the case of the soldiers, most people lived and died without ever having seen any state but their own. And as the mails were irregular and uncertain, and the rates of postage very high, people heard from one another but seldom. Commercial dealings between the different states were inconsiderable. The occupation of the people was chiefly agriculture. Cities were few and small, and each little district for the most part supported itself. Under such circumstances the different parts of the country knew very little about each other, and local prejudices were intense. It was not simply free Massachusetts and

Local jealousies and antipathies, an inheritance from primeval savagery.

slave-holding South Carolina, or English Connecticut and Dutch New York, that misunderstood and ridiculed each the other; but even between such neighbouring states as Connecticut and Massachusetts, both of them thoroughly English and Puritan, and in all their social conditions almost exactly alike, it used often to be said that there was no love lost. These unspeakably stupid and contemptible local antipathies are inherited by civilized men from that far-off time when the clan system prevailed over the face of the earth, and the hand of every clan was raised against its neighbours. They are pale and evanescent survivals from the universal primitive warfare, and the sooner they die out from human society the better for every one. They should be stigmatized and frowned down upon every fit occasion, just as we frown upon swearing as a symbol of anger and contention. But the only thing which can finally destroy them is the widespread and unrestrained intercourse of different groups of people in peaceful social and commercial relations. The rapidity with which this process is now going on is the most encouraging of all the symptoms of our modern civilization. But a century ago the progress made in this direction had been relatively small, and it was a very critical moment for the American people.

The thirteen states, as already observed, had worked in concert for only nine years, during which their coöperation had been feeble and halting. But the several state governments had been in operation since the first settlement of the country, and were regarded with intense loyalty by the people of the states. Under the royal governors the local political life of each state had been vigorous and often stormy, as befitted communities of the sturdy descendants of English freemen. The legislative assembly of each state had stoutly defended its liberties against the encroachments of the governor. In the eyes of the people it was the only power on earth competent to lay taxes upon them, it was as supreme in its own sphere as the British Parliament itself, and in behalf of this rooted conviction the people had gone to war and won their independence from England. During the war the people of all the states, except Con-

necticut and Rhode Island, had carefully remod-
elled their governments, and in the performance of
this work had withdrawn many of their ablest
statesmen from the Continental Congress ; but except for the expulsion of the royal and
proprietary governors, the work had in
no instance been revolutionary in its
character. It was not so much that the American
people gained an increase of freedom by their separation from England, as that they kept the freedom they had always enjoyed, that freedom which
was the inalienable birthright of Englishmen, but
which George III. had foolishly sought to impair.
The American Revolution was therefore in no respect destructive. It was the most conservative
revolution known to history, thoroughly English
in conception from beginning to end. It had no
likeness whatever to the terrible popular convulsion
which soon after took place in France. The mischievous doctrines of Rousseau had found few
readers and fewer admirers among the Americans.
The principles upon which their revolution was
conducted were those of Sidney, Harrington, and
Locke. In remodelling the state governments, as
in planning the union of the states, the precedents
followed and the principles applied were almost
purely English. We must now pass in review the
principal changes wrought in the several states,
and we shall then be ready to consider the general
structure of the Confederation, and to describe the
remarkable series of events which led to the adoption of our Federal Constitution.

It will be remembered that at the time of the

Conservative character of the Revolution.

Declaration of Independence there were three kinds
of government in the colonies. Connecticut and
Rhode Island had always been true republics, with
governors and legislative assemblies elected by the
people. Pennsylvania, Delaware, and Maryland
presented the appearance of limited hereditary
monarchies. Their assemblies were chosen by the
people, but the lords proprietary appointed their
governors, or in some instances acted as governors
themselves. In Maryland the office of lord proprietary was hereditary in the Calvert State govern-
family; in Delaware and Pennsylvania, ments remod-
which, though distinct commonwealths blies continued
with separate legislatures, had the same from colonial
times.
executive head, it was hereditary in the Penn family. The other eight colonies were viceroyalties,
with governors appointed by the king, while in all
alike the people elected the legislatures. Accordingly in Connecticut and Rhode Island no change
was made necessary by the Revolution, beyond the
mere omission of the king's name from legal documents; and their charters, which dated from the
middle of the seventeenth century, continued to do
duty as state constitutions till far into the nineteenth. During the Revolutionary War all the
other states framed new constitutions, but in most
essential respects they took the old colonial charters for their model. The popular legislative body
remained unchanged even in its name. In North
Carolina its supreme dignity was vindicated in its
title of the House of Commons; in Virginia it was
called the House of Burgesses; in most of the
states the House of Representatives. The mem-

bers were chosen each year, except in South Carolina, where they served for two years. In the New England states they represented the townships, in other states the counties. In all the states except Pennsylvania a property qualification was required of them.

In addition to this House of Representatives all the legislatures except those of Pennsylvania and Georgia contained a second or upper house known
Origin of the senates. as the Senate. The origin of the senate is to be found in the governor's council of colonial times, just as the House of Lords is descended from the Witenagemot or council of great barons summoned by the Old-English kings. The Americans had been used to having the acts of their popular assemblies reviewed by a council, and so they retained this revisory body as an upper house. A higher property qualification was required than for membership of the lower house, and, except in New Hampshire, Massachusetts, and South Carolina, the term of service was longer. In Maryland senators sat for five years, in Virginia and New York for four years, elsewhere for two years. In some states they were chosen by the people, in others by the lower house. In Maryland they were chosen by a college of electors, thus affording a precedent for the method of electing the chief magistrate of the union under the Federal Constitution.

Governors were unpopular in those days. There was too much flavour of royalty and high prerogative about them. Except in the two republics of Rhode Island and Connecticut, American political

history during the eighteenth century was chiefly
the record of interminable squabbles between governors and legislatures, down to the moment when
the detested agents of royalty were clapped into
jail, or took refuge behind the bulwarks of a British seventy-four. Accordingly the new constitutions were very chary of the powers to be exercised
by the governor. In Pennsylvania and
Delaware, in New Hampshire and Mas- Governors
viewed with
sachusetts, the governor was at first re- suspicion.
placed by an executive council, and the president
of this council was first magistrate and titular ruler
of the state. His dignity was imposing enough,
but his authority was merely that of a chairman.
The other states had governors chosen by the legislatures, except in New York where the governor
was elected by the people. No one was eligible to
the office of governor who did not possess a specified amount of property. In most of the states
the governor could not be reëlected, he had no veto
upon the acts of the legislature, nor any power of
appointing officers. In 1780, in a new constitution
drawn up by James Bowdoin and the two Adamses,
Massachusetts led the way in the construction of a
more efficient executive department. The president was replaced by a governor elected annually
by the people, and endowed with the power of appointment and a suspensory veto. The first governor elected under this constitution was John
Hancock. In 1783 New Hampshire adopted a
similar constitution. In 1790 Pennsylvania added
an upper house to its legislature, and vested the
executive power in a governor elected by the peo-

ple for a term of three years, and twice reëligible. He was intrusted with the power of appointment to offices, with a suspensory veto, and with the royal prerogative of reprieving or pardoning criminals. In 1792 similar changes were made in Delaware. In 1789 Georgia added the upper house to its legislature, and about the same time in several states the governor's powers were enlarged.

Thus the various state governments were repetitions on a small scale of what was then supposed to be the triplex government of England, with its King, Lords, and Commons. The governor answered to the king with his dignity curtailed by election for a short period, and by narrowly limited prerogatives. The senate answered to the House of Lords, except in being a representative and not a hereditary body. It was supposed to represent more especially that part of the community which was possessed of most wealth and consideration ; and in several states the senators were apportioned with some reference to the amount of taxes paid by different parts of the state. The senate of New York, in direct imitation of the House of Lords, was made a supreme court of errors. On the other hand, the assembly answered to the House of Commons, save that its power was really limited by the senate as the power of the House of Commons is not really limited by the House of Lords. But this peculiarity of the British Constitution was not well understood a century ago ; and the misunderstanding, as we shall hereafter see, exerted a very serious influence upon the form of our federal government, as well as upon the constitutions of the several states.

In all the thirteen states the common law of England remained in force, as it does to this day save where modified by statute. British and colonial statutes made prior to the Revolution continued also in force unless expressly repealed. The system of civil and criminal courts, the remedies in common law and equity, the forms of writs, the functions of justices of the peace, the courts of probate, all remained substantially unchanged. In Pennsylvania, Delaware, and New Jersey, the judges held office for a term of seven years; in all the other states they held office for life or during good behaviour. In all the states save Georgia they were appointed either by the gov- The judiciary. ernor or by the legislature. It was Georgia that in 1812 first set the pernicious example of electing judges for short terms by the people,[1] — a practice which is responsible for much of the degradation that the courts have suffered in many of our states, and which will have to be abandoned before a proper administration of justice can ever be secured.

In bestowing the suffrage, the new constitutions were as conservative as in all other respects. The general state of opinion in America at that time, with regard to universal suffrage, was far more advanced than the general state of opinion in England, but it was less advanced than the opinions of such statesmen as Pitt and Shelburne and the Duke of Richmond. There was a truly English irregularity in the provisions which were made on

[1] In recent years Georgia has been one of the first states to abandon this bad practice.

this subject.   In New Hampshire, Pennsylvania,
The limited   Delaware, and South Carolina, all resi-
suffrage.   dent freemen who paid taxes could vote.
In North Carolina all such persons could vote for
members of the lower house, but in order to vote
for senators a freehold of fifty acres was required.
In Virginia none could vote save those who possessed such a freehold of fifty acres.   To vote for
governor or for senators in New York, one must
possess a freehold of $250, clear of mortgage, and
to vote for assemblymen one must either have a
freehold of $50, or pay a yearly rent of $10.   The
pettiness of these sums was in keeping with the
time when two daily coaches sufficed for the traffic
between our two greatest commercial cities.   In
Rhode Island an unincumbered freehold worth
$134 was required; but in Rhode Island and Penn-
sylvania the eldest sons of qualified freemen could
vote without payment of taxes.   In all the other
states the possession of a small amount of property,
either real or personal, varying from $33 to $200,
was the necessary qualification for voting.   Thus
slowly and irregularly did the states drift toward
universal suffrage; but although the impediments
in the way of voting were more serious than they
seem to us in these days when the community is
more prosperous and money less scarce, they were
still not very great, and in the opinion of conservative people they barely sufficed to exclude from the
suffrage such shiftless persons as had no visible interest in keeping down the taxes.

At the time of the Revolution the succession to
property was regulated in New York and the south-

ern states by the English rule of primogeniture.
The eldest son took all. In New Jersey, Pennsylvania, Delaware, and the four New England states,
the eldest son took a double share. It
was Georgia that led the way in decree- Abolition of
primogeni-
ing the equal distribution of intestate ture, entails,
and manorial
property, both real and personal; and privileges.
between 1784 and 1796 the example was followed
by all the other states. At the same time entails
were either definitely abolished, or the obstacles to
cutting them off were removed. In New York the
manorial privileges of the great patroons were
swept away. In Maryland the old manorial system
had long been dying a natural death through the
encroachments of the patriarchal system of slavery.
The ownership of all ungranted lands within the
limits of the thirteen states passed from the crown
not to the Confederacy, but to the several state
governments. In Pennsylvania and Maryland such
ungranted lands had belonged to the lords proprietary. They were now forfeited to the state. The
Penn family was indemnified by Pennsylvania to
the amount of half a million dollars; but Maryland made no compensation to the Calverts, inasmuch as their claim was presented by an illegiti-
mate descendant of the last Lord Baltimore.

The success of the American Revolution made it
possible for the different states to take measures
for the gradual abolition of slavery and the immediate abolition of the foreign slave-trade. On this
great question the state of public opinion in America was more advanced than in England. So great
a thinker as Edmund Burke, who devoted much

thought to the subject, came to the conclusion that

slavery was an incurable evil, and that there was not the slightest hope that the trade in slaves could be stopped. The most that he thought could be done by judicious legislation was to mitigate the horrors which the poor negroes endured on board ship, or to prevent wives from being sold away from their husbands or children from their parents. Such was the outlook to one of the greatest political philosophers of modern times just eighty-two years before the immortal proclamation of President Lincoln! But how vast was the distance between Burke and Bossuet, who had declared about eighty years earlier that "to condemn slavery was to condemn the Holy Ghost!" It was equally vast between Burke and his contemporary Thurlow, who in 1799 poured out the vials of his wrath upon "the altogether miserable and contemptible" proposal to abolish the slave-trade. George III. agreed with his chancellor, and resisted the movement for abolition with all the obstinacy of which his hard and narrow nature was capable. In 1769 the Virginia legislature had enacted that the further importation of negroes, to be sold into slavery, should be prohibited. But George III. commanded the governor to veto this act, and it was vetoed. In Jefferson's first draft of the Declaration of Independence, this action of the king was made the occasion of a fierce denunciation of slavery, but in deference to the prejudices of South Carolina and Georgia the clause was struck out by Congress. When George III. and his vetoes had been eliminated from the case, it became possible for the states to legislate freely on the subject. In 1776 negro slaves were held in all the thirteen states, but in all except South Carolina and Georgia there was a strong sentiment in favour of emancipation. In North Carolina, which contained a large Quaker population, and in which estates were small and were often cultivated by free labour, the pro-slavery feeling was never so strong as in the southernmost states. In Virginia all the foremost statesmen — Washington, Jefferson, Lee, Randolph, Henry, Madison, and Mason — were opposed to the continuance of slavery ; and their opinions were shared by many of the largest planters. For tobacco-culture slavery did not seem so indispensable as for the raising of rice and indigo ; and in Virginia the negroes, half-civilized by kindly treatment, were not regarded with horror by their masters, like the ill-treated and ferocious blacks of South Carolina and Georgia. After 1808 the policy and the sentiments of Virginia underwent a marked change. The invention of the cotton-gin, taken in connection with the sudden and prodigious development of manufactures in England, greatly stimulated the growth of cotton in the ever-enlarging area of the Gulf states, and created an immense demand for slave-labour, just at the time when the importation of negroes from Africa came to an end. The breeding of slaves, to be sold to the planters of the Gulf states, then became such a profitable occupation in Virginia as entirely to change the popular feeling about slavery. But until 1808 Virginia sympathized with the anti-slavery sentiment which was growing up in the northern states; and the same was true of Maryland. Emancipation was, however, much more easy to accomplish in the north, because the number of slaves was small, and economic circumstances distinctly favoured free labour. In the work of gradual emancipation the little state of Delaware led the way. In its new constitution of 1776 the further introduction of slaves was prohibited, all restraints upon emancipation having already been removed. In the assembly of Virginia in 1778 a bill prohibiting the further introduction of slaves was moved and carried by Thomas Jefferson, and the same measure was passed in Maryland in 1783, while both these states removed all restraints upon emancipation. North Carolina was not ready to go quite so far, but in 1786 she sought to discourage the slave-trade by putting a duty of £5 per head on all negroes thereafter imported. New Jersey followed the example of Maryland and Virginia. Pennsylvania went farther. In 1780 its assembly enacted that no more slaves should be brought in, and that all children of slaves born after that date should be free. The same provisions were made by New Hampshire in its new constitution of 1783, and by the assemblies of Connecticut and Rhode Island in 1784. New York went farther still, and in 1785 enacted that all children of slaves thereafter born should not only be free, but should be admitted to vote on the same conditions as other freemen. In 1788 Virginia, which contained many free negroes, enacted that any person convicted of kidnapping or selling into slavery any free person should suffer death on the gallows. Summing up all these facts, we see that within two years after the independence of the United States had been acknowledged by England, while the two southernmost states had done nothing to check the growth of slavery, North Carolina had discouraged the importation of slaves; Virginia, Maryland, Delaware, and New Jersey had stopped such importation and removed all restraint upon emancipation; and all the remaining states, except Massachusetts, had made gradual emancipation compulsory. Massachusetts had gone still farther. Before the Revolution the anti-slavery feeling had been stronger there than in any other state, and cases brought into court for the purpose of testing the legality of slavery had been decided in favour of those who were opposed to the continuance of that barbarous institution. In 1777 an American cruiser brought into the port of Salem a captured British ship with slaves on board, and these slaves were advertised for sale, but on complaint being made before the legislature they were set free. The new constitution of 1780 contained a declaration of rights which asserted that all men are born free and have an equal and inalienable right to defend their lives and liberties, to acquire property, and to seek and obtain safety and happiness. The supreme court presently decided that this clause worked the abolition of slavery, and accordingly Massachusetts was the first of American states, within the limits of the Union, to become in the full sense of the words a free commonwealth. Of the negro inhabitants, not more than six thousand in number, a large proportion had already for a long time enjoyed freedom; and all were now admitted to the suffrage on the same terms as other citizens.

By the revolutionary legislation of the states some progress was also effected in the direction of a more complete religious freedom. Pennsylvania and Delaware were the only states in which all Christian sects stood socially and politically on an equal footing. In Rhode Island all Protestants enjoyed equal privileges, but Catholics were debarred from voting. In Massachusetts, New Hampshire, and Connecticut, the old Puritan Congregationalism was the established religion. The Congregational church was supported by taxes, and the minister, once chosen, kept his place for life or during good behaviour. He could not be got rid of unless formally investigated and dismissed by an ecclesiastical council. Laws against blasphemy, which were virtually laws against heresy, were in force in these three states. In Massachusetts, Catholic priests were liable to imprisonment for life. Any one who should dare to speculate too freely about the nature of Christ, or the philosophy of the plan of salvation, or to express a doubt as to the plenary inspiration of every word between the two covers of the Bible, was subject to fine and imprisonment. The tithing-man still arrested Sabbath-breakers and shut them up in the town-cage in the market-place; he stopped all unnecessary riding or driving on Sunday, and haled people off to the meeting-house whether they would or not. Such restraints upon liberty were still endured by people who had

Progress toward freedom in religion.

dared and suffered so much for liberty's sake. The men of Boston strove hard to secure the repeal of these barbarous laws and the disestablishment of the Congregational church ; but they were outvoted by the delegates from the rural towns. The most that could be accomplished was the provision that dissenters might escape the church-rate by supporting a church of their own. The nineteenth century was to arrive before church and state were finally separated in Massachusetts. The new constitution of New Hampshire was similarly illiberal, and in Connecticut no change was made. Rhode Island nobly distinguished herself by contrast when in 1784 she extended the franchise to Catholics.

In the six states just mentioned the British government had been hindered by charter, and by the overwhelming opposition of the people, from seriously trying to establish the Episcopal church. The sure fate of any such mad experiment had been well illustrated in the time of Andros. In the other seven states there were no such insuperable obstacles. The Church of England was maintained with languid acquiescence in New York. By the Quakers and Presbyterians of New Jersey and North Carolina, as well as in half-Catholic, half-Puritan Maryland, its supremacy was unwillingly endured ; in the turbulent frontier commonwealth of Georgia it was accepted with easy contempt. Only in South Carolina and Virginia had the Church of England ever possessed any real hold upon the people. The Episcopal clergy of South Carolina, men of learning and high character, elected by their own congregations instead of being appointed to their livings by a patron, were thoroughly independent, and in the late war their powerful influence had been mainly exerted in behalf of the patriot cause. Hence, while they retained their influence after the close of the war, there was no difficulty in disestablishing the church. It felt itself able to stand without government support. As soon as the political separation from England was effected, the Episcopal church was accordingly separated from the state, not only in South Carolina, but in all the states in which it had hitherto been upheld by the authority of the British government; and in the constitutions of New Jersey, Georgia, and the two Carolinas, no less than in those of Delaware and Pennsylvania, it was explicitly provided that no man should be obliged to pay any church rate or attend any religious service save according to his own free and unhampered will.

The case of Virginia was peculiar. At first the Church of England had taken deep root there because of the considerable immigration of members of the Cavalier party after the downfall of Charles I. Most of the great statesmen of Virginia in the Revolution — such as Washington, Madison, Mason, Jefferson, Pendleton, Henry, the Lees, and the Randolphs — were descendants of Cavaliers and members of the Church of England. But for a long time the Episcopal clergy had been falling into discredit. Many of them were appointed by the British government and ordained by the Bishop

Church and state in Virginia.

of London, and they were affected by the irreligious listlessness and low moral tone of the English church in the eighteenth century. The Virginia legislature thought it necessary to pass special laws prohibiting these clergymen from drunkenness and riotous living. It was said that they spent more time in hunting foxes and betting on race-horses than in conducting religious services or visiting the sick; and according to Bishop Meade, many dissolute parsons, discarded from the church in England as unworthy, were yet thought fit to be presented with livings in Virginia. To this general character of the clergy there were many exceptions. There were many excellent clergymen, especially among the native Virginians, whose appointment depended to some extent upon the repute in which they were held by their neighbours. But on the whole the system was such as to illustrate all the worst vices of a church supported by the temporal power. The Revolution achieved the discomfiture of a clergy already thus deservedly discredited. The parsons mostly embraced the cause of the crown, but failed to carry their congregations with them, and thus they found themselves arrayed in hopeless antagonism to popular sentiment in a state which contained perhaps fewer Tories in proportion to its population than any other of the thirteen.

At the same time the Episcopal church itself had gradually come to be a minority in the commonwealth. For more than half a century Scotch and Welsh Presbyterians, German Lutherans, English Quakers, and Baptists, had been working their way southward from Pennsylvania and New Jersey, and had settled in the fertile country west of the Blue Ridge. Daniel Morgan, who had won the most brilliant battle of the Revolution, was one of these men, and sturdiness was a chief characteristic of most of them. So long as these frontier settlers served as a much-needed bulwark against the Indians, the church saw fit to ignore them and let them build meeting-houses and carry on religious services as they pleased. But when the peril of Indian attack had been thrust westward into the Ohio valley, and these dissenting communities had waxed strong and prosperous, the ecclesiastical party in the state undertook to lay taxes on them for the support of the Church of England, and to compel them to receive Episcopal clergymen to preach for them, to bless them in marriage, and to bury their dead. The immediate consequence was a revolt which not only overthrew the established church in Virginia, but nearly effected its ruin. The troubles began in 1768, when the Baptists had made their way into the centre of the state, and three of their preachers were arrested by the sheriff of Spottsylvania. As the indictment was read against these men for "preaching the gospel contrary to law," a deep and solemn voice interrupted the proceedings. Patrick Henry had come on horseback many a mile over roughest roads to listen to the trial, and this phrase, which savoured of the religious despotisms of old, was quite too much for him. "May it please your worships," he exclaimed, "what did I hear read? Did I hear an expression that these men, whom your worships are about to try for misdemeanour, are charged with preaching the gospel of the Son of God!" The shamefast silence and confusion which ensued was of ill omen for the success of an undertaking so unwelcome to the growing liberalism of the time. The zeal of the persecuted Baptists was presently reinforced by the learning and the dialectic skill of the Presbyterian ministers. Unlike the Puritans of New England, the Presbyterians were in favour of the total separation of church from state. It was one of their cardinal principles that the civil magistrate had no right to interfere in any way with matters of religion. By taking this broad ground they secured the powerful aid of Thomas Jefferson, and afterwards of Madison and Mason. The controversy went on through all the years of the Revolutionary War, while all Virginia, from the sea to the mountains, rang with fulminations and arguments. In 1776 Jefferson and Mason succeeded in carrying a bill which released all dissenters from parish rates and legalized all forms of worship. At last in 1785 Madison won the crowning victory in the Religious Freedom Act, by which the Church of England was disestablished and all parish rates abolished, and still more, all religious tests were done away with. Madison and the Religious Freedom Act, 1785. In this last respect Virginia came to the front among all the American states, as Massachusetts had come to the front in the abolition of negro slavery. Nearly all the states still imposed religious tests upon civil office-holders, from simply declaring a general belief in the infallibleness of

the Bible to accepting the doctrine of the Trinity.
The Virginia statute, which declared that " opinion
in matters of religion shall in nowise diminish,
enlarge, or affect civil capacities," was translated
into French and Italian, and was widely read and
commented on in Europe.

It is the historian's unpleasant duty to add that
the victory thus happily won was ungenerously followed up. Theological and political odium combined to overwhelm the Episcopal church in Virginia. The persecuted became persecutors. It
was contended that the property of the church,
having been largely created by unjustifiable taxation, ought to be forfeited. In 1802 its parson-
ages and glebe lands were sold, its parishes wiped
out, and its clergy left without a calling. " A
reckless sensualist," said Dr. Hawks, "administered the morning dram to his guests from the
silver cup " used in the communion service. But
in all this there is a manifest historic lesson. That
it should have been possible thus to deal with the
Episcopal church in Virginia shows forcibly the
moribund condition into which it had been brought
through dependence upon the extraneous aid of a
political sovereignty from which the people of Virginia were severing their allegiance. The lesson
is most vividly enhanced by the contrast with the
church of South Carolina which, rooted in its own
soil, was quite able to stand alone when government aid was withdrawn. In Virginia the church
in which George Washington was reared had so
nearly vanished by the year 1830 that Chief Justice Marshall said it was folly to dream of reviv-

ing so dead a thing. Nevertheless, under the noble ministration of its great bishop, William Meade, the Episcopal church in Virginia, no longer relying upon state aid, but trusting in the divine persuasive power of spiritual truth, was even then entering upon a new life and beginning to exercise a most wholesome influence.

The separation of the English church in America from the English crown was the occasion of a curious difficulty with regard to the ordination of bishops. Until after the Revolution there were no bishops of that church in America, and between 1783 and 1785 it was not clear how candidates for holy orders could receive the necessary consecration. In 1784 a young divinity student from Maryland, named Mason Weems, who had been studying for some time in England, applied to the Bishop of London for admission to holy orders, but was rudely refused. Weems then had recourse to Watson, Bishop of Llandaff, author of the famous reply to Gibbon. Watson treated him kindly and advised him to get a letter of recommendation from the governor of Maryland, but after this had been obtained he referred him to the Archbishop of Canterbury, who said that nothing could be done without the consent of Parliament. As the law stood, no one could be admitted into the ranks of the English clergy without taking the oath of allegiance and acknowledging the king of England as the head of the church. Weems then wrote to John Adams at the Hague, and to Franklin at Paris, to see if there were any Protestant bishops on the Con-

Mason Weems and Samuel Seabury.

tinent from whom he could obtain consecration. A rather amusing diplomatic correspondence ensued, and finally the king of Denmark, after taking theological advice, kindly offered the services of a Danish bishop, who was to perform the ceremony in Latin. Weems does not seem to have availed himself of this permission, probably because the question soon reached a more satisfactory solution.[1] About the same time the Episcopal church in Connecticut sent one of its ministers, Samuel Seabury of New London, to England, to be ordained as bishop. The oaths of allegiance and supremacy stood as much in the way of the learned and famous minister as in that of the young and obscure student. Seabury accordingly appealed to November 14, the non-juring Jacobite bishops of the 1784. Episcopal church of Scotland, and at length was duly ordained at Aberdeen as bishop of the diocese of Connecticut. While Seabury was in England, the churches in the various states

---

[1] I suppose it was this same Mason Weems that was afterward known in Virginia as Parson Weems, of Pohick parish, near Mount Vernon. See *Magazine of American History*, iii. 465–472; v. 85–90. At first an eccentric preacher, Parson Weems became an itinerant violin-player and book-peddler, and author of that edifying work, *The Life of George Washington, with Curious Anecdotes equally Honourable to Himself and Exemplary to his Young Countrymen.* On the title-page the author describes himself as "formerly rector of Mount Vernon Parish," — which Bishop Meade calls preposterous. The book is a farrago of absurdities, reminding one, alike in its text and its illustrations, of an overgrown English chap-book of the olden time. It has had an enormous sale, and has very likely contributed more than any other single book toward forming the popular notion of Washington. It seems to have been this fiddling parson that first gave currency to the everlasting story of the cherry-tree and the little hatchet.

chose delegates to a general convention, which framed a constitution for the "Protestant Episcopal Church of the United States of America." Advowsons were abolished, some parts of the liturgy were dropped, and the tenure of ministers, even of bishops, was to be during good behaviour. At the same time a friendly letter was sent to the bishops of England, urging them to secure, if possible, an act of Parliament whereby American clergymen might be ordained without taking the oaths of allegiance and supremacy. Such an act was obtained without much difficulty, and three American bishops were accordingly consecrated in due form. The peculiar ordination of Seabury was also recognized as valid by the general convention, and thus the Episcopal church in America was fairly started on its independent career.

This foundation of a separate episcopacy west of the Atlantic was accompanied by the further separation of the Methodists as a distinct religious society. Although John Wesley regarded the notion of an apostolical succession as superstitious, he had made no attempt to separate his followers from the national church. He translated the titles of "bishop" and "priest" from Greek into Latin and English, calling them "superintendent" and "elder," but he did not deny the king's headship. Meanwhile during the long period of his preaching there had begun to grow up a Methodist church in America. George Whitefield had come over and preached in Georgia in 1737, and in Massachusetts in 1744, where he encountered much opposition on the part of the Puritan clergy. But the first Methodist church in America was founded in the city of New York in 1766. In 1772 Wesley sent over Francis Asbury, a man of shrewd sense and deep religious feeling, to act as his assistant and representative in this country.

Francis Asbury and the Methodists.

At that time there were not more than a thousand Methodists, with six preachers, and all these were in the middle and southern colonies; but within five years, largely owing to the zeal and eloquence of Asbury, these numbers had increased sevenfold. At the end of the war, seeing the American Methodists cut loose from the English establishment, Wesley in his own house at Bristol, with the aid of two presbyters, proceeded to ordain ministers enough to make a presbytery, and thereupon set apart Thomas Coke to be "superintendent" or bishop for America. On the same day of November, 1784, on which Seabury was consecrated by the non-jurors at Aberdeen, Coke began preaching and baptizing in Maryland, in rude chapels built of logs or under the shade of forest trees. On Christmas Eve a conference assembled at Baltimore, at which Asbury was chosen bishop by some sixty ministers present, and ordained by Coke, and the constitution of the Methodist church in America was organized. Among the poor white people of the southern states, and among the negroes, the new church rapidly obtained great sway; and at a somewhat later date it began to assume considerable proportions in the north.

Four years after this the Presbyterians, who were most numerous in the middle states, organ-

ized their government in a general assembly, which
was also attended by Congregationalist delegates
from New England in the capacity of simple advisers.   The theological difference between these
two sects was so slight that an alliance grew up
between them, and in Connecticut some fifty years
later their names were often inaccurately used as
if synonymous.   Such a difference seemed to vanish
when confronted with the newer differences that
began to spring up soon after the close
of the Revolution.   The revolt against   Presbyterians;
Roman Catholics.
the doctrine of eternal punishment was
already beginning in New England, and among
the learned and thoughtful clergy of Massachusetts
the seeds of Unitarianism were germinating.   The
gloomy intolerance of an older time was beginning
to yield to more enlightened views.   In 1789 the
first Roman Catholic church in New England was
dedicated in Boston.   So great had been the prejudice against this sect that in 1784 there were only
600 Catholics in all New England.   In the four
southernmost states, on the other hand, there were
2,500; in New York and New Jersey there were
1,700; in Delaware and Pennsylvania there were
7,700; in Maryland there were 20,000; while
among the French settlements along the eastern
bank of the Mississippi there were supposed to be
nearly 12,000.   In 1786 John Carroll, a cousin of
Charles Carroll of Carrollton, was selected by the
Pope as his apostolic vicar, and was afterward suc-
cessively made bishop of Baltimore and archbishop
of the United States.   By 1789 all obstacles to the
Catholic worship had been done away with in all
the states.

In this brief survey of the principal changes wrought in the several states by the separation from England, one cannot fail to be struck with their conservative character. Things proceeded just as they had done from time immemorial with the English race. Forms of government were modified just far enough to adapt them to the new situation and no farther. The abolition of entails, of primogeniture, and of such few manorial privileges as existed, were useful reforms of far less sweeping character than similar changes would have been in England; and they were accordingly effected with ease. Even the abolition of slavery in the northern states, where negroes were few in number and chiefly employed in domestic service, wrought nothing in the remotest degree resembling a social revolution. But nowhere was this constitutionally cautious and precedent-loving mode of proceeding more thoroughly exemplified than in the measures just related, whereby the Episcopal and Methodist churches were separated from the English establishment and placed upon an independent footing in the new world. From another point of view it may be observed that all these changes, except in the instance of slavery, tended to assimilate the states to one another in their political and social condition. So far as they went, these changes were favourable to union, and this was perhaps especially true in the case of the ecclesiastical bodies, which brought citizens of different states into coöperation in pursuit of specific ends in common.

Except in the instance of slavery, all these changes were favourable to union.

At the same time this survey most forcibly reminds us how completely the legislation which immediately affected the daily domestic life of the citizen was the legislation of the single state in which he lived. In the various reforms just passed in review the United States government took no part, and could not from the nature of the case. Even to-day our national government has no power over such matters, and it is to be hoped it never will have. But at the present day our national government performs many important functions of common concern, which a century ago were scarcely performed at all. The organization of the single state was old in principle and well understood by everybody. It therefore worked easily, and such changes as those above described were brought about with little friction. On the other hand, the principles upon which the various relations of the states to each other were to be adjusted were not well understood. There was wide disagreement upon the subject, and the attempt to compromise between opposing views was not at first successful. Hence, in the management of affairs which concerned the United States as a nation, we shall not find the central machinery working smoothly or quietly. We are about to traverse a period of uncertainty and confusion, in which it required all the political sagacity and all the good temper of the people to save the half-built ship of state from going to pieces on the rocks of civil contention.

CHAPTER III.

THE LEAGUE OF FRIENDSHIP.

THAT some kind of union existed between the states was doubted by no one. Ever since the assembling of the first Continental Congress in 1774 the thirteen commonwealths had acted in concert, and sometimes most generously, as when Maryland and South Carolina had joined in the Declaration of Independence without any crying grievances of their own, from a feeling that the cause of one should be the cause of all. It has sometimes been said that the Union was in its origin a league of sovereign states, each of which surrendered a specific portion of its sovereignty to the federal government for the sake of the common welfare. Grave political arguments have been based upon this alleged fact, but such an account of the matter is not historically true. There never was a time when Massachusetts or Virginia was an absolutely sovereign state like Holland or France. Sovereign over their own internal affairs they are to-day as they were at the time of the Revolution, but there was never a time when they presented themselves before other nations as sovereign, or were recognized as such. Under the government of England before the Revolution the thirteen commonwealths were independent of one another, and were held together, juxtaposed rather than united, only through their allegiance to the British crown. Had that allegiance been maintained there is no telling how long they might have gone on thus disunited ; and this, it seems, should be one of our chief reasons for rejoicing that the political connection with England was dissolved when it was. A permanent redress of grievances, and even virtual independence such as Canada now enjoys, we might perhaps have gained had we listened to Lord North's proposals after the surrender of Burgoyne; but the formation of the Federal Union would certainly have been long postponed, and when we realize the grandeur of the work which we are now doing in the world through the simple fact of such a union, we cannot fail to see that such an issue would have been extremely unfortunate. However this may be, it is clear that until the connection with England was severed the thirteen commonwealths were not united, nor were they sovereign. It is also clear that in the very act of severing their connection with England these commonwealths entered into some sort of union which was incompatible with their absolute sovereignty taken severally. It was not the people of New Hampshire, Massachusetts, and so on through the list, that declared their independence of Great Britain, but it was the representatives of the United States in Congress assembled, and speaking as a single body in the name of the whole. Three weeks before this declaration was adopted, Congress appointed a committee to draw up the

The several states have never enjoyed complete sovereignty.

" articles of confederation and perpetual union,"
by which the sovereignty of the several states was
expressly limited and curtailed in many important
particulars.   This committee had finished its work
by the 12th of July, but the articles were not
adopted by Congress until the autumn of 1777, and
they were not finally put into operation until the
spring of 1781.   During this inchoate period of
union the action of the United States was that
of a confederation in which some portion of the
several sovereignties was understood to be surrendered to the whole.   It was the business of the
articles to define the precise nature and extent of
this surrendered sovereignty which no state by itself ever exercised.   In the mean time this sovereignty, undefined in nature and extent, was exercised, as well as circumstances permitted, by the
Continental Congress.

A most remarkable body was this Continental

The Continen-
tal Congress;
its extraordi-
nary character.

Congress.   For the vicissitudes through
which it passed, there is perhaps no
other revolutionary body, save the Long
Parliament, which can be compared with it.   For
its origin we must look back to the committees
of correspondence devised by Jonathan Mayhew,
Samuel Adams, and Dabney Carr.   First assembled in 1774 to meet an emergency which was generally believed to be only temporary, it continued
to sit for nearly seven years before its powers were
ever clearly defined ; and during those seven years
it exercised some of the highest functions of sovereignty which are possible to any governing body.
It declared the independence of the United States ;

it contracted an offensive and defensive alliance with France; it raised and organized a Continental army; it borrowed large sums of money, and pledged what the lenders understood to be the national credit for their repayment; it issued an inconvertible paper currency, granted letters of marque, and built a navy. All this it did in the exercise of what in later times would have been called "implied war powers," and its authority rested upon the general acquiescence in the purposes for which it acted and in the measures which it adopted. Under such circumstances its functions were very inefficiently performed. But the articles of confederation, which in 1781 defined its powers, served at the same time to limit them; so that for the remaining eight years of its existence the Continental Congress grew weaker and weaker, until it was swept away to make room for a more efficient government.

John Dickinson is supposed to have been the principal author of the articles of con- The articles of federation; but as the work of the com- confederation. mittee was done in secret and has never been reported, the point cannot be determined. In November, 1777, Congress sent the articles to the several state legislatures, with a circular letter recommending them as containing the only plan of union at all likely to be adopted. In the course of the next fifteen months the articles were ratified by all the states except Maryland, which refused to sign until the states laying claim to the northwestern lands, and especially Virginia, should surrender their claims to the confederation. We shall by and by see, when we come to explain this point in detail, that from this action of Maryland there flowed beneficent consequences that were little dreamed of. It was first in the great chain of events which led directly to the formation of the Federal Union. Having carried her point, Maryland ratified the articles on the first day of March, 1781; and thus in the last and most brilliant period of the war, while Greene was leading Cornwallis on his fatal chase across North Carolina, the confederation proposed at the time of the Declaration of Independence was finally consummated.

According to the language of the articles, the states entered into a firm league of friendship with each other; and in order to secure and perpetuate such friendship, the freemen of each state were entitled to all the privileges and immunities of freemen in all the other states. Mutual extradition of criminals was established, and in each state full faith and credit was to be given to the records, acts, and judicial proceedings of every other state. This universal intercitizenship was what gave reality to the nascent and feeble Union. In all the common business relations of life, the man of New Hampshire could deal with the man of Georgia on an equal footing before the law. But this was almost the only effectively cohesive provision in the whole instrument. Throughout the remainder of the articles its language was largely devoted to reconciling the theory that the states were severally sovereign with the visible fact that they were already merged to some extent in a larger political body. The sovereignty of this larger body was vested in the Congress of delegates appointed yearly by the states. No state was to be represented by less than two or more than seven members; no one could be a delegate for more than three years out of every six ; and no delegate could hold any salaried office under the United States. As in colonial times the states had, to preserve their self-government, insisted upon paying their governors and judges, instead of allowing them to be paid out of the royal treasury, so now the delegates in Congress were paid by their own states. In determining questions in Congress, each state had one vote, without regard to population ; but a bare majority was not enough to carry any important measure. Not only for such extraordinary matters as wars and treaties, but even for the regular and ordinary business of raising money to carry on the government, not a single step could be taken without the consent of at least nine of the thirteen states; and this provision well-nigh sufficed of itself to block the wheels of federal legislation. The Congress assembled each year on the first Monday of November, and could not adjourn for a longer period than six months. During its recess the continuity of government was preserved by an executive committee, consisting of one delegate from each state, and known as the "committee of the states." Saving such matters of warfare or treaty as the public interest might require to be kept secret, all the proceedings of Congress were entered in a journal, to be published monthly ; and the yeas and nays must be entered should any delegate request it. The executive de-

partments of war, finance, and so forth were intrusted at first to committees, until experience soon
showed the necessity of single heads. There was
a president of Congress, who, as representing the
dignity of the United States, was, in a certain
sense, the foremost person in the country, but he
had no more power than any other delegate. Of
the fourteen presidents between 1774 and 1789,
perhaps only Randolph, Hancock, and Laurens are
popularly remembered in that capacity ; Jay, St.
Clair, Mifflin, and Lee are remembered for other
things ; Hanson, Griffin, and Boudinot are scarcely
remembered at all, save by the student of American history.

Between the Congress thus constituted and the
several state governments the attributes of sovereignty were shared in such a way as to produce
a minimum of result with a maximum of effort.
The states were prohibited from keeping up any
naval or military force, except militia, or from entering into any treaty or alliance, either with a
foreign power or between themselves, without the
consent of Congress. No state could engage in
war except by way of defence against a sudden Indian attack. Congress had the sole right of determining on peace and war, of sending and receiving
ambassadors, of making treaties, of adjudicating all
disputes between the states, of managing Indian
affairs, and of regulating the value of coin and fix-
ing the standard of weights and measures. Congress took control of the post-office on condition
that no more revenue should be raised from postage
than should suffice to discharge the expenses of the

service. Congress controlled the army, but was provided with no means of raising soldiers save through requisitions upon the states, and it could only appoint officers above the rank of colonel ; the organization of regiments was left entirely in the hands of the states. The traditional and wholesome dread of a standing army was great, but there was no such deep-seated jealousy of a navy, and Congress was accordingly allowed not only to appoint all naval officers, but also to establish courts of admiralty.

Several essential attributes of sovereignty were thus withheld from the states ; and by assuming all debts contracted by Congress prior to the adoption of the articles, and solemnly pledging the public faith for their payment, it was implicitly declared that the sovereignty here accorded to Congress was substantially the same as that which it had asserted and exercised ever since the severing of the connection with England. The articles simply defined the relations of the states to the Confederation as they had already shaped themselves. Indeed, the articles, though not finally ratified till 1781, had been known to Congress and to the people ever since 1776 as their expected constitution, and political action had been shaped in general accordance with the theory on which they had been drawn up. They show that political action was at no time based on the view of the states as absolutely sovereign, but they also show that the share of sovereignty accorded to Congress was very inadequate even to the purposes of an effective confederation. The position in which they left Congress was hardly more than that of the deliberative head of a league. For the most fundamental of all the attributes of sovereignty — the power of taxation — was not given to Congress. It could neither raise taxes through an excise nor through custom - house duties ; it could only make requisitions upon the thirteen members of the confederacy in proportion to the assessed value of their real estate, and it was not provided with any means of enforcing these requisitions. On this point the articles contained nothing beyond the vague promise of the states to obey. The power of levying taxes was thus retained entirely by the states. They not only imposed direct taxes, as they do to-day, but they laid duties on exports and imports, each according to its own narrow view of its local interests. The only restriction upon this was that such state-imposed duties must not interfere with the stipulations of any foreign treaties such as Congress might make in pursuance of treaties already proposed to the courts of France and Spain. Besides all this, the states shared with Congress the powers of coining money, of emitting bills of credit, and of making their promissory notes a legal tender for debts.

The articles failed to create a federal government endowed with real sovereignty.

Such was the constitution under which the United States had begun to drift toward anarchy even before the close of the Revolutionary War, but which could only be amended by the unanimous consent of all the thirteen states. The historian cannot but regard this difficulty of amendment as a fortunate circumstance ; for in the troubles which

presently arose it led the distressed people to seek
some other method of relief, and thus prepared the
way for the Convention of 1787, which destroyed
the whole vicious scheme, and gave us a form of
government under which we have just completed
a century unparalleled for peace and prosperity.
Besides this extreme difficulty of amendment, the
fatal defects of the Confederation were three in
number. The first defect was the two thirds vote
necessary for any important legislation in Congress;
under this rule any five of the states — as, for example, the four southernmost states with Maryland, or the four New England states with New
Jersey — could defeat the most sorely needed measures. The second defect was the impossibility of
presenting a united front to foreign countries in respect to commerce. The third and greatest defect
was the lack of any means, on the part of Congress,
of enforcing obedience. Not only was there no
federal executive or judiciary worthy of the name,
but the central government operated only upon
states, and not upon individuals. Congress could
call for troops and for money in strict conformity
with the articles; but should any state prove delinquent in furnishing its quota, there were no constitutional means of compelling it to obey the call.
This defect was seen and deplored at the outset
by such men as Washington and Madison, but the
only remedy which at first occurred to them was
one more likely to kill than to cure. Only six
weeks after the ratification of the articles, Madison
proposed an amendment " to give to the United
States full authority to employ their force, as well

by sea as by land, to compel any delinquent state
to fulfil its federal engagements." Washington
approved of this measure, hoping, as he said, that
" a knowledge that this power was lodged in Congress might be the means to prevent its ever being
exercised, and the more readily induce obedience.
Indeed," added Washington, " if Congress were
unquestionably possessed of the power, nothing
should induce the display of it but obstinate disobedience and the urgency of the general welfare."
Madison argued that in the very nature of the
Confederation such a right of coercion was necessarily implied, though not expressed in the articles, and much might have been said in behalf
of this opinion. The Confederation explicitly declared itself to be perpetual, yet how could it perpetuate itself for a dozen years without the right to
coerce its refractory members? Practically, however, the remedy was one which could never have
been applied without breaking the Confederation into fragments. To use the army or navy in
coercing a state meant nothing less than civil war.
The local yeomanry would have turned out against
the Continental army with as high a spirit as that
with which they swarmed about the British enemy
at Lexington or King's Mountain. A government
which could not collect the taxes for its yearly
budget without firing upon citizens or blockading
two or three harbours would have been the absurdest
political anomaly imaginable. No such idea could
have entered the mind of a statesman save from
the hope that if one state should prove refractory,
all the others would immediately frown upon it and

uphold Congress in overawing it. In such case the knowledge that Congress had the power would doubtless have been enough to make its exercise unnecessary. But in fact this hope was disappointed, for the delinquency of each state simply set an example of disobedience for all the others to follow; and the amendment, had it been carried, would merely have armed Congress with a threat which everybody would have laughed at. So manifestly hopeless was the case to Pelatiah Webster that as early as May, 1781, he published an able pamphlet, urging the necessity for a federal convention for overhauling the whole scheme of government from beginning to end.

The military weakness due to this imperfect governmental organization may be illustrated by comparing the number of regular troops which Congress was able to keep in the field during the Revolutionary War with the number maintained by the United States government during the War of Secession. A rough estimate, obtained from averages, will suffice to show the broad contrast. In 1863, the middle year of the War of Secession, the total population of the loyal states was about 23,491,600, of whom about one fifth, or 4,698,320, were adult males of military age. Supposing one adult male out of every five to have been under arms at one time, the number would have been 939,664. Now the total number of troops enlisted in the northern army during the four years of the war, reduced to a uniform standard, was 2,320,272, or an average of 580,068 under arms in any single year. In

Military weakness of the government.

point of fact, this average was reached before the middle of the war, and the numbers went on increasing, until at the end there were more than a million men under arms, — at least one out of every five adult males in the northern states. On the other hand, in 1779, the middle year of the Revolutionary War, the white population of the United States was about 2,175,000, of whom 435,000 were adult males of military age. Supposing one out of every five of these to have been under arms at once, the number would have been 87,000. Now in the spring of 1777, when the Continental Congress was at the highest point of authority which it ever reached, when France was willing to lend it money freely, when its paper currency was not yet discredited and it could make liberal offers of bounties, a demand was made upon the states for 80,000 men, or nearly one fifth of the adult male population, to serve for three years or during the war. Only 34,820 were obtained. The total number of men in the field in that most critical year, including the swarms of militia who came to the rescue at Ridgefield and Bennington and Oriskany, and the Pennsylvania militia who turned out while their state was invaded, was 68,720. In 1781, when the credit of Congress was greatly impaired, although military activity again rose to a maximum and it was necessary for the people to strain every nerve, the total number of men in the field, militia and all, was only 29,340, of whom only 13,292 were Continentals; and it was left for the genius of Washington and Greene, working with desperate energy and most pitiful resources, to save the country. A more impressive contrast to the readiness with which the demands of the government were met in the War of Secession can hardly be imagined. Had the country put forth its strength in 1781 as it did in 1864, an army of 90,000 men might have overwhelmed Clinton at the north and Cornwallis at the south, without asking any favours of the French fleet. Had it put forth its full strength in 1777, four years of active warfare might have been spared. Mr. Lecky explains this difference by his favourite hypothesis that the American Revolution was the work of a few ultra-radical leaders, with whom the people were not generally in sympathy; and he thinks we could not expect to see great heroism or self-sacrifice manifested by a people who went to war over what he calls a "money dispute."[1] But there is no reason for supposing that the loyalists represented the general sentiment of the country in the Revolutionary War any more than the peace party represented the general sentiment of the northern states in the War of Secession. There is no reason for supposing that the people were less at heart in 1781 in fighting for the priceless treasure of self-government than they were in 1864 when they fought for the maintenance of the pacific principles underlying our Federal Union. The differences in the organization of the government, and in its power of operating directly upon the people, are quite enough to explain the difference between the languid conduct of the earlier war and the energetic conduct of the later.

[1] *History of England in the Eighteenth Century*, iii. 447.

Impossible as Congress found it to fill the quotas of the army, the task of raising a revenue by requisitions upon the states was even more discouraging. Every state had its own war-debt, and several were applicants for foreign loans not easy to obtain, so that none could without the greatest difficulty raise a surplus to hand over to Congress. The Continental rag-money had ceased to circulate by the end of 1780, and our foreign credit was nearly ruined. The French government began to complain of the heavy demands which the Americans made upon its exchequer, and Vergennes, in sending over a new loan in the fall of 1782, warned Franklin that no more must be expected. To save American credit from destruction, it was at least necessary that the interest on the public debt should be paid. For this purpose Congress in 1781 asked permission to levy a five per cent. duty on imports. The modest request was the signal for a year of angry discussion. Again and again it was asked, If taxes could thus be levied by any power outside the state, why had we ever opposed the Stamp Act or the tea duties? The question was indeed a serious one, and as an instance of reasoning from analogy seemed plausible enough. After more than a year Massachusetts consented, by a bare majority of two in the House and one in the Senate, reserving to herself the right of appointing the collectors. The bill was then vetoed by Governor Hancock, though one day too late, and so it was saved. But Rhode Island flatly refused her consent, and so did Virginia, though Madison earnestly pleaded the cause

Extreme difficulty of obtaining a revenue.

of the public credit. For the current expenses of the government in that same year $9,000,000 were needed. It was calculated that $4,000,000 might be raised by a loan, and the other $5,000,000 were demanded of the states. At the end of the year $422,000 had been collected, not a cent of which came from Georgia, the Carolinas, or Delaware. Rhode Island, which paid $38,000, did the best of all according to its resources. Of the Continental taxes assessed in 1783, only one fifth part had been paid by the middle of 1785. And the worst of it was that no one could point to a remedy for this state of things, or assign any probable end to it.

Under such circumstances the public credit sank at home as well as abroad. Foreign creditors — even France, who had been nothing if not generous with her loans — might be made to wait; but there were creditors at home who, should they prove ugly, could not be so easily put off. The disbandment of the army in the summer of 1783, before the British troops had evacuated New York, was hastened by the impossibility of paying the soldiers and the dread of what they might do under such provocation. Though peace had been officially announced, Hamilton and Livingston urged that, for the sake of appearances if for no other reason, the army should be kept together so long as the British remained in New York, if not until they should have surrendered the western frontier posts. But Congress could not pay the army, and was afraid of it, — and not without some reason. Discouraged at the length of time which had passed since they had received any

Dread of the army.

money, the soldiers had begun to fear lest, now that their services were no longer needed, their honest claims would be set aside. Among the officers, too, there was grave discontent. In the spring of 1778, after the dreadful winter at Valley Forge, several officers had thrown up their commissions, and others threatened to do likewise. To avert the danger, Washington had urged Congress to promise half-pay for life to such officers as should serve to the end of the war. It was only with great difficulty that he succeeded in obtaining a promise of half-pay for seven years, and even this raised an outcry throughout the country, which seemed to dread its natural defenders only less than its enemies. In the fall of 1780, however, in the general depression which followed upon the disasters at Charleston and Camden, the collapse of the paper money, and the discovery of Arnold's treason, there was serious danger that the army would fall to pieces. At this critical moment Washington had earnestly appealed to Congress, and against the strenuous opposition of Samuel Adams had at length extorted the promise of half-pay for life. In the spring of 1782, seeing the utter inability of Congress to discharge its pecuniary obligations, many officers began to doubt whether the promise would ever be kept. It had been made before the articles of confederation, which required the assent of nine states to any such measure, had been finally ratified. It was well known that nine states had never been found to favour the measure, and it was now feared that it might be repealed or repudiated, so loud was the popular clamour against it. All this comes of republican government, said some of the officers; too many cooks spoil the broth; a dozen heads are as bad as no head; you do not know whose promises to trust; a monarchy, with a good king whom all men can trust, would extricate us from these difficulties. In this mood, Colonel Louis Nicola, of the Pennsylvania line, a foreigner by birth, addressed a long and well-argued letter to Washington, setting forth the troubles of the time, and urging him to come forward as a saviour of society, and accept the crown at the hands of his faithful soldiers. Nicola was an aged man, of excellent character, and in making this suggestion he seemed to be acting as spokesman of a certain clique or party among the officers, — how numerous is not known. Washington instantly replied that Nicola could not have found a person to whom such a scheme could be more odious, and he was at a loss to conceive what he had ever done to have it supposed that he could for one moment listen to a suggestion so fraught with mischief to his country. Lest the affair, becoming known, should enhance the popular distrust of the army, Washington said nothing about it. But as the year went by, and the outcry against half-pay continued, and Congress showed symptoms of a willingness to compromise the matter, the discontent of the army increased. Officers and soldiers brooded alike over their wrongs. " The army," said General Macdougall, " is verging to that state which, we are told, will make a wise man mad." The peril of the situation was increased by the

Supposed scheme for making Washington king.

well-meant but injudicious whisperings of other public creditors, who believed that if the army would only take a firm stand and insist upon a grant of permanent funds to Congress for liquidating all public debts, the states could probably be prevailed upon to make such a grant. Robert Morris, the able secretary of finance, held this opinion, and did not believe that the states could be brought to terms in any other way. His namesake and assistant, Gouverneur Morris, held similar views, and gave expression to them in February, 1783, in a letter to General Greene, who was still commanding in South Carolina. When Greene received the letter, he urged upon the legislature of that state, in most guarded and moderate language, the paramount need of granting a revenue to Congress, and hinted that the army would not be satisfied with anything less. The assembly straightway flew into a rage. "No dictation by a Cromwell!" shouted the members. South Carolina had consented to the five per cent. impost, but now she revoked it, to show her independence, and Greene's eyes were opened at once to the danger of the slightest appearance of military intervention in civil affairs.

At the same time a violent outbreak in the army at Newburgh was barely prevented by the unfailing tact of Washington. A rumour went about the camp that it was generally expected the army would not disband until the question of pay should be settled, and that the public creditors looked to them to make some such demonstration as would overawe the delinquent states. General Gates

had lately emerged from the retirement in which
he had been fain to hide himself after Camden,
and had rejoined the army where there was now
such a field for intrigue. An odious aroma of im-
potent malice clings about his memory on this last
occasion on which the historian needs to notice him.
He plotted in secret with officers of the staff and
others. One of his staff, Major Armstrong, wrote
an anonymous appeal to the troops, and another,
Colonel Barber, caused it to be circulated about
the camp. It named the next day for a meeting
to consider grievances. Its language was inflam-
matory. "My friends!" it said, "after
seven long years your suffering cour- The danger-
age has conducted the United States of March 11.
America through a doubtful and bloody 1783.
war ; and peace returns to bless — whom ? A
country willing to redress your wrongs, cherish
your worth, and reward your services ? Or is it
rather a country that tramples upon your rights,
disdains your cries, and insults your distresses ?
. . . If such be your treatment while the swords
you wear are necessary for the defence of America,
what have you to expect when those very swords,
the instruments and companions of your glory,
shall be taken from your sides, and no mark of
military distinction left but your wants, infirmities,
and scars ? If you have sense enough to discover
and spirit to oppose tyranny, whatever garb it
may assume, awake to your situation. If the present moment be lost, your threats hereafter will be
as empty as your entreaties now. Appeal from
the justice to the fears of government, and sus-

pect the man who would advise to longer forbearance."

Better English has seldom been wasted in a
worse cause. Washington, the man who was aimed
at in the last sentence, got hold of the paper next
day, just in time, as he said, " to arrest the feet
that stood wavering on a precipice." The memory
of the revolt of the Pennsylvania line, which had
so alarmed the people in 1781, was still fresh in
men's minds ; and here was an invitation to more
wholesale mutiny, which could hardly fail to end
in bloodshed, and might precipitate the perplexed
and embarrassed country into civil war. Washington issued a general order, recognizing the existence of the manifesto, but overruling it so far as
to appoint the meeting for a later day, with the
senior major-general, who happened to be Gates,
to preside. This order, which neither discipline
nor courtesy could disregard, in a measure tied
Gates's hands, while it gave Washington time to
ascertain the extent of the disaffection. On the
appointed day he suddenly came into the meeting,
and amid profoundest silence broke forth in a
most eloquent and touching speech. Sympathizing
keenly with the sufferings of his hearers, and fully
admitting their claims, he appealed to their better
feelings, and reminded them of the terrible difficulties under which Congress laboured, and of the
folly of putting themselves in the wrong. He still
counselled forbearance as the greatest of victories,
and with consummate skill he characterized the
anonymous appeal as undoubtedly the work of some
crafty emissary of the British, eager to disgrace

the army which they had not been able to vanquish.
All were hushed by that majestic presence and
those solemn tones. The knowledge that he had
refused all pay, while enduring more than any other
man in the room, gave added weight to every word.
In proof of the good faith of Congress he began
reading a letter from one of the members, when,
finding his sight dim, he paused and took from his
pocket the new pair of spectacles which the astron-
omer David Rittenhouse had just sent him. He
had never worn spectacles in public, and as he put
them on he said, in his simple manner and with
his pleasant smile, " I have grown gray in your
service, and now find myself growing blind."
While all hearts were softened he went on reading
the letter, and then withdrew, leaving the meeting
to its deliberations. There was a sudden and
mighty revulsion of feeling. A motion was reported declaring "unshaken confidence in the justice of Congress ; " and it was added that " the
officers of the American army view with abhorrence
and reject with disdain the infamous proposals contained in a late anonymous address to them." The
crestfallen Gates, as chairman, had nothing to do
but put the question and report it carried unanimously ; for if any still remained obdurate they no
longer dared to show it. Washington immediately
set forth the urgency of the case in an earnest
letter to Congress, and one week later the matter
was settled by an act commuting half-pay for life
into a gross sum equal to five years' full pay, to be
discharged at once by certificates bearing interest
at six per cent. Such poor paper was all that

Congress had to pay with, but it was all ultimately redeemed ; and while the commutation was advantageous to the government, it was at the same time greatly for the interest of the officers, while they were looking out for new means of livelihood, to have their claims adjusted at once, and to receive something which could do duty as a respectable sum of money.

Nothing, however, could prevent the story of the Newburgh affair from being published all over the country, and it greatly added to the distrust with which the army was regarded on general principles. What might have happened was forcibly suggested by a miserable occurrence in June, about two months after the disbanding of the army had begun. Some eighty soldiers of the Pennsylvania line, mutinous from discomfort and want of pay,

Congress driven from Philadelphia by mutinous soldiers, June 21, 1783.

broke from their camp at Lancaster and marched down to Philadelphia, led by a sergeant or two. They drew up in line before the state house, where Congress was assembled, and after passing the grog began throwing stones and pointing their muskets at the windows. They demanded pay, and threatened, if it were not forthcoming, to seize the members of Congress and hold them as hostages, or else to break into the bank where the federal deposits were kept. The executive council of Pennsylvania sat in the same building, and so the federal government appealed to the state government for protection. The appeal was fruitless. President Dickinson had a few state militia at his disposal, but did not dare to summon them, for fear they should side with the rioters. The city government was equally listless, and the townsfolk went their ways as if it were none of their business ; and so Congress fled across the river and on to Princeton, where the college afforded it shelter. Thus in a city of thirty-two thousand inhabitants, the largest city in the country, the government of the United States, the body which had just completed a treaty browbeating England and France, was ignominiously turned out-of-doors by a handful of drunken mutineers. The affair was laughed at by many, but sensible men keenly felt the disgrace, and asked what would be thought in Europe of a government which could not even command the services of the police. The army became more unpopular than ever, and during the summer and fall many town-meetings were held in New England, condemning the Commutation Act. Are we not poor enough already, cried the farmers, that we must be taxed to support in idle luxury a riotous rabble of soldiery, or create an aristocracy of men with gold lace and epaulets, who will presently plot against our liberties ? The Massachusetts legislature protested ; the people of Connecticut meditated resistance. A convention was held at Middletown in December, at which two thirds of the towns in the state were represented, and the best method of overruling Congress was discussed. Much high-flown eloquence was wasted, but the convention broke up without deciding upon any course of action. The matter had become so serious that wise men changed their minds, and disapproved of proceedings calculated to throw Congress into contempt.   Samuel Adams, who had almost violently opposed the grant of half-pay and had been dissatisfied with the Commutation Act, now came completely over to the other side.   Whatever might be thought of the policy of the measures, he said, Congress had an undoubted right to adopt them. The army had been necessary for the defence of our liberties, and the public faith had been pledged to the payment of the soldiers.   States were as much bound as individuals to fulfil their engagements, and did not the sacred Scriptures say of an honest man that, though he sweareth to his own hurt, he changeth not?   Such plain truths prevailed in the Boston town-meeting, which voted that "the commutation is wisely blended with the national debt."   The agitation in New England presently came to an end, and in this matter the course of Congress was upheld.

In order fully to understand this extravagant distrust of the army, we have to take into account another incident of the summer of 1783, which gave rise to a discussion that sent its reverberation all over the civilized world.   Men of the present generation who in childhood rummaged in their grandmothers' cosy garrets cannot fail to have come across scores of musty and worm-eaten pamphlets, their yellow pages crowded with italics and exclamation points, inveighing in passionate language against the wicked and dangerous society of the Cincinnati.   Just before the army was disbanded, the officers, at the suggestion of General Knox, formed themselves into a secret society, for the purpose of keeping up their friendly intercourse and cherishing the heroic memories of the struggle in which they had taken part. With the fondness for classical analogies which characterized that time, they likened themselves to Order of the Cincinnatus, who was taken from the Cincinnati. plough to lead an army, and returned to his quiet farm so soon as his warlike duties were over. They were modern Cincinnati. A constitution and by-laws were established for the order, and Washington was unanimously chosen to be its president. Its branches in the several states were to hold meetings each Fourth of July, and there was to be a general meeting of the whole society every year in the month of May. French officers who had taken part in the war were admitted to membership, and the order was to be perpetuated by descent through the eldest male representatives of the families of the members. It was further provided that a limited membership should from time to time be granted, as a distinguished honour, to able and worthy citizens, without regard to the memories of the war. A golden American eagle attached to a blue ribbon edged with white was the sacred badge of the order; and to this emblem especial favour was shown at the French court, where the insignia of foreign states were generally, it is said, regarded with jealousy. No political purpose was to be subserved by this order of the Cincinnati, save in so far as the members pledged to one another their determination to promote and cherish the union between the states. In its main intent the society was to be a kind of masonic brotherhood, charged with the duty of aiding the widows and the orphan children of its members in time of need.   Innocent as all this was, however, the news of the establishment of such a society was greeted with a howl of indignation all over the country.   It was thought that its founders were inspired by a deep-laid political scheme for centralizing the government and setting up a hereditary aristocracy.   The press teemed with invective and ridicule, and the feeling thus expressed by the penny-a-liners was shared by able men accustomed to weigh their words.   Franklin dealt with it in a spirit of banter, and John Adams in a spirit of abhorrence ; while Samuel Adams pointed out the dangers inherent in the principle of hereditary transmission of honours, and in the admission of foreigners into a secret association possessed of political influence in America.   What ! cried the men of Massachusetts.   Have we thrown overboard the effete institutions of Europe, only to have them straightway introduced among us again, after this plausible and surreptitious fashion ?   At Cambridge it was thought that the general sentiment of the university was in favour of suppressing the order by act of legislature.   One of the members, who was a candidate for senator in the spring of 1784, found it necessary to resign in order to save his chances for election.   Rhode Island proposed to disfranchise such of her citizens as belonged to the order, albeit her most eminent citizen, Nathanael Greene, was one of them.   Ædanus Burke, a judge of the Supreme Court of South Carolina, wrote a violent pamphlet against the society of the Cincinnati under the pseudonym of

Cassius, the slayer of tyrants; and this diatribe, translated and amplified by Mirabeau, awakened dull echoes among readers of Rousseau and haters of privilege in all parts of Europe. A swarm of brochures in rejoinder and rebutter issued from the press, and the nineteenth century had come in before the controversy was quite forgotten.

It is easy for us now to smile •at this outcry against the Cincinnati as much ado about nothing, seeing as we do that in the absence of territorial jurisdiction or especial political privileges an order of nobility cannot be created by the mere inheritance of empty titles or badges. For example, since the great revolution which swept away the landlordship and fiscal exemptions of the French nobility, a marquisate or a dukedom in France is of scarcely more political importance than a doctorate of laws in a New England university. Men were nevertheless not to be blamed in 1783 for their hostility toward that ghost of the hereditary principle which the Cincinnati sought to introduce. In a free industrial society like that of America it had no proper place or meaning; and the attempt to set up such a form might well have been cited in illustration of the partial reversion toward militancy which eight years of warfare had effected. The absurdity of the situation was quickly realized by Washington, and he prevailed upon the society, in its first annual meeting of May, 1784, to abandon the principle of hereditary membership. The agitation was thus allayed, and in the presence of graver questions the much-dreaded brotherhood gradually ceased to occupy popular attention.

The opposition to the Cincinnati is not fully explained unless we consider it in connection with Nicola's letter, the Newburgh address, and the flight of Congress to Princeton. The members of the Cincinnati were pledged to do whatever they could to promote the union between the states; the object of the Newburgh address was to enlist the army in behalf of the public creditors, and in some vaguely-imagined fashion to force a stronger government upon the country; the letter of Nicola shows that at least some of the officers had harboured the notion of a monarchy; and the weakness of Congress had been revealed in the most startling manner by its flight before a squad of mutineers. It is one of the lessons of history that, in the virtual absence of a central government for which a need is felt, the want is apt to be supplied by the strongest organization in the country, whatever that may happen to be. It was in this way that the French army, a few years later, got control of the government of France and made its general emperor. In 1783, if the impotence of Congress were to be as explicitly acknowledged as it was implicitly felt, the only national organization left in the country was the army, and when this was disbanded it seemed nevertheless to prolong its life under a new and dangerous form in the secret brotherhood of the Cincinnati. The cession of western lands to the confederacy was, moreover, completed at about this time, and one of the uses to which the new territory was to be put was the payment of claims due to the soldiers. It was distinctly feared, as is shown in a letter from Samuel Adams to Elbridge

Gerry, that the members of the Cincinnati would acquire large tracts of western land under this arrangement, and, importing peasants from Germany, would grant farms to them on terms of military service and fealty, thus introducing into America the feudal system. In order to forestall any such movement, it was provided by Congress that in any new states formed out of the western territory no person holding a hereditary title should be admitted to citizenship.

From the weakness of Congress as illustrated in its inability to raise money to pay the public debt and meet the current expenses of government, and from the popular dread of military usurpation which went along with the uneasy consciousness of that weakness, we have now to turn to another group of affairs in which the same point is still further illustrated and emphasized. We have seen how the commissioners of the United States in Paris had succeeded in making a treaty of peace with Great Britain on extremely favourable terms. So unpopular was the treaty in England, on account of the great concessions made to the Americans, that, as we have seen, the fall of Lord Shelburne's ministry was occasioned thereby. As an offset to these liberal concessions, of which the most considerable was the acknowledgment of the American claim *Congress finds itself unable to carry out the provisions of the treaty.* to the northwestern territory, our confederate government was pledged to do all in its power to effect certain concessions which were demanded by England. That the American loyalists, whose property had been confiscated by various state governments, should be indemnified for their losses was a claim which, whatever Americans might think of it, England felt bound in honour to urge. That private debts, due from American to British creditors, should be faithfully discharged was the plainest dictate of common honesty. Congress, as we have seen, was bound by the treaty to recommend to the several states to desist from the persecution of Tories, and to give them an opportunity of recovering their estates; and it had been further agreed that all private debts should be discharged at their full value in sterling money. It now turned out that Congress was powerless to carry out the provisions of the treaty upon either of these points. The recommendations concerning the Tories were greeted with a storm of popular indignation. Since the beginning of the war these unfortunate persons Persecution of had been treated with severity both by Tories. the legislatures and by the people. Many had been banished; others had fled the country, and against these refugees various harsh laws had been enacted. Their estates had been confiscated, and their return prohibited under penalty of imprisonment or death. Many others, who had remained in the country, were objects of suspicion and dislike in states where they had not, as in New York and the Carolinas, openly aided the enemy or taken part in Indian atrocities. Now, on the conclusion of peace, in utter disregard of Congress, fresh measures of vengeance were taken against these "fawning spaniels," as they were called, these "tools and minions of Britain." An article in the "Massachusetts Chronicle" expressed the common

feeling: "As Hannibal swore never to be at peace
with the Romans, so let every Whig swear, by
his abhorrence of slavery, by liberty and religion,
by the shades of departed friends who have fallen
in battle, by the ghosts of those of our brethren
who have been destroyed on board of prison-ships
and in loathsome dungeons, never to be at peace
with those fiends the refugees, whose thefts, mur-
ders, and treasons have filled the cup of woe."
Tons of pamphlets, issued under the customary
Latin pseudonyms, were filled with this truculent
bombast ; and like sentiments were thundered from
the pulpit by men who had quite forgotten for the
moment their duty of preaching reconciliation and
forgiveness of injuries. Why should not these
wretches, it was sarcastically asked, be driven at
once from the country ? Of course they could not
desire to live under a free government which they
had been at such pains to destroy. Let them go
forthwith to his majesty's dominions, and live under
the government they preferred. It would never
do to let them stay here, to plot treason at their
leisure ; in a few years they would get control of
all the states, and either hand them over to Great
Britain again, or set up a Tory despotism on American soil. Such was the rubbish that passed current
as argument with the majority of the people. A
small party of moderate Whigs saw its absurdity,
and urged that the Tories had much better remair
at home, where they had lost all political influence,
than go and found unfriendly colonies to the northward. The moderate Whigs were in favour of
heeding the recommendation of Congress, and act

ing in accordance with the spirit of the treaty ; and these humane and sensible views were shared by Gadsden and Marion in South Carolina, by Theodore Sedgwick in Massachusetts, and by Greene Hamilton, and Jay. But any man who held such opinions, no matter how conspicuous his services had been, ran the risk of being accused of Tory sympathies. "Time-serving Whigs " and " trimmers " were the strangely inappropriate epithets hurled at men who, had they been in the slightest degree time-servers, would have shrunk from the thankless task of upholding good sense and humanity in the teeth of popular prejudice.

In none of the states did the loyalists receive severer treatment than in New York, and for obvious reasons. Throughout the war the frontier had been the scene of atrocities such as no other state, save perhaps South Carolina, had witnessed. Cherry Valley and Minisink were names of horror not easily forgotten, and the fate of Lieutenant Boyd and countless other victims called loudly for vengeance. The sins of the Butlers and their bloodthirsty followers were visited in robbery and insult upon unoffending men, who were like them in nothing but in being labelled with the epithet " Tory." During the seven years that the city of New York had been occupied by the British army, many of these loyalists had found shelter there. The Whig citizens, on the other hand, had been driven off the island, to shift as best they might in New Jersey, while their comfortable homes were seized and assigned by military orders to these very Tories. For seven years the refugee Whigs

from across the Hudson had looked upon New York with feelings like those with which the mediæval exile from Florence or Pisa was wont to regard his native city. They saw in it the home of enemies who had robbed them, the prison-house of gallant friends penned up to die of wanton ill-usage in foul ships' holds in the harbour. When at last the king's troops left the city, it was felt that a great day of reckoning had arrived. In September, 1783, two months before the evacuation, more than twelve thousand men, women, and children embarked for the Bahamas or for Nova Scotia, rather than stay and face the troubles that were coming. Many of these were refined and cultivated persons, and not all had been actively hostile to the American cause ; many had simply accepted British protection. Against those who remained in the city the returning Whigs now proceeded with great severity. The violent party was dominant in the legislature, and George Clinton, the governor, put himself conspicuously at its head. A bill was passed disfranchising all such persons as had voluntarily stayed in neighbourhoods occupied by the British troops; their offence was called misprision of treason. But the council vetoed this bill as too wholesale in its operation, for it would have left some districts without voters enough to hold an election. An " iron-clad oath " was adopted instead, and no one was allowed to vote unless he could swear that he had never in anywise abetted the enemy. It was voted that no Tory who had left the state should be permitted to return ; and a bill was passed

The Trespass Act of New York, 1784.

known as the Trespass Act, whereby all persons who had quit their homes by reason of the enemy's presence might recover damages in an action of trespass against such persons as had since taken possession of the premises. Defendants in such cases were expressly barred from pleading a military order in justification of their possession. As there was scarcely a building on the island of New York that had not thus changed hands during the British occupation, it was easy to foresee what confusion must ensue. Everybody whose house had once been, for ever so few days, in the hands of a Tory now rushed into court with his action of trespass. Damages were rated at most exorbitant figures, and it became clear that the misdeeds of the enemy were about to be made the excuse for a carnival of spoliation, when all at once the test case of Rutgers *v.* Waddington brought upon the scene a sturdy defender of order, an advocate who was soon to become one of the foremost personages in American history.

Of all the young men of that day, save perhaps William Pitt, the most precocious was Alexander Hamilton. He had already given promise of a great career before the breaking out of the war.

Alexander Hamilton. He was born on the island of Nevis, in the West Indies, in 1757. His father belonged to that famous Scottish clan from which have come one of the most learned metaphysicians and one of the most original mathematicians of modern times. His mother was a French lady, of Huguenot descent, and biographers have been fond of tracing in his character the various qualities of his parents. To the shrewdness and persistence, the administrative ability, and the taste for abstract reasoning which we are wont to find associated in the highest type of Scottish mind he joined a truly French vivacity and grace. His earnestness, sincerity, and moral courage were characteristic alike of Puritan and of Huguenot. In the course of his short life he exhibited a remarkable many-sidedness. So great was his genius for organization that in many essential respects the American government is moving to-day along the lines which he was the first to mark out. As an economist he shared to some extent in the shortcomings of the age which preceded Adam Smith, but in the special department of finance he has been equalled by no other American statesman save Albert Gallatin. He was a splendid orator and brilliant writer, an excellent lawyer, and a clear-headed and industrious student of political history. He was also eminent as a political leader, although he lacked faith in democratic government, and a generous impatience of temperament sometimes led him to prefer short and arbitrary by-paths toward desirable ends, which can never be securely reached save along the broad but steep and arduous road of popular conviction. But with all Hamilton's splendid qualities, nothing about him is so remarkable as the early age at which these were developed. At the age of fifteen a brilliant newspaper article brought him into such repute in the little island of Nevis that he was sent to New York to avail himself of the best advantages afforded by the King's College, now known

as Columbia. He had at first no definite intention
of becoming an American citizen, but the thrilling
events of the time appealed strongly to the earnest
heart and powerful intelligence of this wonderful
boy. At a gathering of the people of New York
in July, 1774, his generous blood warmed, till a
resistless impulse brought him on his feet to speak
to the assembled multitude. It was no company
of half-drunken idlers that thronged about him, but
an assemblage of grave and responsible citizens,
who looked with some astonishment upon this boy
of seventeen years, short and slight in stature, yet
erect and Cæsar-like in bearing, with firm set
mouth and great, dark, earnest eyes. His eloquent
speech, full of sense and without a syllable of bombast, held his hearers entranced, and from that day
Alexander Hamilton was a marked man. He began publishing anonymous pamphlets, which at
first were attributed by some to Jay, and by others
to Livingston. When their authorship was dis-
covered, the loyalist party tried in vain to buy off
the formidable youth. He kept up the pamphlet-
war, in the course of which he wofully defeated
Dr. Cooper, the Tory president of the college; but
shortly afterward he defended the doctor's house
against an angry mob, until that unpopular gentleman had succeeded in making his escape to a British ship. Hamilton served in the army throughout
the war, for the most part as aid and secretary to
Washington; but in 1781 he was a colonel in the
line, and stormed a redoubt at Yorktown with
distinguished skill and bravery. He married a
daughter of Philip Schuyler, began the practice of

*l*aw, and in 1782, at the age of twenty-five, was chosen a delegate to Congress.

In 1784, when the Trespass Act threw New York into confusion, Hamilton had come to be regarded as one of the most powerful advocates in the country. In the test case which now came before the courts he played a part of consummate boldness and heroism. Elizabeth Rutgers was a widow, who had fled from New York after its capture by General Howe. Her confiscated estate had passed into the hands of Joshua Waddington, a rich Tory merchant, and she now brought suit under the Trespass Act for its recovery. It was a case in which popular sympathy was naturally and strongly enlisted in behalf of the poor widow. That she should have been turned out of house and home was one of the many gross instances of wickedness wrought by the war. On the other hand, the disturbance wrought by the enforcement of the Trespass Act was already creating fresh wrongs much faster than it was righting old ones; and it is for such reasons as this that both in the common law and in the law of nations the principle has been firmly established that "the fruits of immovables belong to the captor as long as he remains in actual possession of them." The Trespass Act contravened this principle, and it also contravened the treaty. It moreover placed the state of New York in an attitude of defiance toward Congress, which had made the treaty and expressly urged upon the states to suspend the legislation against the Tories. On large grounds of public policy, therefore, the Trespass Act de-

The case of
Rutgers *v.*
Waddington.

served to be set aside by the courts, and when Hamilton was asked to serve as counsel for the defendant he accepted the odious task without hesitation. There can be no better proof of his forensic ability than his winning a verdict, in such a case as this, from a hostile court that was largely influenced by the popular excitement. The decision nullified the Trespass Act, and forthwith mass meetings of the people and an extra session of the legislature condemned this action of the court. Hamilton was roundly abused, and his conduct was attributed to unworthy motives. But he faced the people as boldly as he had faced the court, and published a letter, under the signature of Phocion, setting forth in the clearest light the injustice and impolicy of extreme measures against the Tories. The popular wrath and disgust at Hamilton's course found expression in a letter from one Isaac Ledyard, a hot-headed pot-house politician, who signed himself Mentor. A war of pamphlets ensued between Mentor and Phocion. It was genius pitted against dulness, reason against passion; and reason wielded by genius won the day. The more intelligent and respectable citizens reluctantly admitted that Hamilton's arguments were unanswerable. A club of boon companions, to which Ledyard belonged, made the same admission by the peculiar manner in which it proposed to silence him. It was gravely proposed that the members of the club should pledge themselves one after another to challenge Hamilton to mortal combat, until some one of them should have the good fortune to kill him! The scheme met with general favour, but was defeated by the exertions of Ledyard himself, whose zeal was not ardent enough to condone treachery and murder. The incident well illustrates the intense bitterness of political passion at the time, as Hamilton's conduct shows him in the light of a most courageous and powerful defender of the central government. For nothing was more significant in the verdict which he had obtained than its implicit assertion of the rights of the United States as against the legislature of a single state.

In spite of the efforts of such men as Hamilton, life was made very uncomfortable for the Tories. In some states they were subjected to mob violence. Instances of tarring and feathering were not uncommon. The legislature of South Carolina was honourably distinguished for the good faith with which it endeavoured to enforce the recommendation of Congress; but the people, unable to forget the smoking ruins of plundered homes, were less lenient. Notices were posted ordering prominent loyalists to leave the country; the newspapers teemed with savage warnings; and finally, of those who tarried beyond a certain time, many were shot or hanged to trees. This extremity of bitterness, however, did not long continue. The instances of physical violence were mostly confined to the first two or three years after the close of the war. In most of the states the confiscating acts were after a while repealed, and many of the loyalists were restored to their estates. But the emigration which took place between 1783 and 1785 was very large. It has been esti- Emigration of Tories.

mated that 100,000 persons, or nearly three per cent. of the total white population, quit the country. Those from the southern states went mostly to the Bahamas and Florida ; while those from the north laid the foundation of new British states in New Brunswick and Upper Canada. Many of these refugees appealed to the British government for indemnification for their losses, and their claims received prompt attention. A parliamentary commission was appointed to inquire into the matter, and by the year 1790 some $16,000,000 had been distributed among about 4,000 sufferers, while many others received grants of crown-lands, or half-pay as military officers, or special annuities, or appointments in the civil service. On the whole, the compensation which the refugees received from Parliament seems to have been much more ample than that which the ragged soldiers of our Revolutionary army ever received from Congress.

While the political passions resulting in this forced emigration of loyalists were such as naturally arise in the course of a civil war, the historian cannot but regret that the United States should have been deprived of the services of so many excellent citizens. In nearly all such cases of wholesale popular vengeance, it is the wrong individuals who suffer. We could well afford to dispense with the border-ruffians who abetted the Indians in their carnival of burning and scalping, but the refugees of 1784 were for the most part peaceful and unoffending families, above the average in education and refinement. The vicarious suffering inflicted upon them set nothing right, but simply increased the mass of wrong, while to the general interests of the country the loss of such people was in every way damaging. The immediate political detriment wrought at the time, though it is that which here most nearly concerns us, was perhaps the least important. Since Congress was manifestly unable to carry out the treaty, an excuse was furnished to England for declining to fulfil some of its provisions. In regard to the loyalists, indeed, the treaty had recognized that Congress possessed but an advisory power; but in the other provision concerning the payment of private debts, which in the popular mind was very much mixed up with the question of justice to the loyalists, the faith of the United States was distinctly pledged. On this point also Congress was powerless to enforce the treaty. Massachusetts, New York, Pennsylvania, Maryland, Virginia, and South Carolina had all enacted laws obstructing the collection of British debts; and in flat defiance of the treaty these statutes remained in force until after the downfall of the Confederation. The states were aware that such conduct needed an excuse, and one was soon forthcoming. Many negroes had left the country with the British fleet : some doubtless had sought their freedom ; others, perhaps, had been kidnapped as booty, and sold to planters in the West Indies. The number of these black men carried away by the fleet had been magnified tenfold by popular rumour. Complaints had been made to Sir Guy Carleton, but he had replied that any negro who came within his lines was pre-

Congress is unable to enforce payment of debts to British creditors. England retaliates by refusing to surrender the western posts.

sumably a freeman, and he could not lend his aid in remanding such persons to slavery. Jay, as one of the treaty commissioners, gave it as his opinion that Carleton was quite right in this, but he thought that where a loss of slaves could be proved, Great Britain was bound to make pecuniary compensation to the owners. The matter was wrangled over for several years, in the state legislatures, in town and county meetings, at dinner-tables, and in bar-rooms, with the general result that, until such compensation should be made, the statutes hindering the collection of debts would not be repealed. In retaliation for this, Great Britain refused to withdraw her garrisons from the western fortresses, which the treaty had surrendered to the United States. This measure was very keenly felt by the people. As an assertion of superior strength, it was peculiarly galling to our weak and divided confederacy, and it also wrought us direct practical injury. It encouraged the Indian tribes in their depredations on the frontier, and it deprived American merchants of an immensely lucrative trade in furs. In the spring of 1787 there were advertised for sale in London more than 360,000 skins, worth $1,200,-000 at the lowest estimate; and had the posts been surrendered according to the treaty, all this would have passed through the hands of American merchants. The London fur-traders were naturally loth to lose their control over this business, and in the language of modern politics they brought "pressure" to bear on the government to retain the fortresses as long as possible. The American refusal to pay British creditors furnished an excellent excuse, while the weakness of Congress made any kind of reprisal impossible; and it was not until Washington's second term as president, after our national credit had been restored and the strength of our new government made manifest, that England surrendered this chain of strongholds, commanding the woods and waters of our north-western frontier.

CHAPTER IV.

DRIFTING TOWARD ANARCHY.

AT the close of the eighteenth century the bar-barous superstitions of the Middle Ages concerning trade between nations still flourished with scarcely diminished vitality. The epoch-making work of Adam Smith had been published in the same year in which the United States declared their independence. The one was the great scientific event, as the other was the great political event of the age ; but of neither the one nor the other were the scope and purport fathomed at the time. Among the foremost statesmen, those who, like Shelburne and Gallatin, understood the principles of the "Wealth of Nations" were few indeed.

Barbarous su-perstitions about trade. The simple principle that when two parties trade both must be gainers, or one would soon stop trading, was generally lost sight of ; and most commercial legislation proceeded upon the theory that in trade, as in gambling or betting, what the one party gains the other must lose. Hence towns, districts, and nations surrounded themselves with walls of legislative restrictions intended to keep out the monster Trade, or to admit him only on strictest proof that he could do no harm. On this barbarous theory, the use of a colony consisted in its being a customer

which you could compel to trade with yourself,
while you could prevent it from trading with anybody else ; and having secured this point, you
could cunningly arrange things by legislation so as
to throw all the loss upon this enforced customer,
and keep all the gain to yourself. In the seventeenth and eighteenth centuries all the commercial
legislation of the great colonizing states was based
upon this theory of the use of a colony. For effectiveness, it shared to some extent the characteristic features of legislation for making water run
up hill. It retarded commercial development all
over the world, fostered monopolies, made the rich
richer and the poor poorer, hindered the interchange of ideas and the refinement of manners,
and sacrificed millions of human lives in misdi-
rected warfare ; but what it was intended to do it
did not do. The sturdy race of smugglers — those
despised pioneers of a higher civilization — thrived
in defiance of kings and parliaments ; and as it
was impossible to carry out such legislation thoroughly without stopping trade altogether, colonies
and mother countries contrived to increase their
wealth in spite of it. The colonies, however, understood the animus of the theory in so far as it
was directed against them, and the revolutionary
sentiment in America had gained much of its
strength from the protest against this one-sided
justice. In one of its most important aspects, the
Revolution was a deadly blow aimed at the old
system of trade restrictions. It was to a certain
extent a step in realization of the noble doctrines
of Adam Smith. But where the scientific thinker

grasped the whole principle involved in the matter, the practical statesmen saw only the special application which seemed to concern them for the moment. They all understood that the Revolution had set them free to trade with other countries than England, but very few of them understood that, whatever countries trade together, the one cannot hope to benefit by impoverishing the other.

This point is much better understood in England to-day than in the United States; but a century ago there was little to choose between the two countries in ignorance of political economy. England had gained great wealth and power through trade with her rapidly growing American colonies. One of her chief fears, in the event of American independence, had been the possible loss of that trade. English merchants feared that American commerce, when no longer confined to its old paths by legislation, would somehow find its way to France and Holland and Spain and other countries, until nothing would be left for England. The Revolution worked no such change, however. The principal trade of the United States was with England, as before, because England could best supply the goods that Americans wanted; and it is such considerations, and not acts of Parliament, that determine trade in its natural and proper channels. In 1783 Pitt introduced into Parliament a bill which would have secured mutual unconditional free trade between the two countries; and this was what such men as Franklin, Jefferson, and Madison desired. Could this bill have passed, the hard feelings occasioned by the war would soon have

died out, the commercial progress of both countries
would have been promoted, and the stupid measures which led to a second war within thirty years
might have been prevented. But the wisdom of
Pitt found less favour in Parliament than the dense
stupidity of Lord Sheffield, who thought that to
admit Americans to the carrying trade would undermine the naval power of Great Britain. Pitt's
measure was defeated, and the regulation of commerce with America was left to the king in council. Orders were forthwith passed as if upon the
theory that America poor would be a better customer than America rich.

The carrying trade to the West Indies had been
one of the most important branches of American
industry. The men of New England
were famous for seamanship, and better and cheaper ships could be built in
the seaports of Massachusetts than anywhere in
Great Britain. An oak vessel could be built at
Gloucester or Salem for twenty-four dollars per
ton ; a ship of live-oak or American cedar cost not
more than thirty-eight dollars per ton. On the
other hand, fir vessels built on the Baltic cost
thirty-five dollars per ton, and nowhere in England, France, or Holland could a ship be made of
oak for less than fifty dollars per ton. Often the
cost was as high as sixty dollars. It was not
strange, therefore, that before the war more than
one third of the tonnage afloat under the British
flag was launched from American dock-yards. The
war had violently deprived England of this enormous advantage, and now she sought to make the

Shipbuilding in New England.

privation perpetual, in the delusive hope of confining British trade to British keels, and in the belief that it was the height of wisdom to impoverish the nation which she regarded as her best customer. In July, 1783, an order in council proclaimed that henceforth all trade between the United States and the British West Indies must be carried on in British-built ships, owned and navigated by British subjects. A serious blow was thus dealt not only at American shipping, but also at the interchange of commodities between the states and the islands, which was greatly hampered by this restriction. During the whole of the eighteenth century the West India sugar trade with the North American colonies and with Great Britain had been of immense value to all parties, and all had been seriously damaged by the curtailment of it due to the war. Now that the artificial state of things created by the war was to be perpetuated by legislation, the prospect of repairing the loss seemed indefinitely postponed. Moreover, even in trading directly with Great Britain, American ships were only allowed to bring in articles produced in the particular states of which their owners were citizens, — an enactment which seemed to add insult to injury, inasmuch as it directed especial attention to the want of union among the thirteen states. Great indignation was aroused in America, and reprisals were talked of, but efforts were first made to obtain a commercial treaty.

British navigation acts and orders in council directed against American commerce.

In 1785 Franklin returned from France, and Jefferson was sent as minister in his stead, while

John Adams became the first representative of the
United States at the British court.   Adams was
at first very courteously received by George III.,
and presently set to work to convince Lord Car-
marthen, the foreign secretary, of the desirableness
of unrestricted intercourse between the two countries.   But popular opinion in England
was obstinately set against him.   But _{John Adams}
for the Navigation Act and the orders
in council, it was said, all ships would
by and by come to be built in America, and every
time a frigate was wanted for the navy the Lords
of Admiralty would have to send over to Boston
or Philadelphia and order one.   Rather than do
such a thing as this, it was thought that the British
navy should content itself with vessels of inferior
workmanship and higher cost, built in British dock-
yards.   Thirty years after, England gathered an
unexpected fruit of this narrow policy, when, to
her intense bewilderment, she saw frigate after
frigate outsailed and defeated in single combat
with American antagonists.   Owing to her exclusive measures, the rapid improvement in American
shipbuilding had gone on quite beyond her ken,
until she was thus rudely awakened to it.   With
similar short-sighted jealousy, it was argued that
the American share in the whale-fishery and in the
Newfoundland fishery should be curtailed as much
as possible.   Spermaceti oil was much needed in
England : complaints were rife of robbery and
murder in the dimly lighted streets of London and
other great cities.   But it was thought that if
American ships could carry oil to England and

salt fish to Jamaica, the supply of seamen for the British navy would be diminished; and accordingly such privileges must not be granted the Americans unless valuable privileges could be granted in return. But the government of the United States could grant no privileges because it could impose no restrictions. British manufactured goods were needed in America, and Congress, which could levy no duties, had no power to keep them out. British merchants and manufacturers, it was argued, already enjoyed all needful privileges in American ports, and accordingly they asked no favours and granted none.

Such were the arguments to which Adams was obliged to listen. The popular feeling was so strong that Pitt could not have stemmed it if he would. It was in vain that Adams threatened reprisals, and urged that the British measures would defeat their own purpose. "The end of the Navigation Act," said he, "as expressed in its own preamble, is to confine the commerce of the colonies to the mother country; but now we are become independent states, instead of confining our trade to Great Britain, it will drive it to other countries." and he suggested that the Americans might make a navigation act in their turn, admitting to American ports none but American-built ships, owned and commanded by Americans. But under the articles of confederation such a threat was idle, and the British government knew it to be so. Thirteen separate state governments could never be made to adopt any such measure in concert. The weakness of Congress had been fatally revealed in its inability to protect the loyalists or to enforce the payment of debts, and in its failure to raise a revenue for meeting its current expenses. A government thus slighted at home was naturally despised abroad. England neglected to send a minister to Philadelphia, and while Adams was treated politely, his arguments were unheeded. Whether in this behaviour Pitt's government was influenced or not by political as well as economical reasons, it was certain that a political purpose was entertained by the king and approved by many people. There was an intention of humiliating the Americans, and it was commonly said that under a sufficient weight of commercial distress the states would break up their feeble union, and come straggling back, one after another, to their old allegiance. The fiery spirit of Adams could ill brook this contemptuous treatment of the nation which he represented. Though he favoured very liberal commercial relations with the whole world, he could see no escape from the present difficulties save in systematic retaliation. " I should be sorry," he said, " to adopt a monopoly, but, driven to the necessity of it, I would not do things by halves. . . . If monopolies and exclusions are the only arms of defence against monopolies and exclusions, I would venture upon them without fear of offending Dean Tucker or the ghost of Dr. Quesnay." That is to say, certain commercial privileges must be withheld from Great Britain, in order to be offered to her in return for reciprocal privileges. It was a miserable policy to be forced to adopt, for such restrictions upon trade inevitably cut both ways. Like the non-importa tion agreement of 1768 and the embargo of 1808, such a policy was open to the objections familiarly urged against biting off one's own nose. It was injuring one's self in the hope of injuring somebody else. It was perpetuating in time of peace the obstacles to commerce generated by a state of war. In a certain sense, it was keeping up warfare by commercial instead of military methods, and there was danger that it might lead to a renewal of armed conflict. Nevertheless, the conduct of the British government seemed to Adams to leave no other course open. But such " means of preserving ourselves," he said, " can never be secured until Congress shall be made supreme in foreign commerce."

It was obvious enough that the separate action of the states upon such a question was only adding to the general uncertainty and confusion. In 1785 New York laid a double duty on all goods whatever imported in British ships. In the same year Pennsylvania passed the first of the long series of American tariff acts, designed to tax the whole community for the alleged benefit of a few greedy manufacturers. Massachusetts sought to establish committees of correspondence for the purpose of entering into a new non-importation agreement, and its legislature resolved that " the present powers of the Congress of the United States, as contained in the articles of confederation, are not fully adequate to the great purposes they were originally designed to effect." The Massachusetts delegates in Congress — Gerry, Holton, and King

Reprisal impossible; the states impose conflicting duties.

– were instructed to recommend a general convention of the states for the purpose of revising and
amending the articles of confederation; but the
delegates refused to comply with their instructions,
and set forth their reasons in a paper which was
approved by Samuel Adams, and caused the legislature to reconsider its action. It was feared that
a call for a convention might seem too much like
an open expression of a want of confidence in Congress, and might thereby weaken it still further
without accomplishing any good result. For the
present, as a temporary expedient, Massachusetts
took counsel with New Hampshire, and the two
states passed navigation acts, prohibiting British
ships from carrying goods out of their harbours,
and imposing a fourfold duty upon all such goods
as they should bring in. A discriminating tonnage
duty was also laid upon all foreign vessels. Rhode
Island soon after adopted similar measures. In
Congress a scheme for a uniform navigation act,
to be concurred in and passed by all the thirteen
states, was suggested by one of the Maryland delegates; but it was opposed by Richard Henry Lee
and most of the delegates from the far south.
The southern states, having no ships or seamen
of their own, feared that the exclusion of British
competition might enable northern ship-owners to
charge exorbitant rates for carrying their rice and
tobacco, thus subjecting them to a ruinous monopoly; but the gallant Moultrie, then governor of
South Carolina, taking a broader view of the case,
wrote to Bowdoin, governor of Massachusetts, asserting the paramount need of harmonious and

united action. In the Virginia assembly, a hot-headed member, named Thurston, declared himself in doubt " whether it would not be better to encourage the British rather than the eastern marine ; " but the remark was greeted with hisses and groans, and the speaker was speedily put down. Amid such mutual jealousies and misgivings, during the year 1785 acts were passed by ten states granting to Congress the power of regulating commerce for the ensuing thirteen years. The three states which refrained from acting were Georgia, South Carolina, and Delaware. The acts of the other ten were, as might have been expected, a jumble of incongruities. North Carolina granted all the power that was asked, but stipulated that when all the states should have done likewise their acts should be summed up in a new article of confederation. Connecticut, Pennsylvania, and Maryland had fixed the date at which the grant was to take effect, while Rhode Island provided that it should not expire until after the lapse of twenty-five years. The grant by New Hampshire allowed the power to be used only in one specified way, — by restricting the duties imposable by the several states. The grants of Massachusetts, New York, New Jersey, and Virginia were not to take effect until all the others should go into operation. The only thing which Congress could do with these acts was to refer them back to the several legislatures, with a polite request to try to reduce them to something like uniformity.

Meanwhile, the different states, with their different tariff and tonnage acts, began to make commercial war upon one another. No sooner had the other three New England states virtually closed their ports to British shipping than Connecticut threw hers wide open, an act which she followed up by laying duties upon imports from Massachusetts. Penn- Commercial war between different states. sylvania discriminated against Delaware, and New Jersey, pillaged at once by both her greater neigh- bours, was compared to a cask tapped at both ends. The conduct of New York became especially selfish and blameworthy. That rapid growth which was so soon to carry the city and the state to a position of primacy in the Union had already begun. After the departure of the British the revival of business went on with leaps and bounds. The feeling of local patriotism waxed strong, and in no one was it more completely manifested than in George Clin- ton, the Revolutionary general, whom the people elected governor for nine successive terms. From a humble origin, by dint of shrewdness and untir- ing push, Clinton had come to be for the moment the most powerful man in the state of New York. He had come to look upon the state almost as if it were his own private manor, and his life was de- voted to furthering its interests as he understood them. It was his first article of faith that New York must be the greatest state in the Union. But his conceptions of statesmanship were ex- tremely narrow. In his mind, the welfare of New York meant the pulling down and thrusting aside of all her neighbours and rivals. He was the vigor- ous and steadfast advocate of every illiberal and exclusive measure, and the most uncompromising enemy to a closer union of the states. His great popular strength and the commercial importance of the community in which he held sway made him at this time the most dangerous man in America. The political victories presently to be won by Hamilton, Schuyler, and Livingston, without which our grand and pacific federal union could not have been brought into being, were victories won by most desperate fighting against the dogged opposition of Clinton. Under his guidance, the history of New York, during the five years following the peace of 1783, was a shameful story of greedy monopoly and sectional hate. Of all the thirteen states, none behaved worse except Rhode Island.

A single instance, which occurred early in 1787, may serve as an illustration. The city of New York, with its population of 30,000 souls, had long been supplied with firewood from Connecticut, and with butter and cheese, chickens and garden vegetables, from the thrifty farms of New Jersey. This trade, it was observed, carried thousands of dollars out of the city and into the pockets of detested Yankees and despised Jerseymen. It was ruinous to domestic industry, said the men of New York. It must be stopped by those effective remedies of the Sangrado school of economic doctors, a navigation act and a protective tariff. Acts were accordingly passed, obliging every Yankee sloop which came down through Hell Gate, and every Jersey market boat which was rowed across from Paulus Hook to Cortlandt Street, to pay entrance fees and obtain clearances at the custom-house, just as was done by ships from London or

Hamburg; and not a cart-load of Connecticut fire-wood could be delivered at the back-door of a country-house in Beekman Street until it should have paid a heavy duty. Great and just was the wrath of the farmers and lumbermen. The New Jersey legislature made up its mind to retaliate. The city of New York had lately bought a small patch of ground on Sandy Hook, and had built a light-house there. This light-house was the one weak spot in the heel of Achilles where a hostile arrow could strike, and New Jersey gave vent to her indignation by laying a tax of $1,800 a year on it. Connecticut was equally prompt. At a great meeting of business men, held at New London, it was unanimously agreed to suspend all commercial intercourse with New York. Every merchant signed an agreement, under penalty of $250 for the first offence, not to send any goods whatever into the hated state for a period of twelve months. By such retaliatory measures, it was hoped that New York might be compelled to rescind her odious enactment. But such meetings and such resolves bore an ominous likeness to the meetings and resolves which in the years before 1775 had heralded a state of war ; and but for the good work done by the federal convention another five years would scarcely have elapsed before shots would have been fired and seeds of perennial hatred sown on the shores that look toward Manhattan Island.

To these commercial disputes there were added disputes about territory. The chronic quarrel between Connecticut and Pennsylvania over the valley of Wyoming was decided in the autumn of 1782

by a special federal court, appointed in accordance with the articles of confederation.

Disputes about
territory; dis-
asters in the
valley of Wyo-
ming, 1784.
The prize was adjudged to Pennsylvania, and the government of Connecticut submitted as gracefully as possible.
But new troubles were in store for the inhabitants
of that beautiful region. The traces of the massacre of 1778 had disappeared, the houses had been
rebuilt, new settlers had come in, and the pretty
villages had taken on their old look of content-
ment and thrift, when in the spring of 1784 there
came an accumulation of disasters. During a very
cold winter great quantities of snow had fallen,
and lay piled in huge masses on the mountain
sides, until in March a sudden thaw set in. The
Susquehanna rose, and overflowed the valley, and
great blocks of ice drifted here and there, carrying
death and destruction with them. Houses, barns,
and fences were swept away, the cattle were
drowned, the fruit trees broken down, the stores
of food destroyed, and over the whole valley there
lay a stratum of gravel and pebbles. The people
were starving with cold and hunger, and President
Dickinson urged the legislature to send prompt relief to the sufferers. But the hearts of the members were as flint, and their talk was incredibly
wicked. Not a penny would they give to help the
accursed Yankees. It served them right. If they
had stayed in Connecticut, where they belonged,
they would have kept out of harm's way. And
with a blasphemy thinly veiled in phrases of pious
unction, the desolation of the valley was said to
have been contrived by the Deity with the express

object of punishing these trespassers. But the cruelty of the Pennsylvania legislature was not confined to words. A scheme was devised for driving out the settlers and partitioning their lands among a company of speculators. A force of militia was sent to Wyoming, commanded by a truculent creature named Patterson. The ostensible purpose was to assist in restoring order in the valley, but the behaviour of the soldiers was such as would have disgraced a horde of barbarians. They stole what they could find, dealt out blows to the men and insults to the women, until their violence was met with violence in return. Then Patterson sent a letter to President Dickinson, accusing the farmers of sedition, and hinting that extreme measures were necessary. Having thus, as he thought, prepared the way, he attacked the settlement, turned some five hundred people out-of-doors, and burned their houses to the ground. The wretched victims, many of them tender women, or infirm old men, or little children, were driven into the wilderness at the point of the bayonet, and told to find their way to Connecticut without further delay. Heartrending scenes ensued. Many died of exhaustion, or furnished food for wolves. But this was more than the Pennsylvania legislature had intended. Patterson's zeal had carried him too far. He was recalled, and the sheriff of Northumberland County was sent, with a posse of men, to protect the settlers. Patterson disobeyed, however, and withdrawing his men to a fortified lair in the mountains, kept up a guerilla warfare. All the Connecticut men in the neighbouring country flew to arms.

Men were killed on both sides, and presently Patterson was besieged. A regiment of soldiers was then sent from Philadelphia, under Colonel Armstrong, who had formerly been on Gates's staff, the author of the incendiary Newburgh address. On arriving in the valley, Armstrong held a parley with the Connecticut men, and persuaded them to lay down their arms; assuring them on his honour that they should meet with no ill treatment, and that their enemy, Patterson, should be disarmed also. Having thus fallen into this soldier's clutches, they were forthwith treated as prisoners. Seventy-six of them were handcuffed and sent under guard, some to Easton and some to Northumberland, where they were thrown into jail.

Great was the indignation in New England when these deeds were heard of. The matter had become very serious. A war between Connecticut and Pennsylvania might easily grow out of it. But the danger was averted through a very singular feature in the Pennsylvania constitution. In order to hold its legislature in check, Pennsylvania had a council of censors, which was assembled once in seven years in order to inquire whether the state had been properly governed during the interval. Soon after the troubles in Wyoming the regular meeting of the censors was held, and the conduct of Armstrong and Patterson was unreservedly condemned. A hot controversy ensued between the legislature and the censors, and as the people set great store by the latter peculiar institution, public sympathy was gradually awakened for the sufferers. The wickedness of the affair began to dawn upon

people's minds, and they were ashamed of what had
been done. Patterson and Armstrong were frowned
down, the legislature disavowed their acts, and it
was ordered that full reparation should be made to
the persecuted settlers of Wyoming.[1]

In the Green Mountains and on the upper waters
of the Connecticut there had been trouble for
many years. In the course of the Revolutionary
War, the fierce dispute between New York and
New Hampshire for the possession of the Green
Mountains came in from time to time to influence
most curiously the course of events. It was closely
connected with the intrigues against General
Schuyler, and thus more remotely with the Conway
cabal and the treason of Arnold. About the time
of Burgoyne's invasion the association of Green
Mountain Boys endeavoured to cut the Gordian knot
by declaring Vermont an independent
state, and applying to the Continental
Congress for admission into the Union.
The New York delegates in Congress succeeded in
defeating this scheme, but the Vermont people went
on and framed their constitution. Thomas Chittenden, a man of rough manners but very considerable
ability, a farmer and innkeeper, like Israel Putnam, was chosen governor, and held that position
for many years. New Hampshire thus far had not
actively opposed these measures, but fresh grounds
of quarrel were soon at hand. Several towns on
the east bank of the Connecticut River wished to

Troubles in the Green Mountains, 1777-84.

---

[1] A very interesting account of these troubles may be found in
the first volume of Professor McMaster's *History of the People of
the United States.*

escape from the jurisdiction of New Hampshire. They preferred to belong to Vermont, because it was not within the Union, and accordingly not liable to requisitions of taxes from the Continental Congress. It was conveniently remembered that by the original grant, in the reign of Charles II., New Hampshire extended only sixty miles from the coast. Vermont was at first inclined to assent, but finding the scheme unpopular in Congress, and not wishing to offend that body, she changed her mind. The towns on both banks of the river then tried to organize themselves into a middle state, — a sort of Lotharingia on the banks of this New World Rhine, — to be called New Connecticut. By this time New Hampshire was aroused, and she called attention to the fact that she still believed herself entitled to dominion over the whole of Vermont. Massachusetts now began to suspect that the upshot of the matter would be the partition of the whole disputed territory between New Hampshire and New York, and, ransacking her ancient grants and charters, she decided to set up a claim on her own part to the southernmost towns in Vermont. Thus goaded on all sides, Vermont adopted an aggressive policy. She not only annexed the towns east of the Connecticut River, but also asserted sovereignty over the towns in New York as far as the Hudson. New York sent troops to the threatened frontier, New Hampshire prepared to do likewise, and for a moment war seemed inevitable. But here, as in so many other instances, Washington appeared as peacemaker, and prevailed upon Governor Chittenden to use his influence in getting the dangerous claims withdrawn. After the spring of 1784 the outlook was less stormy in the Green Mountains. The conflicting claims were allowed to lie dormant, but the possibilities of mischief remained, and the Vermont question was not finally settled until after the adoption of the Federal Constitution. Meanwhile, on the debatable frontier between Vermont and New York the embers of hatred smouldered. Barns and houses were set on fire, and belated wayfarers were found mysteriously murdered in the depths of the forest.

Incidents like these of Wyoming and Vermont seem trivial, perhaps, when contrasted with the lurid tales of border warfare in older times between half-civilized peoples of mediæval Europe, as we read them in the pages of Froissart and Sir Walter Scott. But their historic lesson is none the less clear. Though they lift the curtain but a little way, they show us a glimpse of the untold dangers and horrors from which the adoption of our Federal Constitution has so thoroughly freed us that we can only with some effort realize how narrowly we have escaped them. It is fit that they should be borne in mind, that we may duly appreciate the significance of the reign of law and order which has been established on this continent during the greater part of a century. When reported in Europe, such incidents were held to confirm the opinion that the American confederacy was going to pieces. With quarrels about trade and quarrels about boundaries, we seemed to be treading the old-fashioned paths of anarchy, even as they had been trodden in other ages and other parts of the world. It was natural that people in Europe should think so, because there was no historic precedent to help them in forming a different opinion. No one could possibly foresee that within five years a number of gentlemen at Philadelphia, containing among themselves a greater amount of political sagacity than had ever before been brought together within the walls of a single room, would amicably discuss the situation and agree upon a new system of government whereby the dangers might be once for all averted. Still less could any one foresee that these gentlemen would not only agree upon a scheme among themselves, but would actually succeed, without serious civil dissension, in making the people of thirteen states adopt, defend, and cherish it. History afforded no example of such a gigantic act of constructive statesmanship. It was, moreover, a strange and apparently fortuitous combination of circumstances that were now preparing the way for it and making its accomplishment possible. No one could forecast the future. When our ministers and agents in Europe raised the question as to making commercial treaties, they were disdainfully asked whether European powers were expected to deal with thirteen governments or with one. If it was answered that the United States constituted a single government so far as their relations with foreign powers were concerned, then we were forthwith twitted with our failure to keep our engagements with England with regard to the loyalists and the collection of private debts. Yes, we see, said the European diplomats; the United States

One nation or thirteen?

are one nation to-day and thirteen to-morrow, according as may seem to subserve their selfish interests. Jefferson, at Paris, was told again and again
that it was useless for the French government to
enter into any agreement with the United States,
as there was no certainty that it would be fulfilled
on our part; and the same things were said all
over Europe. Toward the close of the war most
of the European nations had seemed ready to enter
into commercial arrangements with the United
States, but all save Holland speedily lost interest
in the subject. John Adams had succeeded in
making a treaty with Holland in 1782. Frederick
the Great treated us more civilly than other
sovereigns. One of the last acts of his life was to
conclude a treaty for ten years with the United
States; asserting the principle that free ships
make free goods, taking arms and military stores
out of the class of contraband, agreeing to refrain
from privateering even in case of war between the
two countries, and in other respects showing a
liberal and enlightened spirit.

This treaty was concluded in 1786. It scarcely
touched the subject of international trade in time
of peace, but it was valuable as regarded the matters it covered, and in the midst of the general
failure of American diplomacy in Europe it fell
pleasantly upon our ears. Our diplomacy had
failed because our weakness had been proclaimed
to the world. We were bullied by England, in-
sulted by France and Spain, and looked askance
at in Holland. The humiliating position in which
our ministers were placed by the beggarly poverty

of Congress was something almost beyond credence. It was by no means unusual for the superintendent of finance, when hard pushed for money, to draw upon our foreign ministers, and then sell the drafts for cash.   This was not only not unusual; it was **an** established custom.   It was done again and **again**, when there was not the smallest ground for supposing that the minister upon whom the draft **was** made would have any funds wherewith to meet **it.**   He must go and beg the money.   That was part of his duty as envoy, — to solicit loans without security for a government that could not raise enough money by taxation to defray its current

Failure of American credit; John Adams begging in Holland, 1784. expenses.   It was sickening work.   Just before John Adams had been appointed minister to England, and while he was visiting in London, he suddenly learned that drafts upon him had been presented to his bankers in Amsterdam to the amount of more than **a** million florins.   Less than half a million florins were on hand to meet these demands, and unless something were done at once the greater part of this paper would go back to America protested. Adams lost not a moment in starting for Holland. In these modern days of precision in travel, when we can translate space into time, the distance between London and Amsterdam is eleven hours.   It was accomplished by Adams, after innumerable delays and vexations and no little danger, in fifty-four days.   The bankers had contrived, by ingenious excuses, to keep the drafts from going to protest until the minister's arrival, but the gazettes **were** full of the troubles of Congress and the bick

erings of the states, and everybody was suspicious.
Adams applied in vain to the regency of Amster-
lam. The promise of the American government
was not regarded as valid security for a sum equivalent to about three hundred thousand dollars.
The members of the regency were polite, but inexorable. They could not make a loan on such
terms; it was unbusinesslike and contrary to precedent. Finding them immovable, Adams was
forced to apply to professional usurers and Jew
brokers, from whom, after three weeks of perplexity and humiliation, he obtained a loan at exorbitant interest, and succeeded in meeting the
drafts. It was only too plain, as he mournfully
confessed, that American credit was dead. Such
were the trials of our American ministers in Europe
in the dark days of the League of Friendship. It
was not a solitary, but a typical, instance. John
Jay's experience at the unfriendly court of Spain
was perhaps even more trying.

European governments might treat us with cold
disdain, and European bankers might pronounce
our securities worthless, but there was one quarter
of the world from which even worse measure was
meted out to us. Of all the barbarous communities with which the civilized world has had to deal
in modern times, perhaps none have made so much
trouble as the Mussulman states on the southern
shore of the Mediterranean. After the breaking
up of the great Moorish kingdoms of the Middle
Ages, this region had fallen under the nominal
control of the Turkish sultans as lords paramount
of the orthodox Mohammedan world. Its miser-

able populations became the prey of banditti.
Swarms of half-savage chieftains settled down upon

The Barbary pirates. the land like locusts, and out of such a pandemonium of robbery and murder
as has scarcely been equalled in historic times the
pirate states of Morocco and Algiers, Tunis and
Tripoli, gradually emerged. Of these communities
history has not one good word to say. In these
fair lands, once illustrious for the genius and virtues of a Hannibal and the profound philosophy of
St. Augustine, there grew up some of the most terrible despotisms ever known to the world. The
things done daily by the robber sovereigns were
such as to make a civilized imagination recoil with
horror. One of these cheerful creatures, who
reigned in the middle of the eighteenth century,
and was called Muley Abdallah, especially prided
himself on his peculiar skill in mounting a horse.
Resting his left hand upon the horse's neck, as he
sprang into the saddle he simultaneously swung
the sharp scimiter in his right hand so deftly as to
cut off the head of the groom who held the bridle.
From his behaviour in these sportive moods one
may judge what he was capable of on serious occasions. He was a fair sample of the Barbary mon-
archs. The foreign policy of these wretches was
summed up in piracy and blackmail. Their cor-
sairs swept the Mediterranean and ventured far
out upon the ocean, capturing merchant vessels,
and murdering or enslaving their crews. Of the
rich booty, a fixed proportion was paid over to the
robber sovereign, and the rest was divided among
the gang. So lucrative was this business that it

attracted hardy ruffians from all parts of Europe, and the misery they inflicted upon mankind during four centuries was beyond calculation. One of their favourite practices was the kidnapping of eminent or wealthy persons, in the hope of extorting ransom. Cervantes and Vincent de Paul were among the celebrated men who thus tasted the horrors of Moorish slavery; but it was a calamity that might fall to the lot of any man or woman, and it was but rarely that the victims ever regained their freedom.

Against these pirates the governments of Europe contended in vain. Swift cruisers frequently captured their ships, and from the days of Joan of Arc down to the days of Napoleon their skeletons swung from long rows of gibbets on all the coasts of Europe, as a terror and a warning. But their losses were easily repaired, and sometimes they cruised in fleets of seventy or eighty sail, defying the navies of England and France. It was not until after England, in Nelson's time, had acquired supremacy in the Mediterranean that this dreadful scourge was destroyed. Americans, however, have just ground for pride in recollecting that their government was foremost in chastising these pirates in their own harbours. The exploits of our little navy in the Mediterranean at the beginning of the present century form an interesting episode in American history, but in the weak days of the Confederation our commerce was American citizens kidnapped. plundered with impunity, and American citizens were seized and sold into slavery in the markets of Algiers and Tripoli. One reason for the long survival of this villainy was the low state of humanity among European nations. An Englishman's sympathy was but feebly aroused by the plunder of Frenchmen, and the bigoted Spaniard looked on with approval so long as it was Protestants that were kidnapped and bastinadoed. In 1783 Lord Sheffield published a pamphlet on the commerce of the United States, in which he shamelessly declared that the Barbary pirates were really useful to the great maritime powers, because they tended to keep the weaker nations out of their share in the carrying trade. This, he thought, was a valuable offset to the Empress Catherine's device of the armed neutrality, whereby small nations were protected; and on this wicked theory, as Franklin tells us, London merchants had been heard to say that "if there were no Algiers, it would be worth England's while to build one." It was largely because of such feelings that the great states of Europe so long persisted in the craven policy of paying blackmail to the robbers, instead of joining in a crusade and destroying them.

In 1786 Congress felt it necessary to take measures for protecting the lives and liberties of American citizens. The person who called himself "Emperor" of Morocco at that time was different from most of his kind. He had a taste for reading, and had thus caught a glimmering of the enlightened liberalism which French philosophers were preaching. He wished to be thought a benevolent despot, and with Morocco, accordingly, Congress succeeded in making a treaty. But nothing could be done with the other pirate states without paying black

mail. Few scenes in our history are more amusing, or more irritating, than the interview of John
Adams with an envoy from Tripoli in London.
The oily-tongued barbarian, with his soft voice and
his bland smile, asseverating that his only interest
in life was to do good and make other people happy
stands out in fine contrast with the blunt, straightforward, and truthful New Englander; and their
conversation reminds one of the old story of Cœur-
de-Lion with his curtal-axe and Saladin with the
blade that cut the silken cushion. Adams felt sure
that the fellow was either saint or devil, but could
not quite tell which. The envoy's love <small>Tripoli de-</small>
for mankind was so great that he could <small>mands blackmail, Feb.</small>
not bear the thought of hostility between <small>1786.</small>
the Americans and the Barbary States, and he
suggested that everything might be happily arranged for a million dollars or so. Adams thought
it better to fight than to pay tribute. It would be
cheaper in the end, as well as more manly. At the
same time, it was better economy to pay a million
dollars at once than waste many times that sum in
war risks and loss of trade. But Congress could
do neither one thing nor the other. It was too
poor to build a navy, and too poor to buy off the
pirates ; and so for several years to come American
ships were burned and American sailors enslaved
with utter impunity. With the memory of such
wrongs deeply graven in his heart, it was natural
that John Adams, on becoming president of the
United States, should bend his energies toward
founding a strong American navy.

A government touches the lowest point of ignominy when it confesses its inability to protect the lives and property of its citizens. A government

which has come to this has failed in discharging the primary function of government, and forthwith ceases to have any reason for existing. In March, 1786, Grayson wrote to Madison that several members of Congress thought seriously of recommending a general convention for remodelling the government. "I have not made up my mind," says Grayson, "whether it would not be better to bear the ills we have than fly to those we know not of. I am, however, in no doubt about the weakness of the federal government. If it remains much longer in its present state of imbecility, we shall be one of the most contemptible nations on the face of the earth." "It is clear to me as A, B, C," said Washington, "that an extension of federal powers would make us one of the most happy, wealthy, respectable, and powerful nations that ever inhabited the terrestrial globe. Without them we shall soon be everything which is the direct reverse. I predict the worst consequences from a half-starved, limping government, always moving upon crutches and tottering at every step."

There is no telling how long the wretched state of things which followed the Revolution might have continued, had not the crisis been precipitated by the wild attempts of the several states to remedy the distress of the people by legislation.

That financial distress was widespread and deep-seated was not to be denied. At the beginning of the war the amount of accumulated capital in the country had been very small. The great majority of the people did little more than get from the annual yield of their farms or plantations enough to meet the current expenses of the year. Outside of agriculture the chief resources were the carrying trade, the exchange of commodities with England and the West Indies, and the cod and whale fisheries; and in these occupations many people had grown rich. The war had destroyed all these sources of revenue. Imports and exports had alike been stopped, so that there was a distressing scarcity of some of the commonest household articles. The enemy's navy had kept us from the fisheries. Before the war, the dock-yards of Nantucket were ringing with the busy sound of adze and hammer, rope-walks covered the island, and two hundred keels sailed yearly in quest of spermaceti. At the return of peace, the docks were silent and grass grew in the streets. The carrying trade and the fisheries began soon to revive, but it was some years before the old prosperity was restored. The war had also wrought serious damage to agriculture, and in some parts of the country the direct destruction of property by the enemy's troops had been very great. To all these causes of poverty there was added the hopeless confusion due to an inconvertible paper currency. The worst feature of this financial device is that it not only impoverishes people, but bemuddles their brains by creating a false and fleeting show of prosperity. By violently disturbing apparent values, it always brings on an era of wild speculation and extravagance in living, followed by sudden collapse and protracted suffering. In such

crises the poorest people, those who earn their
bread by the sweat of their brows and have no
margin of accumulated capital, always suffer the
most. Above all men, it is the labouring man who
needs sound money and steady values. We have
seen all these points amply illustrated since the
War of Secession. After the War of Independence, when the margin of accumulated capital was
so much smaller, the misery was much greater.
While the paper money lasted there was marked
extravagance in living, and complaints were loud
against the speculators, especially those who operated in bread-stuffs. Washington said he would
like to hang them all on a gallows higher than that
of Haman ; but they were, after all, but the inevitable products of this abnormal state of things, and
the more guilty criminals were the demagogues who
went about preaching the doctrine that the poor
man needs cheap money. After the collapse of
this continental currency in 1780, it seemed as if
there were no money in the country, and at the
peace the renewal of trade with England seemed at
first to make matters worse. The brisk importation of sorely needed manufactured goods, which
then began, would naturally have been paid for in
the south by indigo, rice, and tobacco, in the middle states by exports of wheat and furs, and in
New England by the profits of the fisheries, the
shipping, and the West India trade. But in the
southern and middle states the necessary revival
of agriculture could not be effected in a moment,
and British legislation against American shipping
and the West India trade fell with crippling force

upon New England. Consequently, we had little
else but specie with which to pay for imports, and
the country was soon drained of what little specie
there was. In the absence of a circulating medium
there was a reversion to the practice of barter, and
the revival of business was thus further impeded.
Whiskey in North Carolina, tobacco in Virginia,
did duty as measures of value ; and Isaiah Thomas,
editor of the Worcester " Spy," announced that he
would receive subscriptions for his paper in salt
pork.

It is worth while, in this connection, to observe
what this specie was, the scarcity of which created
so much embarrassment. Until 1785 no national
coinage was established, and none was issued until
1793. English, French, Spanish, and German
coins, of various and uncertain value, passed from
hand to hand. Beside the ninepences <small>State of the</small>
and fourpence-ha'-pennies, there were <small>coinage.</small>
bits and half-bits, pistareens, picayunes, and fips.
Of gold pieces there were the johannes, or joe, the
doubloon, the moidore, and pistole, with English
and French guineas, carolins, ducats, and chequins.
Of coppers there were English pence and half-
pence and French sous ; and pennies were issued
at local mints in Vermont, Massachusetts, Connecticut, New Jersey, and Pennsylvania. The English shilling had everywhere degenerated in value,
but differently in different localities ; and among
silver pieces the Spanish dollar, from Louisiana
and Cuba, had begun to supersede it as a measure
of value. In New England the shilling had sunk
from nearly one fourth to one sixth of a dollar ; in

New York to one eighth; in North Carolina to one tenth. It was partly for this reason that in devis- ng a national coinage the more uniform dollar was adopted as the unit. At the same time the decimal system of division was adopted instead of the cum- brous English system, and the result was our pres- ent admirably simple currency, which we owe to Gouverneur Morris, aided as to some points by Thomas Jefferson. During the period of the Con- federation, the chaotic state of the currency was a serious obstacle to trade, and it afforded endless opportunities for fraud and extortion. Clipping and counterfeiting were carried to such lengths that every moderately cautious person, in taking payment in hard cash, felt it necessary to keep a small pair of scales beside him and carefully weigh each coin, after narrowly scrutinizing its stamp and deciphering its legend.

In view of all these complicated impediments to business on the morrow of a long and costly war, it was not strange that the whole country was in some measure pauperized. The cost of the war, estimated in cash, had been about $170,000,000 — a huge sum if we consider the circumstances of the country at that time. To meet this crush-

Cost of the war; Robert Morris and his immense ser- vices.

ing indebtedness Mr. Hildreth reckons the total amount raised by the states, whether by means of repudiated paper or of taxes, down to 1784, as not more than $30,- 000,000. No wonder if the issue of such a strug- gle seemed quite hopeless. In many parts of the country, by the year 1786, the payment of taxes had come to be regarded as an amiable eccentri-

city. At one moment, early in 1782, there was not
a single dollar in the treasury. That the government had in any way been able to finish the
war, after the downfall of its paper money, was due
to the gigantic efforts of one great man, — Robert
Morris, of Pennsylvania. This statesman was
born in England, but he had come to Philadelphia
in his boyhood, and had amassed an enormous fortune, which he devoted without stint to the service
of his adopted country. Though opposed to the
Declaration of Independence as rash and premature, he had, nevertheless, signed his name to that
document, and scarcely any one had contributed
more to the success of the war. It was he who
supplied the money which enabled Washington to
complete the great campaign of Trenton and
Princeton. In 1781 he was made superintendent
of finance, and by dint of every imaginable device
of hard-pressed ingenuity he contrived to support
the brilliant work which began at the Cowpens
and ended at Yorktown. He established the Bank
of North America as an instrument by which government loans might be negotiated. Sometimes
his methods were such as doctors call heroic, as
when he made sudden drafts upon our ministers in
Europe after the manner already described. In
every dire emergency he was Washington's chief
reliance, and in his devotion to the common weal
he drew upon his private resources until he became
poor ; and in later years — for shame be it said —
an ungrateful nation allowed one of its noblest and
most disinterested champions to languish in a debt-
or's prison. It was of ill omen for the fortunes of

the weak and disorderly Confederation that in 1784, after three years of herculean struggle with impossibilities, this stout heart and sagacious head could no longer weather the storm. The task of creating wealth out of nothing had become too arduous and too thankless to be endured. Robert Morris resigned his place, and it was taken by a congressional committee of finance, under whose management the disorders only hurried to a crisis.

By 1786, under the universal depression and want of confidence, all trade had well-nigh stopped, and political quackery, with its cheap and dirty remedies, had full control of the field. In the very face of miseries so plainly traceable to the deadly paper currency, it may seem strange that people should now have begun to clamour for a renewal of the experiment which had worked so much evil. Yet so it was. As starving men are said to dream of dainty banquets, so now a craze for fictitious wealth in the shape of paper money ran like an epidemic through the country. There was a Barmecide feast of economic vagaries ; only now it was the several states that sought to apply the remedy, each in its own way. And when we have threaded the maze of this rash legislation, we shall the better understand that clause in our federal constitution which forbids the making of laws impairing the obligation of contracts. The events of 1786 impressed upon men's minds more forcibly than ever the wretched and disorderly condition of the country, and went far toward calling into existence the needful popular sentiment in favour of an overruling central government.

The craze for paper-money, 1786.

The disorders assumed very different forms in the different states, and brought out a great diversity of opinion as to the causes of the distress and the efficacy of the proposed remedies. Only two states out of the thirteen — Connecticut and Delaware — escaped the infection, but, on the other hand, it was only in seven states that the paper money party prevailed in the legislatures. North Carolina issued a large amount of paper, and, in order to get it into circulation as quickly as possible, the state government proceeded to buy tobacco with it, paying double the specie value of the tobacco. As a natural consequence, the paper dollar instantly fell to seventy cents, and went on declining. In South Carolina an issue was tried somewhat more cautiously, but the planters soon refused to take the paper at its face value. Coercive measures were then attempted. Planters and merchants were urged to sign a pledge not to discriminate between paper and gold, and if any one dared refuse the fanatics forthwith attempted to make it hot for him. A kind of "Kuklux" society was organized at Charleston, known as the "Hint Club." Its purpose was to hint to such people that they had better look out. If they did not mend their ways, it was unnecessary to inform them more explicitly what they might expect. Houses were combustible then as now, and the use of firearms was well understood. In Georgia the legislature itself attempted coercion. Paper money was made a legal tender in spite of strong opposition, and a law was passed prohibiting any planter or merchant from exporting any produce without taking affidavit that he had never refused to receive this scrip at its full face value. But somehow people found that the more it was sought to keep up the paper by dint of threats and forcing acts, the faster its value fell. Virginia had issued bills of credit during the campaign of 1781, but it was enacted at the same time that they should not be a legal tender after the next January. The influence of Washington, Madison, and Mason was effectively brought to bear in favour of sound currency, and the people of Virginia were but slightly affected by the craze of 1786. In the autumn of that year a proposition from two counties for an issue of paper was defeated in the legislature by a vote of eighty-five to seventeen, and no more was heard of the matter. In Maryland, after a very obstinate fight, a rag money bill was carried in the house of representatives, but the senate threw it out; and the measure was thus postponed until the discussion over the federal constitution superseded it in popular interest. Pennsylvania had warily begun in May, 1785, to issue a million dollars in bills of credit, which were not made a legal tender for the payment of private debts. They were mainly loaned to farmers on mortgage, and were received by the state as an equivalent for specie in the payment of taxes. By August, 1786, even this carefully guarded paper had fallen some twelve cents below par, — not a bad showing for such a year as that. New York moved somewhat less cautiously. A million dollars were issued in bills of credit receivable for the custom-house duties, which were then paid into the state treasury ; and these bills were made a legal tender for all money received in law- suits. At the same time the New Jersey legisla- ture passed a bill for issuing half a million paper dollars, to be a legal tender in all business trans- actions. The bill was vetoed by the governor in council. The aged Governor Livingston was greatly respected by the people ; and so the mob at Elizabethtown, which had duly planted a stake and dragged his effigy up to it, refrained from inflict- ing the last indignities upon the image, and burned that of one of the members of the council instead. At the next session the governor yielded, and the rag money was issued. But an unforeseen diffi- culty arose. Most of the dealings of New Jersey people were in the cities of New York and Phila- delphia, and in both cities the merchants refused their paper, so that it speedily became worthless.

The business of exchange was thus fast getting into hopeless confusion. It has been said of Brad- shaw's Railway Guide, the indispensable compan- ion of the traveller in England, that no man can study it for an hour without qualifying himself for an insane asylum. But Bradshaw is pellucid clear- ness compared with the American tables of ex- change in 1786, with their medley of dollars and shillings, moidores and pistareens. The addition of half a dozen different kinds of paper created such a labyrinth as no human intellect could ex- plore. No wonder that men were counted wise who preferred to take whiskey and pork instead. No- body who had a yard of cloth to sell could tell how much it was worth. But even worse than all this was the swift and certain renewal of bankruptcy which so many states were preparing for them-selves.

Nowhere did the warning come so quickly or so sharply as in New England. Connecticut, indeed, as already observed, came off scot-free. She had issued a little paper money soon after the battle of Lexington, but had stopped it about the time of the surrender of Burgoyne. In 1780 she had wisely and summarily adjusted all relations be-tween debtor and creditor, and the crisis of 1786 found her people poor enough, no doubt, but able to wait for better times and indisposed to adopt violent remedies. It was far otherwise in Rhode Island and Massachusetts. These were preëmi-nently the maritime states of the Union, and upon them the blows aimed by Eng-land at American commerce had fallen most se-verely. It was these two maritime states that suf-fered most from the cutting down of the carrying trade and the restriction of intercourse with the West Indies. These things worked injury to ship-building, to the exports of lumber and oil and salted fish, even to the manufacture of Medford rum. Nowhere had the normal machinery of busi-ness been thrown out of gear so extensively as in these two states, and in Rhode Island there was the added disturbance due to a prolonged occupa-tion by the enemy's troops. Nowhere, perhaps, was there a larger proportion of the population in debt, and in these preëminently commercial com-munities private debts were a heavier burden and involved more personal suffering than in the some-

Distress in New England.

what patriarchal system of life in Virginia or
South Carolina. In the time of which we are now
treating, imprisonment for debt was common.
High-minded but unfortunate men were carried to
jail, and herded with thieves and ruffians in loathsome dungeons, for the crime of owing a hundred
dollars which they could not promptly pay. Under
such circumstances, a commercial disturbance, in-
volving widespread debt, entailed an amount of
personal suffering and humiliation of which, in
these kinder days, we can form no adequate conception. It tended to make the debtor an outlaw,
ready to entertain schemes for the subversion of
society. In the crisis of 1786, the agitation in
Rhode Island and Massachusetts reached white
heat, and things were done which alarmed the
whole country. But the course of events was different in the two states. In Rhode Island the agitators obtained control of the government, and the
result was a paroxysm of ·tyranny. In Massachusetts the agitators failed to secure control of the
government, and the result was a paroxysm of rebellion.

The debates over paper money in the Rhode Isl-
and legislature began in 1785, but the advocates
of a sound currency were victorious. These men
were roundly abused in the newspapers, and in the
next spring election most of them lost their seats.
The legislature of 1786 showed an overwhelming
majority in favor of paper money. The farmers
from the inland towns were unanimous in supporting the measure. They could not see the difference
between the state making a dollar out of paper and

a dollar out of silver. The idea that the value did not lie in the government stamp they dismissed as an idle crotchet, a wire-drawn theory, worthy only of "literary fellows." What they could see was the glaring fact that they had no money, hard or soft ; and they wanted something that would satisfy their creditors and buy new gowns for their wives, whose raiment was unquestionably the worse for wear. On the other hand, the merchants from seaports like Providence, Newport, and Bristol understood the difference between real money and the promissory notes of a bankrupt government, but they were in a hopeless minority. Half a million dollars were issued in scrip, to be loaned to the farmers on a mortgage of their real estate. No one could obtain the scrip without giving a mortgage for twice the amount, and it was thought that this security would make it as good as gold. But the depreciation began instantly. When the worthy farmers went to the store for dry goods or sugar, and found the prices rising with dreadful rapidity, they were at first astonished, and then enraged. The trouble, as they truly said, was with the wicked merchants, who would not take the paper dollars at their face value. These men were thus thwarting the government, and must be punished. An act was accordingly hurried through the legislature, commanding every one to take paper as an equivalent for gold, under penalty of five hundred dollars fine and loss of the right of suffrage. The merchants in the cities thereupon shut up their shops. During the summer of 1786 all

Rag money victorious in Rhode Island; the "Know Ye" measures.

business was at a standstill in Newport and Providence, except in the bar-rooms. There and about
the market-places men spent their time angrily discussing politics, and scarcely a day passed without
street-fights, which at times grew into riots. In
the country, too, no less than in the cities, the god-
dess of discord reigned. The farmers determined
to starve the city people into submission, and they
entered into an agreement not to send any produce
into the cities until the merchants should open their
shops and begin selling their goods for paper at its
face value. Not wishing to lose their pigs and butter and grain, they tried to dispose of them in Boston and New York, and in the coast towns of Connecticut. But in all these places their proceedings
had awakened such lively disgust that placards
were posted in the taverns warning purchasers
against farm produce from Rhode Island. Disappointed in these quarters, the farmers threw away
their milk, used their corn for fuel, and let their
apples rot on the ground, rather than supply the
detested merchants. Food grew scarce in Providence and Newport, and in the latter city a mob of
sailors attempted unsuccessfully to storm the provision stores. The farmers were threatened with
armed violence. Town-meetings were held all over
the state, to discuss the situation, and how long
they might have talked to no purpose none can say,
when all at once the matter was brought into court.
A cabinet-maker in Newport named Trevett went
into a meat-market kept by one John Weeden, and
selecting a joint of meat, offered paper in payment.
Weeden refused to take the paper except at a

heavy discount. Trevett went to bed supperless, and next morning informed against the obstinate butcher for disobedience to the forcing act. Should the court find him guilty, it would be a good speculation for Trevett, for half of the five hundred dollars fine was to go to the informer. Hard-money men feared lest the court might prove subservient to the legislature, since that body possessed the power of removing the five judges. The case was tried in September amid furious excitement. Huge crowds gathered about the court-house and far down the street, screaming and cheering like a crowd on the night of a presidential election. The judges were clear-headed men, not to be browbeaten. They declared the forcing act unconstitutional, and dismissed the complaint. Popular wrath then turned upon them. A special session of the legislature was convened, four of the judges were removed, and a new forcing-act was prepared. This act provided that no man could vote at elections or hold any office without taking a test oath promising to receive paper money at par. But this was going too far. Many soft-money men were not wild enough to support such a measure; among the farmers there were some who had grown tired of seeing their produce spoiled on their hands; and many of the richest merchants had announced their intention of moving out of the state. The new forcing act accordingly failed to pass, and presently the old one was repealed. The paper dollar had been issued in May; in November it passed for sixteen cents.

These outrageous proceedings awakened disgust

and alarm among sensible people in all the other
states, and Rhode Island was everywhere reviled
and made fun of. One clause of the forcing act
had provided that if a debtor should offer paper to
his creditor and the creditor should refuse to take
it at par, the debtor might carry his rag money to
court and deposit it with the judge ; and the judge
must thereupon issue a certificate discharging the
debt. The form of certificate began with the
words " Know Ye," and forthwith the unhappy little state was nicknamed Rogues' Island, the home
of Know Ye men and Know Ye measures.

While the scorn of the people was thus poured
out upon Rhode Island, much sympathy was felt
for the government of Massachusetts, which was
called upon thus early to put down armed rebellion.
The pressure of debt was keenly felt in the rural
districts of Massachusetts. It is esti-
mated that the private debts in the _{Rag money de-}
state amounted to some $7,000,000, and _{the Shays insur-}
the state's arrears to the federal gov- _{1786 – Feb.}
ernment amounted to some $7,000,000 _{1787.}
more. Adding to these sums the arrears of bounties due to the soldiers, and the annual cost of the
state, county, and town governments, there was
reached an aggregate equivalent to a tax of more
than $50 on every man, woman, and child in this
population of 379,000 souls. Upon every head of a
family the average burden was some $200 at a time
when most farmers would have thought such a sum
yearly a princely income. In those days of scarcity most of them did not set eyes on so much as
$50 in the course of a year, and happy was he who

had tucked away two or three golden guineas or moidores in an old stocking, and sewed up the treasure in his straw mattress or hidden it behind the bricks of the chimney-piece. Under such circumstances the payment of debts and taxes was out of the question; and as the same state of things made creditors clamorous and ugly, the courts were crowded with lawsuits. The lawyers usually contrived to get their money by exacting retainers in advance, and the practice of champerty was common, whereby the lawyer did his work in consideration of a percentage on the sum which was at last forcibly collected. Homesteads were sold for the payment of foreclosed mortgages, cattle were seized in distrainer, and the farmer himself was sent to jail. The smouldering fires of wrath thus kindled found expression in curses aimed at lawyers, judges, and merchants. The wicked merchants bought foreign goods and drained the state of specie to pay for them, while they drank Madeira wine and dressed their wives in fine velvets and laces. So said the farmers; and city ladies, far kinder than these railers deemed them, formed clubs, of which the members pledged themselves to wear homespun, — a poor palliative for the deep-seated ills of the time. In such mood were many of the villagers when in the summer of 1786 they were overtaken by the craze for paper money. At the meeting of the legislature in May, a petition came in from Bristol County, praying for an issue of paper. The petitioners admitted that such money was sure to deteriorate in value, and they doubted the wisdom of trying to keep it up by forcing acts. Instead of this they would have the rate of its deterioration regulated by law, so that a dollar might be worth ninety cents to-day, and presently seventy cents, and by and by fifty cents, and so on till it should go down to zero and be thrown overboard. People would thus know what to expect, and it would be all right. The delicious *naïveté* of this argument did not prevail with the legislature of Massachusetts, and soft money was frowned down by a vote of ninety-nine to nineteen. Then a bill was brought in seeking to reëstablish in legislation the ancient practice of barter, and make horses and cows legal tender for debts; and this bill was crushed by eighty-nine votes against thirty-five. At the same time this legislature passed a bill to strengthen the federal government by a grant of supplementary funds to Congress, and thus laid a further burden of taxes upon the people.

There was an outburst of popular wrath. A convention at Hatfield in August decided that the court of common pleas ought to be abolished, that no funds should be granted to Congress, and that paper money should be issued at once. Another convention at Lenox denounced such incendiary measures, approved of supporting the federal government, and declared that no good could come from the issue of paper money. But meanwhile the angry farmers had resorted to violence. The legislature, they said, had its sittings in Boston, under the influence of wicked lawyers and merchants, and thus could not be expected to do the will of the people. A cry went up that henceforth the law-makers must sit in some small inland town, where jealous eyes might watch their proceedings. Meanwhile the lawyers must be dealt with; and at Northampton, Worcester, Great Barrington, and Concord the courts were broken up by armed mobs. At Concord one Job Shattuck brought several hundred armed men into the town and surrounded the court-house, while in a fierce harangue he declared that the time had come for wiping out all debts. "Yes," squeaked a nasal voice from the crowd, — "yes, Job, we know all about them two farms you can't never pay for!" But this repartee did not save the judges, who thought it best to flee from the town. At first the legislature deemed it wise to take a lenient view of these proceedings, and it even went so far as to promise to hold its next session out of Boston. But the agitation had reached a point where it could not be stayed. In September the supreme court was to sit at Springfield, and Governor Bowdoin sent a force of 600 militia under General Shepard to protect it. They were confronted by some 600 insurgents, under the leadership of Daniel Shays. This man had been a captain in the Continental army, and in his force were many of the penniless veterans whom Gates would fain have incited to rebellion at Newburgh. Shays seems to have done what he could to restrain his men from violence, but he was a poor creature, wanting alike in courage and good faith. On the other hand the militia were lacking in spirit. After a disorderly parley, with much cursing and swearing, they beat a retreat, and the court was prevented from sitting. Fresh riots followed at Worcester and Concord. A regiment of cavalry, sent out by the governor, scoured Middlesex County, and, after a short fight in the woods near Groton, captured Job Shattuck and dispersed his men. But this only exasperated the insurgents. They assembled in Worcester to the number of 1,200 or more, where they lived for two months at free quarters, while Shays organized and drilled them.

Meanwhile the habeas corpus act was suspended for eight months, and Governor Bowdoin called out an army of 4,400 men, who were placed under command of General Lincoln. As the state treasury was nearly empty, some wealthy gentlemen in Boston subscribed the money needed for equipping these troops, and about the middle of January, 1787, they were collected at Worcester. The rebels had behaved shamefully, burning barns and seizing all the plunder they could lay hands on. As their numbers increased they found their military stores inadequate, and accordingly they marched upon Springfield, with the intent to capture the federal arsenal there, and provide themselves with muskets and cannon. General Shepard held Springfield with 1,200 men, and on the 25th of January Shays attacked him with a force of somewhat more than 2,000, hoping to crush him and seize the arsenal before Lincoln could come to the rescue. But his plan of attack was faulty, and as soon as his men began falling under Shepard's fire a panic seized them, and they retreated in disorder to Ludlow, and then to Amherst, setting fire to houses and robbing the inhabitants. On the approach of

Lincoln's army, three days later, Shays retreated
to Pelham, and planted his forces on
The insurrec-
tion suppressed
by state troops. two steep hills protected at the bottom
by huge snowdrifts. Lincoln advanced
to Hadley and sought to open negotiations with
the rebels. They were reminded that a contest
with the state government was hopeless, and that
they had already incurred the penalty of death;
but if they would now lay down their arms and go
home, a free pardon could be obtained for them.
Shays seemed willing to yield, and Saturday, the
3d of February, was appointed for a conference
between some of the leading rebels and some of
the officers. But this was only a stratagem. During the conference Shays decamped and marched
his men through Prescott and North Dana to Petersham. Toward nightfall the trick was discov-
ered, and Lincoln set his whole force in motion
over the mountain ridges of Shutesbury and New
Salem. The day had been mild, but during the
night the thermometer dropped below zero and an
icy, cutting snow began to fall. There was great
suffering during the last ten miles, and indeed the
whole march of thirty miles in thirteen hours over
steep and snow-covered roads was a worthy exploit
for these veterans of the Revolution. Shays and
his men had not looked for such a display of energy, and as they were getting their breakfast on
Sunday morning at Petersham they were taken by
surprise. A few minutes sufficed to scatter them
in flight. A hundred and fifty, including Shays
himself, were taken prisoners. The rest fled in all
directions, most of them to Athol and Northfield,

whence they made their way into Vermont. General Lincoln then marched his troops into the mountains of Berkshire, where disturbances still continued. On the 26th of February one Captain Hamlin, with several hundred insurgents, plundered the town of Stockbridge and carried off the leading citizens as hostages. He was pursued as far as Sheffield, defeated there in a sharp skirmish, with a loss of some thirty in killed and wounded, and his troops scattered. This put an end to the insurrection in Massachusetts.

During the autumn similar disturbances had occurred in the states to the northward. At Exeter in New Hampshire and at Windsor and Rutland in Vermont the courts had been broken up by armed mobs, and at Rutland there had been bloodshed. When the Shays rebellion was put down, Governor Bowdoin requested the neighbouring states to lend their aid in bringing the insurgents to justice, and all complied with the request except Vermont and Rhode Island. The legislature of Rhode Island sympathized with the rebels, and refused to allow the governor to issue a warrant for their arrest. On the other hand, the governor of Vermont issued a proclamation out of courtesy toward Massachusetts, but he caused it to be understood that this was but an empty form, as the state of Vermont could not afford to discourage immigration ! A feeling of compassion for the insurgents was widely spread in Massachusetts. In March the leaders were tried, and fourteen were convicted of treason and sentenced to death ; but Governor Bowdoin,

Conduct of neighbouring states.

whose term was about to expire, granted a reprieve for a few weeks. At the annual election in April the candidates for the governorship were Bowdoin and Hancock, and it was generally believed that the latter would be more likely than the former to pardon the convicted men. So strong was this feeling that, although much gratitude was felt toward Bowdoin, to whose energetic measures the prompt suppression of the rebellion was due, Hancock obtained a large majority. When the question of a pardon came up for discussion, Samuel Adams, who was then president of the senate, was strongly opposed to it, and one of his arguments was very characteristic. " In monarchies," he said, " the crime of treason and rebellion may admit of being pardoned or lightly punished ; but the man who dares to rebel against the laws of a republic ought to suffer death." This was Adams's sensitive point. He wanted the whole world to realize that the rule of a republic is a rule of law and order, and that liberty does not mean license. But in spite of this view, for which there was much to be said, the clemency of the American temperament prevailed, and Governor Hancock pardoned all the prisoners.

Nothing in the history of these disturbances is more instructive than the light incidentally thrown upon the relations between Congress and the state government. Just before the news of the rout at Petersham, Samuel Adams had proposed in the senate that the governor should be requested to write to Congress and inform that body of what was going on in Massachusetts, stating that " al-

though the legislature are firmly persuaded that
. . . in all probability they will be able speedily
and effectively to suppress the rebellion, yet, if any
unforeseen event should take place which may frus-
trate the measures of government, they rely upon
such support from the United States as is expressly
and solemnly stipulated by the articles of confederation." A resolution to this effect was carried in
the senate, but defeated in the house through the
influence of western county members in sympathy
with the insurgents; and incredible as it may seem,
the argument was freely used that it was incompatible with the dignity of Massachusetts to allow
United States troops to set foot upon her soil.
When we reflect that the arsenal at Springfield,
where the most considerable disturbance occurred,
was itself federal property, the climax of absurdity
might seem to have been reached.

It was left for Congress itself, however, to cap
that climax. The progress of the insurrection in
the autumn in Vermont, New Hampshire, and Massachusetts, as well as the troubles in Rhode Island,
had alarmed the whole country. It was feared
that the insurgents in these states might join
forces, and in some way kindle a flame
that would run through the land. Accordingly Congress in October called
upon the states for a continental force, but did not
dare to declare openly what it was to be used for.
It was thought necessary to say that the troops
were wanted for an expedition against the northwestern Indians! National humiliation could go
no further than such a confession, on the part of

Congress afraid to in-terfere.

our central government, that it dared not use force in defence of those very articles of confederation to which it owed its existence.   Things had come to such a pass that people of all shades of opinion were beginning to agree upon one thing, — that something must be done, and done quickly.

CHAPTER V

GERMS OF NATIONAL SOVEREIGNTY.

WHILE the events we have heretofore contemplated seemed to prophesy the speedy dissolution
and downfall of the half-formed American Union,
a series of causes, obscure enough at first, but
emerging gradually into distinctness and then into
prominence, were preparing the way for the foundation of a national sovereignty. The growth of this
sovereignty proceeded stealthily along Creation of a
national do-
such ancient lines of precedent as to main beyond
the Alleghan-
take ready hold of people's minds, al- ies.
though few, if any, understood the full purport of
what they were doing. Ever since the days when
our English forefathers dwelt in village communities in the forests of northern Germany, the idea of
a common land or folkland — a territory belonging
to the whole community, and upon which new communities might be organized by a process analogous
to what physiologists call cell-multiplication — had
been perfectly familiar to everybody. Townships
budded from village or parish folkland in Maryland and Massachusetts in the seventeenth century,
just as they had done in England before the time
of Alfred. The critical period of the Revolution
witnessed the repetition of this process on a gigantic scale. It witnessed the creation of a national

territory beyond the Alleghanies, — an enormous folkland in which all the thirteen old states had a common interest, and upon which new and derivative communities were already beginning to organize themselves. Questions about public lands are often regarded as the driest of historical deadwood. Discussions about them in newspapers and magazines belong to the class of articles which the general reader usually skips. Yet there is a great deal of the philosophy of history wrapped up in this subject, and it now comes to confront us at a most interesting moment; for without studying this creation of a national domain between the Alleghanies and the Mississippi, we cannot understand how our Federal Union came to be formed.

When England began to contend with France and Spain for the possession of North America, she made royal grants of land upon this continent, in royal ignorance of its extent and configuration. But until the Seven Years' War the eastward and westward partitioning of these grants was of little practical consequence; for English dominion was bounded by the Alleghanies, and everything beyond was in the hands of the French. In that most momentous war the genius of the elder Pitt won the region east of the Mississippi for men of English race, while the vast territory of Louisiana, beyond, passed under the control of Spain. During the Revolutionary War, in a series of romantic expeditions, the state of Virginia took military possession of a great part of the wilderness east of the Mississippi, founding towns in the Ohio and Cumberland valleys, and occupying with garrisons of

her state militia the posts at Cahokia, Kaskaskia,
and Vincennes. We have seen how, through the
skill of our commissioners at Paris, this noble country was secured for the Americans in the treaty of
1783, in spite of the reluctance of France   Conflicting
and the hostility of Spain. Throughout   claims to the
  western terri-
the Revolutionary War the Americans   tory.
claimed the territory as part of the United States;
but when once it passed from under the control of
Great Britain, into whose hands did it go? To
whom did it belong? To this question there were
various and conflicting answers. North Carolina,
indeed, had already taken possession of what was
afterward called Tennessee, and at the beginning
of the war Virginia had annexed Kentucky. As
to these points there could be little or no dispute.
But with the territory north of the Ohio River it
was very different. Four states laid claim either
to the whole or to parts of this territory, and these
claims were not simply conflicting, but irreconcilable.

The charters of Massachusetts and Connecticut
were framed at a time when people had not got over
the notion that this part of the continent was not
much wider than Mexico, and accordingly these
colonies had received the royal permission to extend from sea to sea. The existence of a foreign
colony of Dutchmen in the neighbourhood was a
trifle about which these documents did   Claims of Mas-
not trouble themselves; but when   sachusetts and
  Connecticut.
Charles II. conquered this colony and
bestowed it upon his brother, the province of New
York became a stubborn fact, which could not

be disregarded. Massachusetts and Connecticut peaceably settled their boundary line with New York, and laid no claims to land within the limits of that state; but they still continued to claim what lay beyond it, as far as the Mississippi River, where the Spanish dominion now began. The regions claimed by Massachusetts have since become the southern halves of the states of Michigan and Wisconsin. The region claimed by Connecticut was a narrow strip running over the northern portions of Pennsylvania, Ohio, Indiana, and Illinois; and we have seen how much trouble was occasioned in Pennsylvania by this circumstance.

But New York laughed to scorn these claims of Connecticut. In the seventeenth century all the Algonquin tribes between Lake Erie and the Cumberland Mountains had become tributary to the Iroquois; and during the hundred years' struggle between France and England for the supremacy of this continent the Iroquois had put themselves under the protection of England, which thenceforth always treated them as an appurtenance to New York. For a hundred years before the Revolution, said New York, she had borne the expense of protecting the Iroquois against the French, and by various treaties she had become lawful suzerain over the Six Nations and their lands and the lands of their Algonquin vassals. On such grounds New York claimed pretty much everything north of the Ohio and east of the Miami.

But according to Virginia, it made little difference what Massachusetts and Connecticut and New

Claims of New York.

York thought about the matter, for every acre of land, from the Ohio River up to Lake Superior, belonged to her. Was not she the lordly Virginia's claims. " Old Dominion," out of which every one of the states had been carved? Even Cape Cod and Cape Ann were said to be in " North Virginia," until, in 1614, Captain John Smith invented the name " New England." It was a fair presumption that any uncarved territory belonged to Virginia ; and it was further held that the original charter of 1609 used language which implicitly covered the northwestern territory, though, as Thomas Paine showed, in a pamphlet entitled " Public Good," this was very doubtful. But besides all this, it was Virginia that had actually conquered the disputed territory, and held every military post in it except those which the British had not surrendered ; and who could doubt that possession was nine points in the law ?

Of these conflicting claims, those of New York and Virginia were the most grasping and the most formidable, because they concerned a region into which immigration was beginning rapidly to pour. They were regarded with strong disfavour by the small states, Rhode Island, New Jersey, Delaware, and Maryland, which were so situated that they never could expand in any direction. They looked forward with dread to a future in which New York and Virginia might wax powerful Maryland's novel and beneficent suggestion, Oct. 15, 1777. enough to tyrannize over their smaller neighbours. But of these protesting states it was only Maryland that fairly rose to the occasion, and suggested an idea which seemed startling at first, but from which mighty and unforeseen consequences were soon to follow.[1] It was on the 15th of October, 1777, just two days before Burgoyne's surrender, that this path-breaking idea first found expression in Congress. The articles of confederation were then just about to be presented to the several states to be ratified, and the question arose as to how the conflicting western claims should be settled. A motion was then made that " the United States in Congress assembled shall have the sole and exclusive right and power to ascertain and fix the western boundary of such states as claim to the Mississippi, . . . and lay out the land beyond the boundary so ascertained into separate and independent states, from time to time, as the numbers and circumstances of the people may require." To carry out such a motion, it would be necessary for the four claimant states to surrender their claims into the hands of the United States, and thus create a domain which should be owned by the confederacy in common. So bold a step towards centralization found no favour at the time. No other state but Maryland voted for it.

But Maryland's course was well considered : she pursued it resolutely, and was rewarded with complete success. By February, 1779, all the other states had ratified the articles of confederation. In the following May, Maryland declared that she

[1] This subject has been treated in a masterly manner by Mr. H. B. Adams, in an essay on Maryland's Influence upon Land Cessions to the United States, published in the Third Series of the admirable *Johns Hopkins University Studies in History and Politics.* I am indebted to Mr. Adams for many valuable suggestions.

would not ratify the articles until she should receive some definite assurance that the northwestern
territory should become the common property of
the United States, "subject to be parcelled out by
Congress into free, convenient, and independent
governments." The question, thus boldly brought
into the foreground, was earnestly discussed in Congress and in the state legislatures, until in February, 1780, partly through the influence of General
Schuyler, New York decided to cede all her claims
to the western lands. This act of New York set
things in motion, so that in September Congress
recommended to all states having west- The several
ern claims to cede them to the United states yield
their claims in
States. In October, Congress, still pur- favour of the
United States,
suing the Maryland idea, went farther, 1780–85.
and declared that all such lands as might be ceded
should be sold in lots to immigrants and the money
used for federal purposes, and that in due season
distinct states should be formed there, to be admitted into the Union, with the same rights of sovereignty as the original thirteen states. As an in-
ducement to Virginia, it was further provided that
any state which had incurred expense during the
war in defending its western possessions should
receive compensation. To this general invitation
Connecticut immediately responded by offering to
cede everything to which she laid claim, except
3,250,000 acres on the southern shore of Lake
Erie, which she wished to reserve for educational
purposes. Washington disapproved of this reser-
vation, but it was accepted by Congress, though
the business was not completed until 1786. This

part of the state of Ohio is still commonly spoken of as the " Connecticut Reserve." Half a million acres were given to citizens of Connecticut whose property had been destroyed in the British raids upon her coast towns, and the rest were sold, in 1795, for $1,200,000, in aid of schools and colleges.

In January, 1781, Virginia offered to surrender all the territory northwest of the Ohio, provided that Congress would guarantee her in the possession of Kentucky. This gave rise to a discussion which lasted nearly three years, until Virginia withdrew her proviso and made the cession absolute. It was accepted by Congress on the 1st of March, 1784, and on the 19th of April, in the following year, — the tenth anniversary of Lexington, — Massachusetts surrendered her claims ; and the whole north-western territory — the area of the great states of Michigan, Wisconsin, Illinois, Indiana, and Ohio (excepting the Connecticut Reserve) — thus became the common property of the half-formed nation. Maryland, however, did not wait for this. As soon as New York and Virginia had become thoroughly committed to the movement, she ratified the articles of confederation, which thus went into operation on the 1st of March, 1781.

This acquisition of a common territory speedily led to results not at all contemplated in the theory of union upon which the articles of confederation were based. It led to " the exercise of national sovereignty in the sense of eminent domain," as shown in the ordinances of 1784 and 1787, and prepared men's minds for the work of the Federal Convention. Great credit is due to Maryland for her resolute course in setting in motion this train of events. It aroused fierce indignation at the time, as to many people it looked unfriendly to the Union. Some hot-heads were even heard to say that if Maryland should persist any longer in her refusal to join the confederation, she ought to be summarily divided up between the neighbouring states, and her name erased from the map. But the brave little state had earned a better fate than that of Poland. When we have come to trace out the results of her action, we shall see that just as it was Massachusetts that took the decisive step in bringing on the Revolutionary War when she threw the tea into Boston harbour, so it was Maryland that, by leading the way toward the creation of a national domain, laid the corner-stone of our Federal Union. Equal credit must be given to Virginia for her magnanimity in making the desired surrender. It was New York, indeed, that set the praiseworthy example; but New York, after all, surrendered only a shadowy claim, whereas Virginia gave up a magnificent and princely territory of which she was actually in possession. She might have held back and made endless trouble, just as, at the beginning of the Revolution, she might have refused to make common cause with Massachusetts; but in both instances her leading statesmen showed a far-sighted wisdom and a breadth of patriotism for which no words of praise can be too strong. In the later instance, as in the earlier, Thomas Jefferson played an important part. He, who in after years, as president of the United States, was destined, by

Magnanimity of Virginia.

the purchase of Louisiana, to carry our western frontier beyond the Rocky Mountains, had, in 1779, done more than any one else to support the romantic campaign in which General Clark had taken possession of the country between the Alleghanies and the Mississippi. He had much to do with the generous policy which gave up the greater part of that country for a national domain, and on the very day on which the act of cession was completed he presented to Congress a remarkable plan for the government of the new territory, which was only partially successful because it attempted too much, but the results of which were in many ways notable.

In this plan, known as the Ordinance of 1784, Jefferson proposed to divide the northwestern territory into ten states, or just twice as many as have actually grown out of it. In each of these states the settlers might establish a local government, under the authority of Congress ; and when in any one of them the population should come to equal that of the least populous of the original states, it might be admitted into the Union by the consent of nine states in Congress. The new states were to have universal suffrage ; they must have republican forms of government ; they must pay their shares of the federal debt ; they must forever remain a part of the United States ; and after the year 1800 negro slavery must be prohibited within their limits. The names of these ten states have afforded much amusement to Jefferson's biographers. In those days the schoolmaster was abroad in the land after a peculiar fashion. Just as we are now in the full

Jefferson proposes a scheme of government for the northwestern territory, 1784.

tide of that Gothic revival which goes back for its
beginnings to Sir Walter Scott; as we admire mediæval things, and try to build our houses after old
English models, and prefer words of what people
call " Saxon " origin, and name our children Ro-
land and Herbert, or Edith and Winifred, so our
greatgrandfathers lived in a time of classical revival. They were always looking for precedents
in Greek and Roman history; they were just beginning to try to make their wooden houses look
like temples, with Doric columns; they preferred
words of Latin origin; they signed their pamphlets
" Brutus " and " Lycurgus," and in sober earnest
baptized their children as Cæsar, or Marcellus, or
Darius. The map of the United States was just
about to bloom forth with towns named Ithaca and
Syracuse, Corinth and Sparta; and on the Ohio
River, opposite the mouth of Licking Creek, a city
had lately been founded, the name of which was
truly portentous. " Losantiville " was this wonderful compound, in which the initial *L* stood for
" Licking," while *os* signified " mouth," *anti* " opposite," and *ville* " town; " and the whole read
backwards as " Town-opposite-mouth-of-Licking."
In 1790 General St. Clair, then governor of the
northwest territory, changed this name to Cincinnati, in honor of the military order to which he belonged. With such examples in mind, we may see
that the names of the proposed ten states, from
which the failure of Jefferson's ordinance has delivered us, illustrated the prevalent taste of the
time rather than any idiosyncrasy of the man. The
proposed names were Sylvania, Michigania, Cher-

sonesus, Assenisipia, Metropotamia, Illinoia, Sara-
toga, Washington, Polypotamia, and Pelisipia.

It was not the nomenclature that stood in the
way of Jefferson's scheme, but the wholesale way
in which he tried to deal with the slavery question.
He wished to hem in the probable extension of
slavery by an impassable barrier, and accordingly
he not only provided that it should be extinguished
He wishes to
prohibit slav-
ery in the na-
tional do-
main. in the northwestern territory after the
year 1800, but at the same time his anti-
slavery ardour led him to try to extend
the national dominion southward. He
did his best to persuade the legislature of Virginia
to crown its work by giving up Kentucky to the
United States, and he urged that North Carolina
and Georgia should also cede their western territories. As for South Carolina, she was shut in between the two neighbouring states in such wise that
her western claims were vague and barren. Jefferson would thus have drawn a north-and-south line
from Lake Erie down to the Spanish border of the
Floridas, and west of this line he would have had
all negro slavery end with the eighteenth century.
The policy of restricting slavery, so as to let it die
a natural death within a narrowly confined area, —
the policy to sustain which Mr. Lincoln was elected
president in 1860, — was thus first definitely outlined by Jefferson in 1784. It was the policy of
forbidding slavery in the national territory. Had
this policy succeeded then, it would have been an
ounce of prevention worth many a pound of cure.
But it failed because of its largeness, because it
had too many elements to deal with. For the

moment, the proposal to exclude slavery from the northwestern territory was defeated, because of the two thirds vote required in Congress for any important measure. It got only seven states in its favour, where it needed nine. This defeat, however, was retrieved three years later, when the famous Ordinance of 1787 prohibited slavery forever from the national territory north of the Ohio River. But Jefferson's scheme had not only to deal with the national domain as it was, but also to extend that domain southward to Florida; and in this it failed. Virginia could not be persuaded to give up Kentucky until too late. When Kentucky came into the Union, after the adoption of the Federal Constitution, she came as a sovereign state, with all her domestic institutions in her own hands. With the western districts of North Carolina the case was somewhat different, and the story of this region throws a curious light upon the affairs of that disorderly time.

In surrendering her western territory, North Carolina showed praiseworthy generosity. But the frontier settlers were too numerous to be handed about from one dominion to another, without saying something about it themselves; and their action complicated the matter, until it was too late for Jefferson's scheme to operate upon them. In June, 1784, North Carolina ceded the region since known as Tennessee, and allowed Congress two years in which to accept the grant. Meanwhile, her own authority was to remain supreme there. But the settlers grumbled and protested. Some of them were sturdy pioneers of the finest type, but

along with these there was a lawless population of
"white trash," ancestors of the peculiar race of
men we find to-day in rural districts of Missouri
and Arkansas. They were the refuse of North
Carolina, gradually pushed westward by the advance of an orderly civilization. Crime was rife
in the settlements, and, in the absence of courts, a
rough-and-ready justice was administered by vigi-
lance committees. The Cherokees, moreover, were
troublesome neighbours, and people lived in dread
of their tomahawks. Petitions had again and
again gone up to the legislature, urging the establishment of courts and a militia, but had passed unheeded, and now it seemed that the state had withdrawn her protection entirely. The settlers did
not wish to have their country made a national domain. If their own state could not protect them,
it was quite clear to them that Congress could not.
What was Congress, any way, but a roomful of
men whom nobody heeded? So these backwoodsmen held a convention in a log-cabin at Jonesbor-
ough, and seceded from North Carolina. They
declared that the three counties between the Bald
Mountains and the Holston River constituted an
independent state, to which they gave the name of
John Sevier, Franklin ; and they went on to frame
and the state a constitution and elect a legislature
of Franklin,
1784–87. with two chambers. For governor they
chose John Sevier, one of the heroes of King's
Mountain, a man of Huguenot ancestry, and such
dauntless nature that he was generally known as
the "lion of the border." Having done all this,
the seceders, in spite of their small respect for

Congress, sent a delegate to that body, requesting that the new state of Franklin might be admitted into the Union. Before this business had been completed, North Carolina repealed her act of cession, and warned the backwoodsmen to return to their allegiance. This at once split the new state into two factions: one party wished to keep on as they had now started, the other wished for reunion with North Carolina. In 1786 the one party in each county elected members to represent them in the North Carolina legislature, while the other party elected members of the legislature of Franklin. Everywhere two sets of officers claimed authority, civil dudgeon grew very high, and pistols were freely used. The agitation extended into the neighbouring counties of Virginia, where some discontented people wished to secede and join the state of Franklin. For the next two years there was something very like civil war, until the North Carolina party grew so strong that Sevier fled, and the state of Franklin ceased to exist. Sevier was arrested on a warrant for high treason, but he effected an escape, and after men's passions had cooled down his great services and strong character brought him again to the front. He sat in the senate of North Carolina, and in 1796, when Tennessee became a state in the Union, Sevier was her first governor.

These troubles show how impracticable was the attempt to create a national domain in any part of the country which contained a considerable population. The instinct of self-government was too strong to allow it. Any such population would have refused to submit to ordinances of Congress. To obey the parent state or to set up for one's self, — these were the only alternatives which ordinary men at that time could understand. Experience had not yet ripened their minds for comprehending a temporary condition of semi-independence, such as exists to-day under our territorial governments. The behaviour of these Tennessee backwoodsmen was just what might have been expected. The land on which they were living was not common land: it had been appropriated; it belonged to them, and it was for them to make laws for it. Such is the lesson of the short-lived state of Franklin. It was because she perceived that similar feelings were at work in Kentucky that Virginia did not venture to loosen her grasp upon that state until it was fully organized and ready for admission into the Union. It was in no such partly settled country that Congress could do such a thing as carve out boundaries and prohibit slavery by an act of national sovereignty. There remained the magnificent territory north of the Ohio, — an empire in itself, as large as the German Empire, with the Netherlands thrown in, — in which the collective wisdom of the American people, as represented in Congress, might autocratically shape the future; for it was still a wilderness, watched by frontier garrisons, and save for the Indians and the trappers and a few sleepy old French towns on the eastern bank of the Mississippi, there were no signs of human life in all its vast solitude. Here, where there was nobody to grumble or secede, Congress, in 1787, proceeded to carry out the work which Jefferson had outlined three years before.

It is interesting to trace the immediate origin of
the famous Ordinance of 1787. At the close of
the war General Rufus Putnam, from the mountain village of Rutland in Massachusetts, sent to
Congress an outline of a plan for colonizing the region between Lake Erie and the Ohio Origin of the
with veterans of the army, who were Ohio company.
well fitted to protect the border against Indian attacks. The land was to be laid out in townships
six miles square, " with large reservations for the
ministry and schools ; " and by selling it to the
soldiers at a merely nominal price, the penniless
Congress might obtain an income, and at the same
time recognize their services in the only substan-
tial way that seemed practicable. Washington
strongly favoured the scheme, but, in order to carry
it out, it was necessary to wait until the cession of
the territory by the various claimant states should
be completed. After this had been done, a series
of treaties were made with the Six Nations, as over-
lords, and their vassal tribes, the Wyandots, Chip-
pewas, Ottawas, Delawares, and Shawnees, whereby
all Indian claims to the lands in question were forever renounced. The matter was then formally
taken up by Holden Parsons of Connecticut, and
Rufus Putnam, Manasseh Cutler, Winthrop Sar-
gent, and others, of Massachusetts, and a joint-
stock company was formed for the purchase of
lands on the Ohio River. A large number of settlers — old soldiers of excellent character, whom
the war had impoverished — were ready to go and
take possession at once ; and in its petition the
Ohio company asked for nothing better than that

its settlers should be " under the immediate gov. ernment of Congress in such mode and for such time as Congress shall judge proper." Such a proposal, affording a means at once of replenishing the treasury and satisfying the soldiers, could not but be accepted ; and thus were laid the founda- tions of a state destined within a century to equal in population and far surpass in wealth the whole Union as it was at that time. It became necessary at once to lay down certain general principles of government applicable to the northwestern terri- tory ; and the result was the Ordinance of 1787, which was chiefly the work of Edward Carrington and Richard Henry Lee of Virginia, and Nathan Dane of Massachusetts, in committee, following the outlines of a draft which is supposed to have been made by Manasseh Cutler. Jefferson was no longer on the ground, having gone on his mission to Paris, but some of the principles of his proposed Ordin..ace of 1784 were adopted.

It was provided that the northwestern territory should ultimately be carved into states, not exceed- ing five in number, and any one of these might be admitted into the Union as soon as its population should reach 60,000. In the mean time, the whole

The Ordinance territory was to be governed by officers of 1787. appointed by Congress, and required to take an oath of allegiance to the United States. Under this government there was to be unqualified freedom of religious worship, and no religious tests should be required of any public official. Intestate property should descend in equal shares to children of both sexes. Public schools were to be established. Suffrage was not yet made universal, as a freehold in fifty acres was required. No law was ever to be made which should impair the obligation of contracts, and it was thoroughly agreed that this provision especially covered and prohibited the issue of paper money. The future states to be formed from this territory must make their laws conform to these fundamental principles, and under no circumstances could any one of them ever be separated from the Union. In such wise, the theory of peaceful secession was condemned in advance, so far as it was possible for the federal government to do so. Jefferson's principle, that slavery should not be permitted in the national domain, was also adopted so far as the northwest was concerned; and it is interesting to observe the names of the states which were present in Congress when this clause was added to the ordinance. They were Georgia, the two Carolinas, Virginia, Delaware, New Jersey, New York, and Massachusetts; and the vote was unanimous. No one was more active in bringing about this result than William Grayson of Virginia, who was earnestly supported by Lee. The action of Virginia and North Carolina at that time need not surprise us. But the movements in favour of emancipation in these two states, and the emancipation actually effected or going on at the north, had already made Georgia and South Carolina extremely sensitive about slavery; and their action on this occasion can be explained only by supposing that they were willing to yield a point in this remote territory, in order by and by to be able to insist upon an equivalent in the case of the territory lying west of Georgia. Nor would they have yielded at all had not a fugitive slave law been enacted, providing that slaves escaping beyond the Ohio should be arrested and returned to their owners. These arrangements having been made, General St. Clair was appointed governor of the territory; surveys were made; land was put up for sale at sixty cents per acre, payable in certificates of the public debt; and settlers rapidly came in. The westward exodus from New England and Pennsylvania now began, and only fourteen years elapsed before Ohio, the first of the five states, was admitted into the Union.

"I doubt," says Daniel Webster, "whether one single law of any law-giver, ancient or modern, has produced effects of more distinct, marked, and lasting character than the Ordinance of 1787." Nothing could have been more emphatically an exercise of national sovereignty; yet, as Madison said, while warmly commending the act, Congress did it "without the least colour of constitutional authority." The ordinance was never submitted to the states for ratification. The articles of confederation had never contemplated an occasion for such a peculiar assertion of sovereignty. "A great and independent fund of revenue," said Madison, "is passing into the hands of a single body of men, who can raise troops to an indefinite number, and appropriate money to their support for an indefinite period of time. . . . Yet no blame has been whispered, no alarm has been sounded," even by men most zealous for state rights and most suspicious of Congress. Within a few months this argument was to be cited with telling effect against those who hesitated to accept the Federal Constitution because of the great powers which it conferred upon the general government. Unless you give a government specific powers, commensurate with its objects, it is liable on occasions of public necessity to exercise powers which have not been granted. Avoid the dreadful dilemma between dissolution and usurpation, urged Madison, by clothing the government with powers that are ample but clearly defined. In a certain sense, the action of Congress in 1787 was a usurpation of authority to meet an emergency which no one had foreseen, as in the cases of Jefferson's purchase of Louisiana and Lincoln's emancipation of the slaves. Each of these instances marked, in one way or another, a brilliant epoch in American history, and in each case the public interest was so unmistakable that the people consented and applauded. The theory upon which the Ordinance of 1787 was based was one which nobody could fail to understand, though perhaps no one would then have known just how to put it into words. It was simply the thirteen states, through their delegates in Congress, dealing with the unoccupied national domain as if it were the common land or folkland of a stupendous township.

The vast importance of the lands between the Alleghanies and the Mississippi was becoming more apparent every year, as the westward movement of population went on. But at this time their value was much more clearly seen by the

southern than by the northern states. In the
north the westward emigration was only just beginning to pass the Alleghanies; in the south, as
we have seen, it had gone beyond them several
years ago. The southern states, accordingly, took
a much sounder view than the northern states of
the importance to the Union of the free navigation
of the Mississippi River. The difference was forcibly illustrated in the dispute with Spain, which
came to a crisis in the summer of 1786. It will
be remembered that by the treaties which closed

Spain, hearing
of the secret
article in the
treaty of 1783,
loses her tem-
per and threat-
ens to shut up
the Mississippi
River.

the Revolutionary War the provinces of
East and West Florida were ceded by
England to Spain. West Florida was
the region lying between the Appalach-
icola and the Mississippi rivers, including the southernmost portions of the
present states of Alabama and Mississippi. By
the treaty between Great Britain and the United
States, the northern boundary of this province was
described by the thirty-first parallel of latitude;
but Spain denied the right of these powers to place
the boundary so low. Her troops still held Natchez,
and she maintained that the boundary must be
placed a hundred miles farther north, starting
from the Mississippi at the mouth of the Yazoo
River, near the present site of Vicksburg. Now
the treaty between Great Britain and the United
States contained a secret article, wherein it was
provided that if England could contrive to keep
West Florida, instead of surrendering it to Spain,
then the boundary should start at the Yazoo. This
showed that both England and the United States

were willing to yield the one to the other a strip of territory which both agreed in withholding from Spain. Presently the Spanish court got hold of the secret article, and there was great indignation. Here was England giving to the Americans a piece of land which she knew, and the Americans knew was recently a part of West Florida, and therefore belonged to Spain! Castilian grandees went to bed and dreamed of invincible armadas. Congress was promptly informed that, until this affair should be set right, the Americans need not expect the Spanish government to make any treaty of commerce with them; and furthermore, let no American sloop or barge dare to show itself on the Mississippi below the Yazoo, under penalty of confiscation. When these threats were heard in America, there was great excitement everywhere, but it assumed opposite phases in the north and in the south. The merchants of New York and Boston cared little more about the Mississippi River than about Timbuctoo, but they were extremely anxious to see a commercial treaty concluded with Spain. On the other hand, the backwoodsmen of Kentucky and the state of Franklin cared nothing for the trade on the ocean, but they would not sit still while their corn and their pork were confiscated on the way to New Orleans. The people of Virginia sympathized with the backwoodsmen, but her great statesmen realized the importance of both interests and the danger of a conflict between them.

The Spanish envoy, Gardoqui, arrived in the summer of 1784, and had many interviews with

Jay, who was then secretary for foreign affairs. Gardoqui set forth that his royal master was graciously pleased to deal leniently with the Americans, and would confer one favour upon them, but could not confer two. He was ready to enter into a treaty of commerce with us, but not until we should have renounced all claim to the navigation of the Mississippi River below the Yazoo. Here the Spaniard was inexorable. A year of weary argument passed by, and he had not budged an inch. At last, in despair, Jay advised Congress, for the sake of the commercial treaty, to consent to the closing of the Mississippi, but only for twenty-five years. As the rumour of this went abroad among the settlements south of the Ohio, there was an outburst of wrath, to which an incident that now occurred gave added virulence. A North Carolinian trader, named Amis, sailed down the Mississippi with a cargo of pots and kettles and barrels of flour. At Natchez his boat and his goods were seized by the Spanish officers, and he was left to make his way home afoot through several hundred miles of wilderness. The story of his wrongs flew from one log-cabin to another, until it reached the distant northwestern territory. In the neighbourhood of Vincennes there were Spanish traders, and one of them kept a shop in the town. The shop was sacked by a band of American soldiers, and an attempt was made to incite the Indians to attack the Spaniards. Indignation meetings were held in Kentucky. The people threatened to send a force of militia down the river and capture Natchez and New Orleans ; and a more

Gardoqui and Jay.

dangerous threat was made. Should the northeastern states desert them and adopt Jay's suggestion, they vowed they would secede, and throw
themselves upon Great Britain for protection. On
the other hand, there was great agitation
in the seaboard towns of Massachusetts.
They were disgusted with the backwoodsmen for making such a fuss about

Threats of
secession in
Kentucky and
in New Eng-
land, 1786.

nothing, and with the people of the southern states
for aiding and abetting them; and during this turbulent summer of 1786, many persons were heard
to declare that, in case Jay's suggestion should not
be adopted, it would be high time for the New
England states to secede from the Union, and form
a confederation by themselves. The situation was
dangerous in the extreme. Had the question been
forced to an issue, the southern states would never
have seen their western territories go and offer
themselves to Great Britain. Sooner than that,
they would have broken away from the northern
states. But New Jersey and Pennsylvania now
came over to the southern side, and Rhode Island,
moving in her eccentric orbit, presently joined
them; and thus the treaty was postponed for the
present, and the danger averted.

This lamentable dispute was watched by Washington with feelings of gravest concern. From an
early age he had indulged in prophetic dreams of
the grandeur of the coming civilization in America,
and had looked to the country beyond the mountains as the field in which the next generation was
to find room for expansion. Few had been more
efficient than he in aiding the great scheme of Pitt

for overthrowing the French power in America, and he understood better than most men of his time how much that scheme implied. In his early journeys in the wilderness he had given especial attention to the possibilities of water connection between the east and west, and he had bought for himself and surveyed many extensive tracts of land beyond the mountains. The subject was a favourite one with him, and he looked at it from both a commercial and a political point of view. What we most needed, he said in 1770, were easy transit lines be-

Washington's views on the importance of canals between east and west. tween east and west, as " the channel of conveyance of the extensive and valuable trade of a rising empire." Just before resigning his commission in 1783 Washington had explored the route through the Mohawk Valley, afterward taken first by the Erie Canal, and then by the New York Central Railroad, and had prophesied its commercial importance in the present century. Soon after reaching his home at Mount Vernon, he turned his attention to the improvement of intercourse with the west through the valley of the Potomac. The east and west, he said, must be cemented together by interests in common; otherwise they will break asunder. Without commercial intercourse they will cease to understand each other, and will thus be ripe for disagreement. It is easy for mental habits, as well as merchandise, to glide down stream, and the connections of the settlers beyond the mountains all centre in New Orleans, which is in the hands of a foreign and hostile power. No one can tell what complications may arise from this, argued Washington ; " let us bind these people to us by a chain that can never be broken ; " and with characteristic energy he set to work at once to establish that line of communication that has since grown into the Chesapeake and Ohio Canal, and into the Baltimore and Ohio Railroad. During the three years preceding the meeting of the Federal Convention he was largely occupied with this work. In 1785 he became president of a company for extending the navigation of the Potomac and James rivers, and the legislature of Virginia passed an act vesting him with one hundred and fifty shares in the stock of the company, in order to testify their " sense of his unexampled merits." But Washington refused the testimonial, and declined to take any pay for his services, because he wished to arouse the people to the political importance of the undertaking, and felt that his words would have more weight if he were known to have no selfish interest in it. His sole purpose, as he repeatedly said, was to strengthen the spirit of union by cementing the eastern and western regions together. At this time he could ill afford to give his services without pay, for his long absence in war-time had sadly impaired his estate. But such was Washington.

His far-sighted genius and self-devotion.

In order to carry out the enterprise of extending the navigation of the Potomac, it became necessary for the two states Virginia and Maryland to act in concert ; and early in 1785 a joint commission of the two states met for consultation at Washington's house at Mount Vernon. A compact insur-

Maryland confers with Virginia regarding the navigation of the Potomac, 1785.

ing harmonious coöperation was prepared by the commissioners ; and then, as Washington's scheme involved the connection of the head waters of the Potomac with those of the Ohio, it was found necessary to invite Pennsylvania to become a party to the compact. Then Washington took the occasion to suggest that Maryland and Virginia, while they were about it, should agree upon a uniform system of duties and other commercial regulations, and upon a uniform currency ; and these suggestions were sent, together with the compact, to the legislatures of the two states. Great things were destined to come from these modest beginnings. Just as in the Yorktown campaign, there had come into existence a multifarious assemblage of events, apparently unconnected with one another, and all that was needed was the impulse given by Washington's far-sighted genius to set them all at work, surging, swelling, and hurrying straight forward to a decisive result.

Late in 1785, when the Virginia legislature had wrangled itself into imbecility over the question of clothing Congress with power over trade, Madison hit upon an expedient. He prepared a motion to the effect that commissioners from all the states should hold a meeting, and discuss the best method of securing a uniform treatment of commercial questions ; but as he was most conspicuous among the advocates of a more perfect union, he was careful not to present the motion himself. Keeping in the background, he persuaded another member — John Tyler, father of the president of that name, a fierce

Madison's motion; a step in advance, 1785.

zealot for state rights — to make the motion. The plan, however, was " so little acceptable that it was not then persisted in," and the motion was laid on the table. But Madison knew what was coming from Maryland, and bided his time. After some weeks it was announced that Maryland had adopted the compact made at Mount Vernon concerning jurisdiction over the Potomac. Virginia instantly replied by adopting it also. Then it was suggested, in the report from Maryland, that Delaware, as well as Pennsylvania, ought to be consulted, since the scheme should rightly include a canal between the Delaware River and the Chesapeake Bay. And why not also consult with these states about a uniform system of duties? If two states can agree upon these matters, why not four? And still further, said the Maryland message, — dropping the weightiest part of the proposal into a subordinate clause, just as women are said to put the quintessence of their letters into the postscript, — might it not be well enough, if we are going to have such a conference, to invite commissioners from all the thirteen states to attend it? An informal discussion can hurt nobody. The conference of itself can settle nothing ; and if four states can take part in it, why not thirteen? Here was the golden opportunity. The Madison-Tyler motion was taken up from the table and carried. Commissioners from all the states were invited to meet on the first Monday of September, 1786, at Annapolis, — a safe place, far removed from the influence of that dread tyrant, the Congress, and from wicked centres of trade, such as New York and Boston. It was the governor of Virginia who sent the invitations. It may not amount to much, wrote Madison to Monroe, but " the expedient is better than nothing ; and, as the recommendation of additional powers to Congress is within the purview of the commission, it may possibly lead to better consequences than at first occur."

The seed dropped by Washington had fallen on fruitful soil. At first it was to be just a little meeting of two or three states to talk about the Potomac River and some projected canals, and already it had come to be a meeting of all the states to discuss some uniform system of legislation on the subject of trade. This looked like progress, yet when the convention was gathered at Annapolis, on the 11th of September, the outlook was most discouraging.

Convention at Annapolis, Sept. 11, 1786.

Commissioners were there from Virginia, Delaware, Pennsylvania, New Jersey, and New York. Massachusetts and New Hampshire, Rhode Island and North Carolina, had duly appointed commissioners, but they were not there. It is curious to observe that Maryland, which had been so earnest in the matter, had nevertheless now neglected to appoint commissioners ; and no action had been taken by Georgia, South Carolina, or Connecticut. With only five states represented, the commissioners did not think it worth while to go on with their work. But before adjourning they adopted an address, written by Alexander Hamilton, and sent it to all the states. All the commissioners present had been empowered to consider how far a uniform commercial system might be essential to the permanent harmony of the states. But New Jersey had taken a step in advance, and instructed her delegates " to consider how far a uniform system in their commercial regulations *and other important matters* might be necessary to the common interest and permanent harmony of the several states." *And other important matters,* — thus again was the weightiest part of the business relegated to a subordinate clause. So gingerly was the great question — so dreaded, yet so inevitable — approached ! This reference to "other matters" was pronounced by the commissioners to be a vast improvement on the original plan ; and Hamilton's address now urged that commissioners be appointed by all the states, to meet in convention at Philadelphia on the second Monday of the following May, " to devise such further provisions as shall appear to them necessary to render the constitution of the federal government adequate to the exigencies of the Union, and to report to Congress such an act as, when agreed to by them, and confirmed by the legislatures of every state, would effectually provide for the same." The report of the commissioners was brought before Congress in October, in the hope that Congress would earnestly recommend to the several states the course of action therein suggested. But Nathan Dane and Rufus King of Massachusetts, intent upon technicalities, succeeded in preventing this. According to King, a convention was an irregular body, which had no right to propose changes in the organic law of the land, and the state legislatures could not properly

Hamilton's address; a further step in advance.

confirm the acts of such a body, or take notice of them. Congress was the only source from which such proposals could properly emanate. These arguments were pleasing to the self-love of Congress, and it refused to sanction the plan of the Annapolis commissioners.

In an ordinary season this would perhaps have ended the matter, but the winter of 1786–87 was not an ordinary season. All the troubles above described seemed to culminate just at this moment. The paper-money craze in so many of the states, the shameful deeds of Rhode Island, the riots in Vermont and New Hampshire, the Shays rebellion in Massachusetts, the dispute with Spain, and the consequent imminent danger of separation between north and south had all come together; and the feeling of thoughtful men and women throughout the country was one of real consternation. The last ounce was now to be put upon the camel's back in the failure of the impost amendment. In 1783, when the cessions of western lands were creating a national domain, a promising plan had been devised for relieving the country of its load of debt, and furnishing Congress with money for its current expenses. All the money coming from sales of the western folkland was to be applied to reducing and wiping out the principal of the public debt. Then the interest of this debt must be provided for; and to that end Congress had recommended an impost, or system of custom-house duties, upon liquors, sugars, teas, coffees, cocoa, molasses, and pepper. This impost was to be kept up for twenty-five years only, and

New York defeats the impost amendment.

the collectors were to be appointed by the several states, each for its own ports. Then for the current expenses of the government, supplementary funds were needed; and these were to be assessed upon the several states, each of which might raise its quota as it saw fit. Such was the original plan; but it soon turned out that the only available source of revenue was the national domain, which had thus been nothing less than the principal thread which had held the Union together. As for the impost, it had never been possible to get a sufficient number of states to agree upon it, and of the quotas for current expenses, as we have seen, very little had found its way to the federal treasury. Under these difficulties, it had been proposed that an amendment to the articles of confederation should endow Congress with the power of levying customs-duties and appointing the collectors; and by the summer of 1786, after endless wrangling, twelve states had consented to the amendment. But, in order that an amendment should be adopted, unanimous consent was necessary. The one delinquent state, which thus blocked the wheels of the confederacy, was New York. She had her little system of duties all nicely arranged for what seemed to be her own interests, and she would not surrender this system to Congress. Upon the neighbouring states her tariff system bore hard, and especially upon New Jersey. In 1786 this little state flatly refused to pay her quota until New York should stop discriminating against her trade. Nothing which occurred in that troubled year caused more alarm than this, for it could not be denied that such a declaration seemed little less than an act of secession on the part of New Jersey. The arguments of a congressional committee at last prevailed upon the state to rescind her declaration. At the same time there came the final struggle in New York over the impost amendment, against which Governor Clinton had firmly set his face. There was a fierce fight, in which Hamilton's most strenuous efforts succeeded in carrying the amendment in part, but not until it had been clogged with a condition that made it useless. Congress, it was declared, might have the revenue, but New York must appoint the collectors; she was not going to have federal officials rummaging about her docks. The legislature well knew that to grant the amendment in such wise was not to grant it at all, but simply to reopen the whole question. Such was the result. Congress expostulated in vain. On the 15th of February, 1787, the matter was reconsidered in the New York legislature, and the impost amendment was defeated.

Thus, only three months before the Federal Convention was to meet, if indeed it was ever to meet, Congress was decisively informed that it would not be allowed to take any effectual measures for raising a revenue. There now seemed nothing left for Congress to do but adopt the recommendation of the Annapolis commissioners, and give its sanction to the proposed convention. Madison, however, had not waited for this, but had prevailed upon the Virginia legislature to go on and appoint its delegates to the convention. The events of the year had worked a change in the popular sentiment in Virginia; people were more afraid of anarchy, and not quite so much afraid of centralization; and now, under Madison's lead, Virginia played her trump card and chose George Washington as one of her delegates. As soon as this was known, there was an outburst of joy throughout the land. Sudden changes in popular senti- ment.

All at once the people began everywhere to feel an interest in the proposed convention, and presently Massachusetts changed her attitude. Up to this time Massachusetts had been as obstinate in her assertion of local independence, and as unwilling to strengthen the hands of Congress, as any of the thirteen states, except New York and Rhode Island. But the Shays rebellion had served as a useful object-lesson. Part of the distress in Massachusetts could be traced to the inability of Congress to pay debts which it owed to her citizens. It was felt that the time had come when the question of a national revenue must be seriously considered. Every week saw fresh converts to the party which called for a stronger government. Then came the news that Virginia had chosen delegates, and that Washington was one of them; then that New Jersey had followed the example; then that Pennsylvania, North Carolina, Delaware, had chosen delegates. It was time for Massachusetts to act, and Rufus King now brought the matter up in Congress. His scruples as to the legality of the proceeding had not changed, and accordingly he moved that Congress should of itself propose a convention at Philadelphia, identical with the one which the Annapolis commissioners had already recommended. The motion was carried, and in this way Congress formally approved and adopted what was going on. Massachusetts immediately chose delegates, and was followed by New York. In April, Georgia and South Carolina followed suit. Connecticut and Maryland came on in May, and New Hampshire, somewhat tardily, in June. Of the thirteen states, Rhode Island alone refused to take any part in the proceedings.

The convention held its meetings in that plain brick building in Philadelphia already immortalized as the place from which the Declaration of Independence was published to the world.

The Federal Convention meets at Philadelphia, May 14–25, 1787.

The work which these men were undertaking was to determine whether that Declaration had been for the blessing or the injury of America and of mankind. That they had succeeded in assembling here at all was somewhat remarkable, when we think of the curious medley of incidents that led to it. At no time in this distressed period would a frank and abrupt proposal for a convention to remodel the government have found favour. Such proposals, indeed, had been made, beginning with that of Pelatiah Webster in 1781, and they had all failed to break through the crust of a truly English conservatism and dread of centralized power. Now, through what some might have called a strange chapter of accidents, before the element of causal sequence in it all had become so manifest as it is to us to-day, this remarkable group of men had been brought together in a single room, while even yet but few of them realized how thoroughly and exhaustively

reconstructive their work was to be. To most of
them it was not clear whether they were going
merely to patch up the articles of confederation,
or to strike out into a new and very different path.
There were a few who entertained far-reaching
purposes; the rest were intelligent critics rather
than constructive thinkers; the result was surpris-
ing to all. It is worth our while to pause for a
moment, and observe the character and composition
of one of the most memorable assemblies the world
has ever seen. Mr. Gladstone says that just " as
the British Constitution is the most subtle organ-
ism which has proceeded from progressive history,
so the American Constitution is the most wonderful work ever struck off at a given time by the
brain and purpose of man." [1] Let us now see who
the men were who did this wonderful work, — this
Iliad, or Parthenon, or Fifth Symphony, of statesmanship. We shall not find that they were all
great geniuses. Such is never the case in such an
assembly. There are not enough great geniuses to
go around ; and if there were, it is questionable if
the result would be satisfactory. In such discussions the points which impress the more ordinary
and less far-sighted members are sure to have great
value ; especially when we bear in mind that the
object of such an assembly is not merely to elaborate a plan, but to get the great mass of people,
including the brick-layers and hod-carriers, to un-

[1] It would be in the highest degree erroneous, however, to
suppose that the Constitution of the United States is not, as
much as any other, an instance of evolution from precedents.
See, in this connection, the very able article by Prof. Alexander
Johnston, *New Princeton Review*, Sept., 1887, pp. 175–190.

derstand it well enough to vote for it. An ideally perfect assembly of law-makers will therefore contain two or three men of original constructive genius, two or three leading spirits eminent for shrewdness and tact, a dozen or more excellent critics representing various conflicting interests, and a rank and file of thoroughly respectable, commonplace men, unfitted for shining in the work of the meeting, but admirably competent to proclaim its results and get their friends and neighbours to adopt them. And in such an assembly, even if it be such as we call ideally perfect, we must allow something for the presence of a few hot-headed and irreconcilable members, — men of inflexible mind, who cannot adapt themselves to circumstances, and will refuse to play when they see the game going against them.

All these points are well illustrated in the assemblage of men that framed our Federal Constitution. In its composition, this group of men left nothing to be desired. In its strength and in its weakness, it was an ideally perfect assembly.

The men who were assembled.

There were fifty-five men, all of them respectable for family and for personal qualities, — men who had been well educated, and had done something whereby to earn recognition in these troubled times. Twenty-nine were university men, graduates of Harvard, Yale, Columbia, Princeton, William and Mary, Oxford, Glasgow, and Edinburgh. Twenty-six were not university men, and among these were Washington and Franklin. Of the illustrious citizens who, for their public services, would naturally have been

here, John Adams and Thomas Jefferson were in
Europe; Samuel Adams, Patrick Henry, and Richard Henry Lee disapproved of the convention, and
remained at home ; and the greatest man of Rhode
Island, Nathanael Greene, who — one likes to think
— might have succeeded in bringing his state into
the convention, had lately died of a sun-stroke, at
the early age of forty-four.

Of the two most famous men present little need
be said. The names of Washington and Franklin
stood for supreme intelligence and consummate
tact. Franklin had returned to this country two
years before, and was now president of Pennsylvania. He was eighty-one years of age, the oldest
man in the convention, as Jonathan Dayton of New
Jersey, aged twenty-six, was the youngest. The
two most profound and original thinkers in the
company were but little older than Dayton. Alexander Hamilton was thirty, James Madison thirty-
six. Among political writers, these two men must
be ranked in the same order with Aristotle, Montesquieu, and Locke; and the " Federalist," their
joint production, is the greatest treatise on government that has ever been written. John Jay, who
contributed a few pages to this immortal volume,
had not been sent to the convention, because New
York did not wish to have it succeed. Along with
Hamilton, New York sent two commonplace men,
Robert Yates and John Lansing, who were extreme and obstinate Antifederalists ; and the action of Hamilton, who was thus prevented from
carrying the vote of his own state for any measure
which he might propose, was in this way sadly en-

barrassed. For another reason, Hamilton failed to exert as much influence in the convention as one would have expected from his profound thought and his brilliant eloquence. Scarcely any of these men entertained what we should now call extreme democratic views. Scarcely any, perhaps, had that intense faith in the ultimate good sense of the people which was the most powerful characteristic of Jefferson. But Hamilton went to the other extreme, and expressed his distrust of popular government too plainly. His views were too aristocratic and his preference for centralization was too pronounced to carry conviction to his hearers. The leading part in the convention fell, therefore, to James Madison, a young man somewhat less brilliant than Hamilton, but superior to him in sobriety and balance of powers. Madison James Madison. used to be called the "Father of the Constitution," and it is true that the government under which we live is more his work than that of any other one man. From early youth his life had been devoted to the study of history and the practice of statesmanship. He was a graduate of Princeton College, an earnest student, familiar with all the best literature of political science from Aristotle down to his own time, and he had given especial attention to the history of federal government in ancient Greece, and in Switzerland and Holland. At the age of twenty-five he had taken part in the Virginia convention which instructed the delegates from that state in Congress to bring forward the Declaration of Independence. During the last part of the war he was an active and

influential member of Congress, where no one
equalled or approached him for knowledge of English history and constitutional law. In 1784 he
had returned to the Virginia legislature, and been
foremost in securing the passage of the great act
which gave complete religious freedom to the people of that state. No man understood better than
he the causes of the alarming weakness of the federal government, and of the commercial disturbances and popular discontent of the time ; nor
had any one worked more zealously or more
adroitly in bringing about the meeting of this convention. As he stood here now, a leader in the
debate, there was nothing grand or imposing in his
appearance. He was small of stature and slight
in frame, like Hamilton, but he had none of Hamilton's personal magnetism. His manner was shy
and prim, and blushes came often to his cheeks.
At the same time, he had that rare dignity of un-
conscious simplicity which characterizes the earnest
and disinterested scholar. He was exceedingly
sweet-tempered, generous, and kind, but very hard
to move from a path which, after long reflection,
he had decided to be the right one. He looked at
politics judicially, and was so little of a party man
that on several occasions he was accused (quite
wrongfully, as I hope hereafter to prove) of gross
inconsistency. The position of leadership, which
he won so early and kept so long, he held by sheer
force of giant intelligence, sleepless industry, and
an integrity which no man ever doubted. But he
was above all things a man of peace. When in
after years, as president of the United States, he

was called upon to manage a great war, he was out of place, and his reputation for supreme ability was temporarily lowered. Here in the Federal Convention we are introduced to him at the noblest and most useful moment of his life.

Of the fifty-five men here assembled, Washington, Franklin, Hamilton, and Madison were of the first order of ability. Many others in the room were gentlemen of more than ordinary talent and culture. Other leading There was John Dickinson, who had members. moved from Pennsylvania into Delaware, and now came to defend the equal rights of the smaller states. There was James Wilson of Pennsylvania, born and educated in Scotland, one of the most learned jurists this country has ever seen. Beside him sat the financier, Robert Morris, and his namesake Gouverneur Morris of Morrisania, near the city of New York, the originator of our decimal currency, and one of the far-sighted projectors of the Erie Canal. Then there was John Rutledge of South Carolina, who ever since the Stamp Act Congress had been the mainstay of his state; and with him were the two able and gallant Pinckneys. Caleb Strong, afterward ten times governor of Massachusetts, was a typical Puritan, hard-headed and supremely sensible; his colleague, Rufus King, already distinguished for his opposition to negro slavery, was a man of brilliant attainments. And there were George Wythe, the chancellor of Virginia, and Daniel Carroll of Maryland, who had played a prominent part in the events which led to the creation of a national domain. Oliver Ellsworth of Connecticut, afterward chief justice of

the United States, was one of the ablest lawyers
of his time; with him were Roger Sherman and
William Johnson, the latter a Fellow of the Royal
Society, and afterward president of Columbia College. The New Jersey delegation, consisting of
William Livingston, David Brearley, William Paterson, and Jonathan Dayton, was a very strong
one; and as to New Hampshire, it is enough to
mention the name of John Langdon. Besides all
these there were some twenty of less mark, men
who said little, but listened and voted. And then
there were the irreconcilables, Yates and Lansing, the two Antifederalists from New York; and
four men of much greater ability, who took an important part in the proceedings, but could not be
induced to accept the result. These four were
Luther Martin of Maryland; George Mason and
Edmund Randolph of Virginia; and Elbridge
Gerry of Massachusetts.

When these men had assembled in Independence
Hall, they chose George Washington president of
the convention. The doors were locked, and an
injunction of strict secrecy was put upon every one.
The results of their work were known in the following September, when the draft of the Federal
Constitution was published. But just what was
said and done in this secret conclave was not revealed until fifty years had passed, and the aged
James Madison, the last survivor of those who sat
there, had been gathered to his fathers. He kept
a journal of the proceedings, which was published
after his death, and upon the interesting story told
in that journal we have now to enter.

CHAPTER VI.

THE FEDERAL CONVENTION.

THE Federal Convention did wisely in withholding its debates from the knowledge of the people.
It was felt that discussion would be more untrammelled, and that its result ought to go before the
country as the collective and unanimous voice of
the convention. There was likely to be wrangling
enough among themselves; but should their scheme
be unfolded, bit by bit, before its parts could be
viewed in their mutual relations, popular excitement would become intense, there might be riots,
and an end would be put to that attitude of mental
repose so necessary for the constructive work that
was to be done. It was thought best that the
scheme should be put forth as a completed whole,
and that for several years, even, until the new system of government should have had a fair trial,
the traces of the individual theories and preferences
concerned in its formation should not be revealed.

Difficult prob-
lem before the
convention.
For it was generally assumed that a system of government new in some important respects would be proposed by the
convention, and while the people awaited the result
the wildest speculations and rumours were current.
A few hoped, and many feared, that some scheme
of monarchy would be established. Such surmises

found their way across the ocean, and hopes were expressed in England that, should a king be chosen, it might be a younger son of George III. It was even hinted, with alarm, that, through gratitude to our recent allies, we might be persuaded to offer the crown to some member of the royal family of France. No such thoughts were entertained, however, by any person present in the convention. Some of the delegates came with the design of simply amending the articles of confederation by taking away from the states the power of regulating commerce, and intrusting this power to Congress. Others felt that if the work were not done thoroughly now another chance might never be offered ; and these men thought it necessary to abolish the confederation, and establish a federal republic, in which the general government should act directly upon the people. The difficult problem was how to frame a plan of this sort which people could be made to understand and adopt. At the very outset some of the delegates began to exhibit symptoms of that peculiar kind of moral cowardice which is wont to afflict free governments, and of which American history furnishes so many instructive examples. It was suggested that palliatives and half measures would be far more likely to find favour with the people than any thorough-going reform, when Washington suddenly interposed with a brief but immortal speech, which ought to be blazoned in letters of gold, and posted on the wall of every American assembly that shall meet to nominate a candidate, or declare a policy, or pass a law, so long as the weakness of human nature shall endure.   Rising from his president's chair, his Washington's solemn appeal. tall figure drawn up to its full height, he exclaimed in tones unwontedly solemn with suppressed emotion, " It is too probable that no plan we propose will be adopted.   Perhaps another dreadful conflict is to be sustained.   If, to please the people, we offer what we ourselves disapprove, how can we afterward defend our work?   Let us raise a standard to which the wise and the honest can repair;   the event is in the hand of God."

This outburst of noble eloquence carried conviction to every one, and henceforth we do not hear that any attempt was avowedly made to avoid the issues as they came up.   It was a most wholesome tonic.   It braced up the convention to high resolves, and impressed upon all the delegates that they were in a situation where faltering or trifling was both wicked and dangerous.   From that moment the mood in which they worked caught something from the glorious spirit of Washington.   There was need of such high purpose, for two plans were presently laid before the meeting, which, for a moment, brought out one of the chief elements of antagonism existing between the states, and which at first seemed irreconcilable.   It was the happy compromise which united and harmonized these two plans that smoothed the further work of the convention, and made it possible for a stable and powerful government to be constructed.

The first of these plans was known as the Virginia plan.   It was agreed upon in a committee of the delegates of that state, and was brought for ward by Edmund Randolph, governor of Virginia, in the name of the state, but its chief author was Madison. It struck instantly at the root of the difficulties under which the country had been staggering ever since the Declaration of Independence. The federal government had possessed no means of enforcing obedience to its laws. Its The root of all edicts were without a sanction; and this the difficulties. was because they operated upon states, and not upon individuals. When an individual defies the law, you can lock him up in jail, or levy an execution upon his property. The immense force of the community is arrayed against him, and he is as helpless as a straw on the billows of the ocean. He cannot raise a militia to protect himself. But when the law is defied by a state, it is quite otherwise. You cannot put a state into jail, nor seize its goods; you can only make war on it, and if you try that expedient you find that the state is not helpless. Its local pride and prejudices are aroused against you, and its militia will turn out in full force to uphold the infraction of law. Against this obstinate and exasperated military force what superior force can you bring? Under some rare combination of circumstances you might get the military force of several of the other states; but ordinarily, when what you are trying to do is simply to enforce every-day laws, and when you simply represent a distrusted general government in conflict with a local government, you cannot do this. The other states will sympathize with the delinquent state; they will feel that the very same condition of things which leads you to attack that state to-

day will lead you to attack some other state to-
morrow. Hence you cannot get any military help,
and you are powerless.

Such was the case with the Continental Congress.
A novel and distrusted institution, it was called
upon to enforce its laws upon long-established communities, full of sturdy independence and obstinate
local prejudices. It was able to act, though with
clumsy slowness, as long as there was an enemy in
the field who was even more dreaded. But as soon
as this enemy had been beaten out of sight it could
not act at all. This had been because it did not
represent the American people, but only the American states. The vital force which moved it was
not the resistless force of a whole people, but only
a shadowy semblance of force, derived from a theoretical consent of thirteen corporate bodies, which
in their corporate capacity could never be compelled
to agree about anything under the sun ; and unless
compelled they would not agree. Four years of
disturbance in every part of the country, in the
course of which troops had been called out in several states, and civil war had been narrowly averted
at least half a dozen times, had proved this beyond
all cavil. With almost any other people than the
Americans civil war would have come already.
With all the vast future interests that were involved in these quarrels looming up before their
keen, sagacious minds, it was a wonder that they
had been kept from coming to blows. Such self-
restraint had been greatly to their credit. It was
the blessed fruit of more than a century of government by free discussion, while yet these states were

colonies, peopled by the very cream of English freemen who had fought the decisive battle of civil and
religious freedom for mankind in that long crisis
when the Invincible Armada was overwhelmed and
the Long Parliament won its triumphs. Such self-
restraint had this people shown in days of trial,
under a vicious government adopted in a time of
hurry and sore distress. But late events had gone
far to show that it could not endure.

The words of Randolph's opening speech are
worth quoting in this connection. "The confederation," he said, "was made in the infancy of the
science of constitutions, when the inefficiency of
requisitions was unknown; when no commercial
discord had arisen among states; when no rebellion like that in Massachusetts had broken out;
when foreign debts were not urgent; when the
havoc of paper money had not been foreseen;
when treaties had not been violated; and when
nothing better could have been conceded by states
jealous of their sovereignty. But it offered no
security against foreign invasion, for Congress
could neither prevent nor conduct a war, nor punish infractions of treaties or of the law of nations,
nor control particular states from provoking war.
The federal government has no constitutional
power to check a quarrel between separate states;
nor to suppress a rebellion in any one of them;
nor to establish a productive impost; nor to coun-
teract the commercial regulations of other nations;
nor to defend itself against the encroachments of
the states. From the manner in which it has been
ratified in many of the states, it cannot be claimed

to be paramount to the state constitutions; so that there is a prospect of anarchy from the inherent laxity of the government. As the remedy, the government to be established must have for its basis the republican principle."

Having thus tersely stated the whole problem, Randolph went on to present the Virginia plan. To make the federal government operate directly upon individuals, one provision was absolutely necessary. It did not solve the whole problem, but it was an indispensable beginning. This was the proposal that there should be a national legislature, in which the American *people* instead of the American states should be represented. For the purposes of federal legislation, there must be an assembly elected directly by the people, and with its members apportioned according to population. There must be such an assembly as our present House of Representatives, standing in the same immediate relation to the people of the whole country as was sustained by the assembly of each separate state to the people of that state. Without such direct representation of the whole people in the Federal Congress, it would be impossible to achieve one secure step toward the radical reform of the weaknesses and vices of the confederation. It was the only way in which the vexed question of one nation or thirteen could be made to yield a satisfactory answer. At the same time it could not be denied that such a proposal was revolutionary in character. It paved the way for a national consolidation which might go further than any one could foresee, and much

The Virginia plan; a radical cure.

further than was desirable. The moribund Congress of the Confederation, with its delegates chosen by the state assemblies, and casting its vote simply by states, had utterly failed to serve as a national legislature. There was a good deal of truth in what John Adams once said of it, that it was more a diplomatic than a legislative body. It was, indeed, because of this consciously felt diplomatic character that it was called a Congress, and not a Parliament. In its lack of coercive power it resembled the international congresses of Europe rather than the supreme legislature of any country. To substitute abruptly for such a body a truly national legislature, based not upon states but upon population, was quietly to inaugurate a revolution of no less magnitude than that which had lately severed us from Great Britain. So bold a step, while all-essential in order to complete that revolution, and make its victorious issue fortunate instead of disastrous to the American people, was sufficiently revolutionary to awaken the fears of many members of the Federal Convention. To the familiar state governments which had so long possessed their love and allegiance, it was superadding a new and untried government, which it was feared would swallow up the states and everywhere extinguish local independence. Nor can it be said that such fears were unreasonable. Our federal government has indeed shown a strong tendency to encroach upon the province of the state governments, especially since our late Civil War. Too much centralization is our danger to-day, as the weakness of the federal tie was our danger a century ago. The rule of the Federalist party was needed in 1789 as the rule of the Republican party was needed in 1861, to put a curb upon the centrifugal tendencies. But after Federalism had fairly done its great work, at the beginning of the nineteenth century, it was well that the administration of our national affairs should pass into the hands of the party to which Thomas Jefferson and Samuel Adams belonged, and which Madison, in his calm statesmanlike wisdom, had come to join. And now that, in our own day, the disruptive forces have been even more thoroughly and effectually overcome, it is time for the principles of that party to be reasserted with fresh emphasis. If the day should ever arrive (which God forbid !) when the people of the different parts of our country shall allow their local affairs to be administered by prefects sent from Washington, and when the self-government of the states shall have been so far lost as that of the departments of France, or even so far as that of the counties of England, — on that day the progressive political career of the American people will have come to an end, and the hopes that have been built upon it for the future happiness and prosperity of mankind will be wrecked forever.

I do not think that the historian writing at the present day need fear any such direful calamity, for the past century has shown most instructively how, in such a society as ours, the sense of political dangers slowly makes its way through the whole mass of the people, until movements at length are made to avert them, and the pendulum swings in the opposite direction. The history of political parties in the United States is especially rich in lessons of this sort. Compared with the statesmen of the Federal Convention, we are at a great advantage in studying this question of national consolidation; and we have no excuse for failing to comprehend the attitude of the men who dreaded the creation of a national legislature as the entering wedge which would by and by rend asunder the structure of our liberties. The great mind of Madison was one of the first to entertain distinctly the noble conception of two kinds of government operating at one and the same time upon the same individuals, harmonious with each other, but each supreme in its own sphere. Such is the fundamental conception of our partly federal, partly national, government, which appears throughout the Virginia plan as well as in the Constitution which grew out of it. It was a political conception of a higher order than had ever before been entertained; it took a great deal of discussion to make it clear to the minds of the delegates generally; and the struggle over this initial measure of a national legislature was so bitter as to come near breaking up the convention.

In its original shape the Virginia plan went much further toward national consolidation than the Constitution as adopted. The reaction against the evils of the loose-jointed confederation, which Randolph so ably summed up, was extreme. According to the Virginia plan, the national legislature was to be composed of two houses, like the legislatures of the several states. The members of the lower house should be chosen directly by the people ; members of the upper house, or Senate, should be elected by the lower house out of persons nominated by the state legislatures. In both the lower and the upper branches of this national legislature the votes were to be the votes of individuals, and no longer the votes of states, as in the Continental Congress. Under the articles of confederation each state had an equal vote, and two thirds were required for every important measure. Under the proposed Constitution each state was to have a number of representatives proportionate either to its wealth or to the number of its free inhabitants, and a bare majority of votes was to suffice to pass all measures in the ordinary course of business ; and these rules were to apply both to the lower house and to the Senate. To adopt such a plan would overthrow the equality of the states altogether. It would give Virginia, the greatest state, sixteen representatives, where Georgia, the smallest state, had but one ; and besides, as the votes were no longer to be taken by states, individual members could combine in any way they pleased, quite irrespective of state lines. It was not strange that to many delegates in the convention such a beginning should have seemed revolutionary. This impression was deepened when it was further proposed not only to clothe this national legislature with original powers of legislation in all cases to which the several states are incompetent, but also to allow it to set aside at discretion such state laws as it might deem unconstitutional. It is interesting to find Madison, whose Federalism afterward came to be so moderate, now appearing as the earnest defender of this extreme provision, so incompatible with state rights. But in Madison's mind at this moment, in the actual presence of the anarchy of the confederation, the only alternative which seemed to present itself was that of armed coercion. " A negative on state laws," he said, " is the mildest expedient that can be devised for enforcing a national decree. Should no such precaution be engrafted, the only remedy would be coercion. The negative would render the use of force unnecessary. This prerogative of the general government is the great pervading principle that must control the centrifugal tendency of the states, which, without it, will continually fly out of their proper orbits, and destroy the order and harmony of the political system." But these views were not destined to find favour with the convention, which finally left the matter to be much more satisfactorily adjusted through the medium of the federal judiciary.

Such were the fundamental provisions of the Virginia plan with regard to the national legislature. To carry out the laws, it was proposed that there should be a national executive, to be chosen by the national legislature for a short term, and ineligible a second time. Whether the executive power should be invested in a single person or in several was not specified. As will be seen hereafter, this was regarded as an extremely delicate point, with which it was thought best not to embarrass the Virginia plan at the outset. Passing lightly over this, it was urged that, in order to com-

plete the action of the government upon individuals, there must be a national judiciary to determine
cases arising under the Constitution, cases in admiralty, and cases in which different states or their
citizens appear as parties. The judges were to be
chosen by the national legislature, to hold office
during good behaviour.

Such, in its main outlines, was the plan which
Randolph laid before the convention,
First reception
of the Virginia in the name of the Virginia delegation.
plan.
An audacious scheme! exclaimed some
of the delegates ; it was enough to take your breath
away. If they were going to begin like this, they
might as well go home, for all discussion would be
time wasted. They were not sent there to set on
foot a revolution, but to amend and strengthen the
articles of confederation. But this audacious plan
simply abolished the Confederation in order to substitute for it a consolidated national government.
Foremost in urging this objection were Yates and
Lansing of New York, with Luther Martin of
Maryland. Dickinson said it was pushing things
altogether too far, and his colleague, George Read,
hinted that the delegation from Delaware might
feel obliged to withdraw from the convention if the
election of representatives according to population
should be adopted. By the tact of Madison and
Gouverneur Morris this question was postponed for
a few days. After some animated discussion, the
issues became so narrowed and defined that they
could be taken up one by one. It was first decided
that the national legislature should consist of two
branches. Then came a warm discussion as to

whether the members of the lower house should be elected directly by the people. Curiously enough, in a country where the principle of popular election had long since taken such deep root, where the assemblies of the several states had been chosen by the people from the very beginning, there was some doubt as to whether the same principle could safely be applied to the national House of Representatives. Gerry, with his head full of the Shays rebellion and the " Know Ye " measures of the neighbouring state, thought the people could not be trusted. " The people do not want virtue," said he, " but are the dupes of pretended patriots." Roger Sherman took a similar view, and was supported by Martin, Rutledge, and both the Pinckneys ; but the sounder opinion prevailed. On this point Hamilton was at one with Mason, Wilson, and Dickinson. The proposed assembly, said Mason, was to be, so to speak, our House of Commons, and ought to know and sympathize with every part of the community. It ought to have at heart the rights and interests of every class of the people, and in no other way could this end be so completely attained as by popular election. " Yes," added Wilson, " without the confidence of the people no government, least of all a republican government, can long subsist. . . . The election of the first branch by the people is not the corner-stone only, but the foundation of the fabric." " It is essential to the democratic rights of the community," said Hamilton, " that the first branch be directly elected by the people." Madison argued powerfully on the same side, and the question was finally decided in favour of popular election.

It was now the 4th of June, when the great question came up which nearly wrecked the convention before it was settled, after a whole month of stormy debate. This was the question as to how the states should be represented in the new Congress. On the Virginia plan, the smaller states would be virtually swamped. Unless they could have equal votes, without regard to wealth or population, they would be at the mercy of the great states. In the division which ensued, the four most populous states — Virginia, Massachusetts, Pennsylvania, and North Carolina — favoured the Virginia plan ; and they succeeded in carrying South Carolina with them. Georgia, too, which, though weak at that moment, possessed considerable room for expansion, voted upon the same side. On the other hand, the states of Connecticut, New Jersey, Delaware, and Maryland — which were not only small in area, but were cut off from further expansion by their geographical situation — were not inclined to give up their equal vote in either branch of the national legislature. At this stage of the proceedings the delegation from New Hampshire had not yet arrived upon the scene. On several occasions the majority of the Maryland delegation went with the larger states, but Luther Martin, always opposed to the Virginia plan, usually succeeded in dividing the vote of the delegation. Of the New York members, Yates and Lansing, here as always, thwarted Hamilton by voting with the smaller states. Their policy throughout was one of obstruction. The members from Connecti-

Antagonism between large states and small states.

cut were disposed to be conciliatory ; but New Jersey was obstinate and implacable. She knew what it was to be tyrannized over by powerful neighbours. The wrongs she had suffered from New York and Pennsylvania rankled in the minds of her delegates. Accordingly, in the name of the smaller states, William Paterson laid before the conven' tion the so-called " New Jersey plan " for the amendment of the articles of confederation. This scheme admitted

The New Jersey plan ; a feeble palliative.

a federal legislature, consisting of a single house, an executive in the form of a council to be chosen by Congress, and likewise a federal judiciary, with powers less extensive than those contemplated by the Virginia plan. It gave to Congress the power to regulate foreign and domestic commerce, to levy duties on imports, and even to raise internal revenue by means of a Stamp Act. But with all this apparent liberality on the surface, the New Jersey plan was vicious at bottom. It did not really give Congress the power to act immediately upon individuals. The federal legislature which it proposed was to represent states, and not individuals, and the states were to vote equally, without regard to wealth or population. If things were to be left in this shape, there was no security that the powers granted to Congress could ever be really exercised. Nay, it was almost certain that they could not be put into operation. It was easy enough on paper to give Congress the permission to levy duties and regulate commerce, but such a permission would amount to nothing unless Congress were armed with the power of enforcing its decrees upon individuals. And it could in no wise acquire such power unless as the creature of the people, and not of the states. The New Jersey plan, therefore, furnished no real remedy for the evils which afflicted the country. It was vigorously opposed by Hamilton, Madison, Wilson, and King. Hamilton, indeed, took this occasion to offer a plan of his own, which, in addition to Madison's scheme of a purely national legislature, contained the features of a tenure for life or good behaviour, for the executive and the members of the upper house. But to most of the delegates this scheme seemed too little removed from a monarchy, and Hamilton's brilliant speech in its favour, while applauded by many, was supported by none. The weighty arguments of Wilson, King, and Madison prevailed, and the New Jersey plan lost its original shape when it was decided that Congress should consist of two houses. The principle of equal state representation, however, remained as a stumbling-block. Paterson, supported by his able colleague Brearley, as well as by Martin and the two irreconcilables from New York, stoutly maintained that to depart from this principle would be to exceed the powers of the convention, which assuredly was not intended to remodel the government from beginning to end. But Randolph answered, " When the salvation of the republic is at stake, it would be treason to our trust not to propose what we find necessary;" and Hamilton pithily reminded the delegates that as they were there only for the purpose of recommending a scheme which would have to be submitted to the states for accept-

ance, they need not be deterred by any false scruples from using their wits to the best possible advantage. The debate on the merits of the question
was an angry one. According to the Virginia
plan, said Brearly, the three states of Virginia,
Massachusetts, and Pennsylvania will carry everything before them. " It was known to him, from
facts within New Jersey, that where large and
small counties were united into a district for electing representatives for the district, the large counties always carried their point, and consequently
the large states would do so. . . . Was it fair,
on the other hand, that Georgia should have an
equal vote with Virginia ? He would not say it
was What remedy, then ? One only : that a
map of the United States be spread out, that all
the existing boundaries be erased, and that a new
partition of the whole be made into thirteen equal
parts." " Yes," said Paterson, " a confederacy
supposes sovereignty in the members composing it,
and sovereignty supposes equality. If we are to
be considered as a nation, all state distinctions
must be abolished, the whole must be thrown into
hotchpot, and when an equal division is made then
there may be fairly an equality of representation."
This argument was repeated with a triumphant
air, as seeming to reduce the Virginia plan to absurdity. Paterson went on to say that " there
was no more reason that a great individual state,
contributing much, should have more votes than a
small one, contributing little, than that a rich individual citizen should have more votes than an in-
digent one. If the ratable property of A was to

that of B as forty to one, ought A, for that reason, to have forty times as many votes as B ? . . . Give the large states an influence in proportion to their magnitude, and what will be the consequence ? Their ambition will be proportionally increased, and the small states will have everything to fear. It was once proposed by Galloway [in the first Continental Congress] that America should be represented in the British Parliament, and then be bound by its laws. America could not have been entitled to more than one third of the representatives which would fall to the share of Great Britain: would American rights and interests have been safe under an authority thus constituted ? " Then, warming with the subject, he exclaimed, If the great states wish to unite on such a plan, " let them unite if they please, but let them remember that they have no authority to compel the others to unite. . . . Shall I submit the welfare of New Jersey with five votes in a council where Virginia has sixteen ? . . . I will never consent to the proposed plan. I will not only oppose it here, but on my return home will do everything in my power to defeat it there. Neither my state nor myself will ever submit to tyranny."

Paterson was ably answered by James Wilson, of Pennsylvania, who pointed out the absurdity of giving 180,000 men in one part of the country as much weight in the national legislature as 750,000 in another part. It is unjust, he said. "The gentleman from New Jersey is candid. He declares his opinions boldly. I commend him for it. I will be equally candid. . . . I never will con-

federate on his principles." The convention grew
nervous and excited over this seemingly irreconcilable antagonism. The discussion was kept up with
much learning and acuteness by Madison, Ellsworth, and Martin, and history was ransacked for
testimony from the Amphiktyonic Council to Old
Sarum, and back again to the Lykian League.
Madison, rightly reading the future, declared that
if once the proposed union should be formed, the
real danger would come not from the rivalry between large and small states, but from the antago-
nistic interests of the slaveholding and non-slave-
holding states. Hamilton pointed out that in the
state of New York five counties had a majority of
the representatives, and yet the citizens of the other
counties were in no danger of tyranny, as the laws
have an equal operation upon all. Rufus King
called attention to the fact that the rights of Scotland were secure from encroachments, although
her representation in Parliament was necessarily
smaller than that of England. But New Jersey and
Delaware, mindful of recent grievances, were not
to be argued down or soothed. Gunning Bedford
of Delaware was especially violent. "Pretences
to support ambition," said he, "are never wanting.
The cry is, Where is the danger? and it is insisted
that although the powers of the general government
will be increased, yet it will be for the good of the
whole; and although the three great states form
nearly a majority of the people of America, they
never will injure the lesser states. *Gentlemen, I
do not trust you.* If you possess the power, the
abuse of it could not be checked; and what then

would prevent you from exercising it to our destruction? . . . Sooner than be ruined, *there are foreign powers who will take us by the hand.* I say this not to threaten or intimidate, but that we should reflect seriously before we act." This language called forth a rebuke from Rufus King. " I am concerned," said he, " for what fell from the gentleman from Delaware, — *take a foreign power by the hand!* I am sorry he mentioned it, and I hope he is able to excuse it to himself on the score of passion."

The situation had become dangerous. " The convention," said Martin, " was on the verge of dissolution, scarce held together by the strength of a hair." When things were looking darkest, Oliver Ellsworth and Roger Sherman suggested a compromise. " Yes," said Franklin, " when a joiner wishes to fit two boards, he sometimes pares off a bit from both." The famous Connecticut compromise led the way to the arrangement which

The Connecticut compromise.

was ultimately adopted, according to which the national principle was to prevail in the House of Representatives, and the federal principle in the Senate. But at first the compromise met with little favour. Neither party was willing to give way. " No compromise for us," said Luther Martin. " You must give each state an equal suffrage, or our business is at an end." " Then we are come to a full stop," said Roger Sherman. " I suppose it was never meant that we should break up without doing something." When the question as to allowing equality of suffrage to the states in the Federal Senate was put to vote, the result was a tie. Connecticut, New York, New Jersey, Delaware, and Maryland — five states — voted in the affirmative ; Massachusetts, Pennsylvania, Virginia, North Carolina, and South Carolina — five states — voted in the negative ; the vote of Georgia was divided and lost. It was Abraham Baldwin, a native of Connecticut and lately a tutor in Yale College, a recent emigrant to Georgia, who thus divided the vote of that state, and prevented a decision which would in all probability have broken up the convention. His state was the last to vote, and the house was hushed in anxious expectation, when this brave and wise young man yielded his private conviction to what he saw to be the paramount necessity of keeping the convention together. All honour to his memory !

The moral effect of the tie vote was in favour of the Connecticut compromise ; for no one could doubt that the little states, New Hampshire and Rhode Island, had they been represented in the division, would have voted upon that side. The matter was referred to a committee as impartially constituted as possible, with Elbridge Gerry as chairman ; and on the 5th of July, after a recess of three days, the committee reported in favour of the compromise. Fresh objections on the part of the large states were now offered by Wilson and Gouverneur Morris, and gloom again overhung the convention. Gerry said that, while he did not fully approve of the compromise, he had nevertheless supported it, because he felt sure that if nothing were done war and confusion must ensue, the old confederation being already virtually at an end. George Mason observed that "it could not be more inconvenient for any gentleman to remain absent from his private affairs than it was for him; but he would bury his bones in that city rather than expose his country to the consequences of a dissolution of the convention." Mason's subsequent behaviour was hardly in keeping with the promise of this brave speech, and in Gerry we shall observe like inconsistency. At present a timely speech from Madison soothed the troubled waters; but it was only after eleven days of somewhat more tranquil debate that the compromise was adopted on the 16th of July. Even then it was but narrowly secured. The ayes were Connecticut, New Jersey, Delaware, Maryland, and North Carolina, — five states; the noes were Pennsylvania, Virginia, South Carolina, and Georgia, — four states; Gerry and Strong against King and Gorham divided the vote of Massachusetts, which was thus lost. New York, for reasons presently to be stated, was absent. It is accordingly to Elbridge Gerry and Caleb Strong that posterity are indebted for here preventing a tie, and thus bringing the vexed question to a happy issue.

According to the compromise secured with so much difficulty, it was arranged that in the lower house population was to be represented, and in the upper house the states, each of which, without regard to size, was forever to be entitled to two senators. In the lower house there was to be one representative for every 40,000 inhabitants, but at Washington's suggestion the number was changed to 30,000, so as to increase the house, which then seemed likely to be too small in numbers. Some one suggested that with the growth of population that rate would make an unwieldy house within a hundred and fifty years from that time, whereat Gorham of Massachusetts laughed to scorn the idea that any system of government they could devise in that room could possibly last a hundred and fifty years. The difficulty has been surmounted by enlarging from time to time the basis of representation. It now seemed inadvisable that the senators should be chosen by the lower house out of persons nominated by the state legislatures ; and it was accordingly decided that they should be not merely nominated, but elected, by the state legislatures. Thus the Senate was made quite independent of the lower house. At the same time, the senators were to vote as individuals, and thus the old practice of voting by states, except in certain peculiar emergencies, was finally done away with.

It is seldom, if ever, that a political compromise leaves things evenly balanced. Almost every such arrangement, when once set working, weighs down the scales decidedly to the one side or the other. The Connecticut compromise was really a decisive victory for Madison and his party, although it modified the Virginia plan so considerably. They could well afford to defer to the fears and prejudices of the smaller states in the struc- It was a deci- ture of the Senate, for by securing a sive victory for Madison's lower house, which represented the scheme. American people, and not the American states, they won the whole battle in so far as the question of radically reforming the government was con-

cerned. As soon as the foundation was thus laid
for a government which should act directly upon
individuals, it obviously became necessary to abandon the articles of confederation, and work out a
new constitution in all its details. The plan, as
now reported, omitted the obnoxious adjective
"national," and spoke of the *federal* legislature
and *federal* courts. But to the men who were still
blindly wedded to the old confederation this sooth-
ing change of phraseology did not conceal their
defeat. On the very day that the compromise was
favourably reported by the committee, Yates and
Lansing quit the convention in disgust, and went
home to New York. After the departure of these
uncongenial colleagues, Hamilton might have acted
with power, had he not known too well that the
sentiment of his state did not support him. As a
mere individual he could do but little, and accordingly he went home for a while to attend to press-
ing business, returning just in time to take part in
the closing scenes. His share in the work of fram-
Irreconcilables ing the Federal Constitution was very
to home.   small. About the time that Hamilton
returned, Luther Martin, whose wrath had waxed
hotter every day, as he saw power after power extended to the federal government, at length gave
way and went back to Maryland, vowing that he
would have nothing more to do with such high-
handed proceedings.

While the Connecticut compromise thus scattered a few scintillations of discontent, and re-
lieved the convention of some of its most discordant
elements, its general effect was wonderfully har-

monizing. The men who had opposed the Virginia plan only through their dread of the larger states were now more than conciliated. The concession of equal representation in the Senate turned out to have been a master stroke of diplomacy. As soon as the little states were assured of an equal share in the control of one of the two central legislative bodies, they suddenly forgot their scruples about thoroughly overhauling the government, and none were readier than they to intrust extensive powers to the new Congress. Paterson of New Jersey, the fiercest opponent of the Virginia plan, became from that time forth to the end of his life the most devoted of Federalists.

That first step which proverbially gives the most trouble had now been fairly taken. But other compromises were needed before the work of construction could properly be carried out. As the antagonism between great and small states disappeared from the scene, other antagonisms appeared. It is worth noting that just for a moment there was revealed a glimmering of jealousy and dread on the part of the eastern states toward those of which the foundations were laid in the northwestern territory. Many *Other antagonisms; vague dread of the future west.* people in New England feared that their children would be drawn westward in such numbers as to create immense states beyond the Ohio; and thus it was foreseen that the relative political weight of New England in the future would be diminished. To a certain extent this prediction has been justified by events, but Roger Sherman rightly maintained that it afforded no just grounds for dread.

King and Gerry introduced a most illiberal and
mischievous motion, that the total number of representatives from new states must never be allowed
to exceed the total number from the original thirteen. Such an arrangement, which would surely
have been enough to create that antagonism between east and west which it sought to forestall
and avoid, was supported by Massachusetts and
Connecticut, with Delaware and Maryland; but it
was defeated by the combination of New Jersey
with the four states south of Maryland. The
ground was thus cleared for a very different kind
of sectional antagonism, — that which, as Madison
truly said, would prove the most deep-seated and
enduring of all, — the antagonism between north
and south. The first great struggle between the
pro-slavery and anti-slavery parties began in the Federal Convention, and it
resulted in the first two of the long series
of compromises by which the irrepressible conflict
was postponed until the north had waxed strong
enough to confront the dreaded spectre of secession,
and, summoning all its energies in one stupendous
effort, exorcise it forever. From this moment down
to 1865 we shall continually be made to realize
how the American people had entered into the
shadow of the coming Civil War before they had
fairly emerged from that of the Revolution; and
as we pass from scene to scene of the solemn story,
we shall learn how to be forever grateful for the
sudden and final clearing of the air wrought by
that frightful storm which men not yet old can still
so well remember.

Antagonism
between slave
states and free
states.

The first compromise related to the distribution of representatives between north and south. Was representation in the lower house of Congress to be proportioned to wealth, or to population; and if the latter, were all the inhabitants, or only all the free inhabitants, to be counted? It was soon agreed that wealth was difficult to reckon and population easy to count; and to an extent sufficient for all ordinary purposes, population might serve as an index of wealth. A state with 500,000 inhabitants would be in most cases richer than one with 400,000. In those days, when cities were few and small, this was approximately true. In our day it is not at all true. A state with large commercial and manufacturing cities is sure to be much richer than a state in which the population is chiefly rural. The population of Massachusetts is somewhat smaller than that of Indiana; but her aggregate wealth is more than double that of Indiana. Disparities like this, which do not trouble us to-day, would have troubled the Federal Convention. We no longer think it desirable to give political representation to wealth, or to anything but persons. We have become thoroughly democratic, but our great-grandfathers had not. To them it seemed quite essential that wealth should be represented as well as persons; but they got over the main difficulty easily, because under the economic conditions of that time population could serve roughly as an index to wealth, and it was much easier to count noses than to assess the value of farms and stock.

But now there was in all the southern states,

and in most of the northern, a peculiar species of collective existence, which might be described either as wealth or as population. As human beings the slaves might be described as population, but in the eye of the law they were chattels. In the northern states slavery was rapidly disappearing, and the property in negroes was so small as to be hardly worth considering; while south of Mason and Dixon's line this peculiar kind of property was the chief wealth of the states. But clearly, in apportioning representation, in sharing political power in the federal assembly, the same rule should have been applied impartially to all the states. At this point, Pierce Butler and Cotesworth Pinckney of South Carolina insisted that slaves were part of the population, and as such must be counted in ascertaining the basis of representation. A fierce and complicated dispute ensued. The South Carolina proposal suggested a uniform rule, but it was one that would scarcely alter the political weight of the north, while it would vastly increase the weight of the south; and it would increase it most in just the quarter where slavery was most deeply rooted. The power of South Carolina, as a member of the Union, would be doubled by such a measure. Hence the northern delegates maintained that slaves, as chattels, ought no more to be reckoned as part of the population than houses or ships "Has a man in Virginia," exclaimed Paterson "a number of votes in proportion to the number of his slaves? And if negroes are not represented in the states to which they belong, why should they

Were slaves to be reckoned as persons or as chattels?

be represented in the general government? . . . If a meeting of the people were to take place in a slave state, would the slaves vote? They would not. Why then should they be represented in a federal government?" "I can never agree," said Gouverneur Morris, "to give such encouragement to the slave-trade as would be given by allowing the southern states a representation for their ne- groes. . . . I would sooner submit myself to a tax for paying for all the negroes in the United States than saddle posterity with such a constitution."

The attitude taken by Virginia was that of peace-maker. On the one hand, such men as Washington, Madison, and Mason, who were ear- nestly hoping to see their own state soon freed from the curse of slavery, could not fail to perceive that if Virginia were to gain an increase of politi- cal weight from the existence of that institution, the difficulty of getting the state legislature to abolish it would be enhanced. But on the other hand, they saw that South Carolina was inexorable, and that her refusal to adopt the Constitution for this reason would certainly carry Georgia with her, and probably North Carolina, also. Even had South Carolina alone been involved, it was not simply a question of forming a Union which should either include her or leave her out in the cold. The case was much more complicated than that. It was really doubtful if, without the cordial as- sistance of South Carolina, a Union could be formed at all. A Federal Constitution had not only to be framed, but it had to be presented to the thirteen states for adoption. It was by no means clear that enough states would ratify it to enable the experiment of the new government to go into operation. New York and Rhode Island were known to be bitterly opposed to it; Massachusetts could not be counted on as sure; to add South Carolina to this list would be to endanger everything. The event justified this caution. We shall hereafter see that it was absolutely necessary to satisfy South Carolina, and that but for her ratification, coming just at the moment when it did, the work of the Federal Convention would probably have been done in vain. It was a clear perception of the wonderful complication of interests involved in the final appeal to the people that induced the Virginia statesmen to take the lead in a compromise. Four years before, in 1783, when Congress was endeavouring to apportion the quotas of revenue to be required of the several states, a similar dispute had arisen. If taxation were to be distributed according to population, it made a great difference whether slaves were to be counted as population or not. If slaves were to be counted, the southern states would have to pay more than their equitable share into the federal treasury; if slaves were not to be counted, it was argued at the north that they would be paying less than their equitable share. Consequently, at that time the north had been inclined to maintain that the slaves were population, while the south had preferred to regard them as chattels. Thus we see that in politics, as well as in algebra, it makes all the difference in the world whether you start with *plus* or with *minus*. On that occasion Madison had offered a successful compromise, in which a slave figured as three fifths of a freeman; and Rutledge of South Carolina, who was now present in the convention, had supported the measure. Madison now proposed the same method of getting over the diffi

culty about representation, and his compromise was adopted. It was agreed that in counting population, whether for direct taxation or for representation in the lower house of Congress, five slaves should be reckoned as three individuals.

All this was thoroughly illogical, of course; it left the question whether slaves are population or chattels for theorizers to wrangle over, and for future events to decide. It was easy for James Wilson to show that there was neither rhyme nor reason in it: but he subscribed to it, nevertheless, just as the northern abolitionists, Rufus King and Gouverneur Morris, joined with Washington and Madison, and with the pro-slavery Pinckneys, in subscribing to it, because they all believed that without such a compromise the Constitution would not be adopted; and in this there can be little doubt that they were right. The evil consequences were unquestionably very serious indeed. Henceforth, so long as slavery lasted, the vote of a southerner counted for more than the vote of a northerner; and just where negroes were most numerous the power of their masters became greatest. In South Carolina there soon came to be more blacks than whites, and the application of the rule therefore went far toward doubling the vote of South Carolina in the House of Representatives and in the electoral college. Every five slaveholders down there were equal in political weight to not less than eight farmers or merchants in the north; and thus this troublesome state acquired a power of working mischief out of all proportion to her real size. At a later date the operation of the rule in Mississippi was similar; and in general it was just the most backward and barbarous parts of the Union that were thus favoured at the expense of the most civilized parts. Admitting all this, how-

In other words, it was the best solution attainable under the circumstances.

ever, it remains undeniable that the Constitution saved us from anarchy; and there can be little doubt that slavery and every other remnant of barbarism in American society would have thriven far more lustily under a state of chronic anarchy than was possible under the Constitution. Four years of concentrated warfare, animated by an intense and lofty moral purpose, could not hurt the character or mar the fortunes of the people, like a century of aimless and miscellaneous squabbling over a host of petty local interests. The War of Secession was a terrible ordeal to pass through; but when one tries to picture what might have happened in this fair land without the work of the Federal Convention, the imagination stands aghast.

The second great compromise between north-

Compromise between New England and South Carolina as to the foreign slave-trade.

ern and southern interests related to the abolition of the foreign slave-trade and the power of the federal government over commerce. All the states except South Carolina and Georgia wished to stop the importation of slaves; but the physical condi-

tions of rice and indigo culture exhausted the
negroes so fast that these two states felt that their
industries would be dried up at the very source
if the importation of fresh negroes were to be
stopped. Cotesworth Pinckney accordingly declared that South Carolina would consider a vote
to abolish the slave-trade as simply a polite way of
telling her that she was not wanted in the Union.
On the other hand, the three New England states
present in the convention had made up their minds
that it would not do to allow the several states any
longer to regulate commerce each according to its
own whim. It was of vital importance that this
power should be taken from the states and lodged
in Congress; otherwise, the Union would soon be
rent in pieces by commercial disputes. The policy
of New York had thoroughly impressed this lesson
upon all the neighbouring states. But none of the
southern states were in favour of granting this power
unreservedly to Congress. If a navigation act
could be passed by a simple majority in Congress,
it was feared that the New Englanders would get
all the carrying trade into their own hands, and
then charge ruinous freights for carrying rice, indigo, and tobacco to the north and to Europe. On
this point, accordingly, the southern delegates acted
as a unit in insisting that Congress should not be
empowered to pass navigation acts, except by a two
thirds vote of both houses. This would have tied
the hands of the federal government most unfortunately; and the New Englanders, enlightened by
their own interests, saw it to be so. Here were the
materials ready for a compromise, or, as the stout

abolitionist, Gouverneur Morris, truly called it, a " bargain " between New England and the far south. New Hampshire, Massachusetts, and Connecticut consented to the prolonging of the foreign slave-trade for twenty years, or until 1808; and in return South Carolina and Georgia consented to the clause empowering Congress to pass navigation acts and otherwise regulate commerce by a simple majority of votes. At the same time, as a concession to rice and indigo, the New Englanders agreed that Congress should be forever prohibited from taxing exports ; and thus one remnant of mediæval political economy was neatly swept away.

This compromise was carried against the sturdy opposition of Virginia. The language of George Mason of Virginia is worth quoting, for it was such as Theodore Parker might have used. He called the slave-trade " this infernal traffic." " Slavery," said he, " discourages arts and manufactures. The poor despise labour when performed by slaves. They prevent the immigration of whites, who really strengthen and enrich a country. They produce the most pernicious effect on manners. Every master of slaves is born a petty tyrant. They bring the judgment of Heaven on a country. As nations cannot be rewarded or punished in the next world, they must be in this. By an inevitable chain of causes and effects, Providence punishes national sins by national calamities." But these prophetic words were powerless against the combination of New England with the far south. One thing was now made certain, — that the vast in-

This last compromise seems to make the adhesion of Virginia doubtful.

fluence of Rutledge and the Pinckneys would be thrown unreservedly in behalf of the new Constitution. "I will confess," said Cotesworth Pinckney, "that I had prejudices against the eastern states before I came here, but I have found them as liberal and candid as any men whatever." But this compromise, which finally secured South Carolina and Georgia, made Virginia for the moment doubtful ; for Mason and Randolph were so disgusted at the absolute power over commerce conceded to Congress that, when the Constitution was finished and engrossed on paper, they refused to sign it.

It is difficult to read this or any other episode in our history whereby negro slavery was extended and fostered without burning indignation. But this is not the proper mood for the historian, whose aim is to interpret men's actions by the circumstances of their time, in order to judge their motives correctly. In 1787 slavery was the cloud like unto a man's hand which portended a deluge, but those who could truly read the signs were few. From north to south, slavery had been slowly dying out for nearly fifty years. It had become extinct in Massachusetts, it was nearly so in all the other northern states, and it had just been forever prohibited in the national domain. In Maryland and Virginia there was a strong and growing party in favour of abolition. The movement had even gathered strength in North Carolina. Only the rice-swamps of the far south remained wedded to their idols. It was quite generally believed that slavery was destined speedily to expire, to give place to a better system of labour, without any great danger or disturbance; and this opinion was distinctly set forth by many delegates in the convention.[1] Even Charles Pinckney went so far as to express a hope that South Carolina, if not too much meddled with, would by and by voluntarily rank herself among the emancipating states; but his older cousin declared himself bound in candour to acknowledge that there was very little likelihood indeed of so desirable an event. Not even these South Carolinians ventured to defend slavery on principle. This belief in the moribund condition of slavery prevented the convention from realizing the actual effect of the concessions which were made. Scarcely any cotton was grown at that time, and none was sent to England. The industrial revolution about to be wrought by the inventions of Arkwright and Hargreaves, Cartwright and Watt and Whitney, could not be foreseen. Nor could it be foreseen that presently, when there should thus arise a great demand for slaves from Virginia as a breeding-ground, the abolitionist

---

[1] The slave-population of the United States, according to the census of 1790, was thus distributed among the states : —

North.			*South.*	
New Hampshire	. . . 158	Delaware	8,887
Vermont	17	Maryland . . .	103,036
Massachusetts	—	Virginia . . .	293,427
Rhode Island	952	North Carolina .	100,572
Connecticut	2,759	South Carolina .	107,094
New York	21,324	Georgia	29,264
New Jersey	11,423	Kentucky . . .	11,830
Pennsylvania	3,737	Tennessee . . .	3,417
	40,370		657,527

Total . . . . 697,897.

party in that state would disappear, leaving her to join in the odious struggle for introducing slavery into the national domain. Though these things were so soon to happen, the wisest man in 1787 could not foresee them. The convention hoped that twenty years would see not only the end of the foreign slave-trade, but the restriction and diminution of slavery itself. It was in such a mood that they completed the compromise by recommending a tariff of ten dollars a head upon all negroes imported, while at the same time a clause was added for insuring the recovery of fugitive slaves, quite similar to the clause in the ordinance for the government of the northwestern territory.

It was the three great compromises here described that laid the foundations of our Federal Constitution. The first compromise, by conceding equal representation to the states in the Senate, enlisted the small states in favour of the new scheme, and by establishing a national system of representation in the lower house, prepared the way for a government that could endure. This was Madison's great victory, secured by the aid of Sherman and Ellsworth, without which nothing could have been effected. The second compromise, at the cost of giving disproportionate weight to the slave states, gained their support for the more perfect union that was about to be formed. The third compromise, at the cost of postponing for twenty years the abolition of the foreign slave-trade, secured absolute free-trade between the states, with the surrender of all control over commerce into the hands

The foundations of the Constitution were thus laid in compromise.

of the federal government. After these steps had been taken, the most difficult and dangerous part of the road had been travelled; the remainder, though extremely important, was accomplished far more easily. It was mainly the task of building on the foundations already laid.

In the grants to the federal government of powers hitherto reserved to the several states, the diversity of opinion among the members of the convention was but slight compared to the profound antagonism which had been allayed by the three initial compromises. It was admitted, as a matter of course, that the federal government alone *Powers grant-* could coin money, fix the standard of *ed to the fed-* weights and measures, establish post- *eral govern-* *ment.* offices and post-roads, and grant patents and copyrights. To it alone was naturally intrusted the whole business of war and of international relations. It could define and punish felonies committed on the high seas; it could maintain a navy and issue letters of marque and reprisal; it could support an army and provide for calling forth the militia to execute the laws of the Union, to suppress insurrections, and to repel invasions. But in relation to this question of the army and the militia there was some characteristic discussion. It was at first proposed that Congress should have the power "to subdue a rebellion in any state on the application of its legislature." The Shays rebellion was then fresh in the memory of all the delegates, and their arguments simply reflected the impression which that unpleasant affair had left upon them. Charles Pinckney, Gouverneur

Morris, and John Langdon wished to have the power given to Congress unconditionally, without waiting for an application from the legislature. But Gerry, who had been on the ground, spoke sturdily against such a needless infraction of state rights. He was utterly opposed, he said, to " letting loose the myrmidons of the United States on a state without its own consent. The states will be the best judges in such cases. More blood would have been spilt in Massachusetts in the late insurrection if the general authority had intermeddled." Ellsworth suggested that Congress should use its discretion only in cases where the legislature of the state could not meet; but Randolph forcibly replied that if Congress is to judge whether a state legislature can or cannot meet, the difficulty is in no wise surmounted. Gerry's view at last prevailed, and in accordance therewith it was decided that the federal power should guarantee to every state a republican form of government, and should protect each of them against invasion; and on application of the legislature, or of the executive (if the legislature could not be convened), it should protect them against domestic violence. This arrangement did not fully provide against such an emergency as that of rival and hostile executives in the same state, as under the so-called " carpetbag " governments which followed after the War of Secession, but it was doubtless as sound a provision as any general constitution could make.

The federal government was further empowered to borrow money on the credit of the United States; and it was declared that all debts contracted and engagements entered into before the adoption of this constitution should be as valid against the United States under this constitution as under the confederation. There was to be no repudiation or readjustment of debts on the ground of inability to pay. Congress was further empowered to establish a uniform rule of naturalization and a uniform law of bankruptcy. But it was prohibited from passing bills of attainder or *ex post facto* laws, or suspending the writ of *habeas corpus*, except under the stress of rebellion or invasion. It was provided that all duties, imposts, or excises should be uniform throughout the United States. The federal government could not give preference to one state over another in its commercial regulations. It could not tax exports. It could not draw money from the treasury save by due process of appropriation, and all bills relating to the raising of revenue must originate in the lower house, which directly represented the people. Congress was empowered to admit new states into the Union, but it was not allowed to interfere with the territorial areas of states already existing without the express consent of the local legislatures. To insure the independence of the federal government, it was provided that senators and representatives should be paid out of the federal treasury, and not by their respective states, as had been the case under the confederation. Except for such offences as treason, felony, or breach of the peace, they should be "privileged from arrest during their attendance at the session of their respective houses, and in going to or returning from the same; and for any

speech or debate in either house " they were not to
be "questioned in any other place." It was further provided that a territory not exceeding ten
miles square should be ceded to the United States,
and set apart as the site of a federal city, in which
the general government should ever after hold its
meetings, erect its buildings, and exercise exclusive
jurisdiction. During the past four years the Continental Congress had skipped about from Philadelphia to Princeton, to Annapolis, to Trenton, to
New York, until it had become a laughing-stock,
and the newspapers were full of squibs about it.
Verily, said one facetious editor, the Lord shall
make this government like unto a wheel, and keep
it rolling back and forth betwixt Dan and Beer-
sheba, and grant it no rest this side of Jordan.
This inconvenience was now to be remedied. Congress was hereafter to have a federal police force
at its disposal, and was never more to be reduced
to the humiliation of a fruitless appeal to the protecting arm of a state government, as at Philadelphia in the summer of 1783. Furthermore, the
Continental Congress had of late years commanded
so little respect, and had offered so few temptations to able men in quest of political distinction,
that its meetings were often attended by no more
than eight or ten members. It was actually on the
point of dying a natural death through sheer lack
of public interest in it. To prevent any possible
continuance of such a disgraceful state of things,
it was agreed that the Federal Congress should be
"authorized to compel the attendance of absent
members, in such manner and under such penalties

as each house may provide." Had the political
life of the country continued to go on as under the
confederation, it is very doubtful whether such a
provision as this would have remedied the evil.
But the new Federal Congress, drawing its life
directly from the people, was destined to afford far
greater opportunities for a political career than
were afforded by the feeble body of delegates which
preceded it ; and a penal clause, compelling members to attend its meetings, was hardly needed
under the new circumstances which arose.

While the powers of the federal government
were thus carefully defined, at the same time several powers were expressly denied to the states. No
state was allowed, without explicit authority from

Powers de-
nied to the
states.

Congress, to lay any tonnage or custom-
house duties, " keep troops or ships of
war in time of peace, enter into any
agreement or compact with another state or with
a foreign power, or engage in war unless actually
invaded, or in such imminent danger as will not
admit of delays." The following clause provided
against a recurrence of some of the worst evils
which had been felt under the " league of friendship : " " No state shall enter into any treaty,
alliance, or confederation ; grant letters of marque
and reprisal; coin money ; emit bills of credit;
make anything but gold and silver coin a tender in
payment of debts ; pass any bill of attainder, *ex
post facto* law, or law impairing the obligation of
contracts ; or grant any title of nobility." Hence
forth there was to be no repetition of such dis
graceful scenes as had lately been witnessed in

Rhode Island. So far as the state legislatures were concerned, paper money was to be ruled out forever. But how was it with the federal government? By the articles of confederation the United States were allowed to issue bills of credit, and make them a tender in payment of debts. In the Federal Convention the committee of detail suggested that this permission might remain under the new constitution; but the suggestion was almost unanimously condemned. All the ablest men in the convention spoke emphatically against it. Gouverneur Morris urged that the federal government, no less than the state governments, should be expressly prohibited from issuing bills of credit, or in any wise making its promissory notes a legal tender. He went over the history of the past ten years; he called attention to the obstinacy with which the wretched device had been resorted to again and again, after its evils had been thrust before everybody's eyes; and he proved himself a true prophet when he said that if the United States should ever again have a great war to conduct, people would have forgotten all about these things, and would call for fresh issues of inconvertible paper, with similar disastrous results. Now was the time to stop it once for all. " Yes," echoed Roger Sherman, " this is the favourable crisis for crushing paper money." "This is the time," said his colleague, Ellsworth, " to shut and bar the door against paper money, which can in no case be necessary. Give the government credit, and other resources will offer. The power may do harm, never good."

Emphatic condemnation of paper money.

There was no way, he added, in which powerful
friends could so soon be gained for the new constitution as by withholding this power from the government. James Wilson took the same view. "It
will have the most salutary influence on the credit
of the United States," said he, "to remove the possibility of paper money." "Rather than grant the
power to Congress," said John Langdon, "I would
reject the whole plan." "The words which grant
this power," said George Read of Delaware, "if
not struck out, will be as alarming as the mark of
the Beast, in the Apocalypse." On none of the
subjects that came up for discussion during that
summer was the convention more nearly unanimous
than in its condemnation of paper money. The
only delegate who ventured to speak in its favour
was Mercer of Maryland. What Hamilton would
have said, if he had been present that day, we may
judge from his vigorous words published some time
before. The power to emit an inconvertible paper
as a sign of value ought never hereafter to be used ;
for in its very nature, said he, it is "pregnant with
abuses, and liable to be made the engine of impo-
sition and fraud, holding out temptations equally
pernicious to the integrity of government and to
the morals of the people." Paterson called it
"sanctifying iniquity by law." The same views
were entertained by Washington and Madison.
There were a few delegates, however, who thought
it unsafe to fetter Congress absolutely. To use
Luther Martin's expression, they did not set themselves up to be "wise beyond every event." George
Mason said he "had a mortal hatred to paper

money, yet, as he could not foresee all emergencies, he was unwilling to tie the hands of the legislature. The late war," he thought, " could not have been carried on had such a prohibition existed." Randolph spoke to the same effect. It was finally decided, by the vote of nine states against New Jersey and Maryland, that the power to issue inconvertible paper should not be granted to the federal government. An express prohibition, such as had been adopted for the separate states, was thought unnecessary. It was supposed that it was enough to withhold the power, since the federal government would not venture to exercise it unless expressly permitted in the Constitution. " Thus," says Madison, in his narrative of the proceedings, " the pretext for a paper currency, and particularly for making the bills a tender, either for public or private debts, was cut off." Nothing could be more clearly expressed than this. As Mr. Justice Field observes, in his able dissenting opinion in the recent case of Juilliard *vs.* Greenman, " if there be anything in the history of the Constitution which can be established with moral certainty, it is that the framers of that instrument intended to prohibit the issue of legal-tender notes both by the general government and by the states, and thus prevent interference with the contracts of private parties." Such has been the opinion of our ablest constitutional jurists, Marshall, Webster, Story, Curtis, and Nelson. There can be little doubt that, according to all sound principles of interpretation, the Legal Tender Act of 1862 was passed in fla‑ grant violation of the Constitution. Could Ells‑

worth and Morris, Langdon and Madison, have foreseen the possibility of such extraordinary judgments as have lately emanated from the Supreme Court of the United States, they would doubtless have insisted upon the express prohibition, instead of leaving it to posterity to root out the plague, as it will apparently some time have to do, by the cumbrous process of an amendment to the Constitution.

The work of the convention, as thus far considered, related to the legislative department of the new government. While these discussions were going on, much attention had been paid, from time to time, to the characteristics of the proposed federal executive. The debates on this question, though long kept up, were far less acrimonious than the debates on representation and the power of Congress over trade, because here there was no obvious clashing of local interests. But for this very reason the convention had no longer so clear a chart to steer by. On the question of the slave-trade, the Pinckneys knew accurately just what South Carolina wanted, how much it would do to claim, and how far it would be necessary to yield. As to the regulation of commerce by a bare majority of votes in Congress, King and Sherman on the one hand, Mason and Randolph on the other, were able to pursue a thoroughly definite course of action in behalf of what were supposed to be the special interests of New England or of Virginia. Consequently, the debates kept close to the point; the controversy was keen, and sometimes, as we have seen, angry.

It was very different with the question as to the federal executive. Upon this point the discussions were guided rather by general speculations as to what would be most likely to work well, and accordingly they wandered far and wide. Some of the delegates seemed to think we should sooner or later come to adopt a hereditary monarchy, and that the chief thing to be done was to postpone the event as long as possible. Many wild ideas were broached : such, for example, as a triple-headed executive, to represent the eastern, middle, and southern states, somewhat as associated Roman emperors at times administered affairs in the different portions of an undivided empire.

Debates as to the federal executive.

The Virginia plan had not stated whether its proposed executive was to be single or plural, because the Virginia delegates could not agree. Madison wished it to be single, to insure greater efficiency, but to Randolph and Mason a tyranny seemed to lurk in such an arrangement. When James Wilson and Charles Pinckney suggested that the executive power should be intrusted into the hands of one man, a profound silence fell upon the convention. No one spoke for several minutes, until Washington, from the chair, asked if he should put the question. Franklin then got up, and said it was an interesting subject, and he should like to hear what the members had to say ; and so the ball was set rolling. Rutledge said there was no need of their being so shy. A man might frankly express his opinions, and afterwards change them if he saw good reason for so doing. For his part, he was in favour of vesting the executive power in a

single person, to secure efficiency of administration
and concentration of responsibility ; but he would
not give him the power to declare war and make
peace.   Sherman then made the far-reaching suggestion, that the executive magistracy was really
" nothing more than an institution for carrying the
will of the legislature into effect ; that the person
or persons ought to be appointed by and account-
able to the legislature only, which was the deposi-
tory of the supreme will of the society.   As they
were the best judges of the business which ought
to be done by the executive department, . . . he
wished the number might not be fixed, but that
the legislature should be at liberty to appoint one
or more, as experience might dictate."   It would
greatly have astonished the convention had they
been told that this suggestion of Sherman's was a
move in the very same line of development which
the British government had been following for
more than half a century ; yet such, as we shall
presently see, was the case.   Had this point been
understood then as we understand it now, the proceedings of the convention could not have failed to
be profoundly affected by it.   As it was, the suggestion did not receive due attention, and the
stream of discussion was turned into a very different channel.   Wilson argued powerfully in favour
of a single chief magistrate, and this view finally
prevailed.

After it had been decided that there should be
one man set in so high a position, there was endless discussion as to whether he should be elected
by the people or by Congress, and whether he

should serve for one, or two, or three, or four, or
ten, or fifteen years. "Better call it There should
be a president,
but how should
he be elected.
twenty," said Rufus King, sarcastically;
"it is the average reign of princes."
Hamilton and Gouverneur Morris would have had
him chosen for life, subject to removal for misbe-
haviour; but the preference for a short term of
service was soon manifest. As to the method of
election, opinions oscillated back and forth for several weeks. Wilson said " he was almost unwilling
to declare the mode which he wished to take place,
being apprehensive that it might appear chimerical. He would say, however, at least, that in
theory he was for an election by the people. Experience, particularly in New York and Massachusetts, showed that an election of the first magistrate by the people at large was both a convenient
and a successful mode. The objects of choice in
such cases must be persons whose merits have general notoriety." Mason, Rutledge, and Strong
agreed with Sherman that the executive should
be chosen by the legislature; but Washington,
Madison, Gerry, and Gouverneur Morris strongly
disapproved of this. Morris argued that an election by the national legislature would be the work
of intrigue and corruption, like the election of the
king of Poland by a diet of nobles; but Mason
declared, on the other hand, that " to refer the
choice of a proper character for a chief magistrate
to the people would be as unnatural as to refer a
trial of colours to a blind man." A decision was
first reached against an election by Congress, because it was thought that if the chief magistrate

should prove himself thoroughly competent he ought to be reëligible; but if reëligible he would be exposed to the temptation of truckling to the most powerful party or cabal in Congress, in order to secure his reëlection. It did not occur to any one to suggest that under ordinary circumstances the executive ought to follow the policy of the most powerful party in Congress, and that he might at the same time preserve all needful independence by being clothed with the power of dissolving Congress and making an appeal to the people in a new election. It is interesting to consider what might have come of such a suggestion, following upon the heels of that made by Roger Sherman. As we shall presently see, it would have immeasurably simplified the machinery of our government, besides making the executive what it ought to be, the arm of the legislature, instead of a separate and coördinate power. Upon this point the minds of nearly all the members were so far under the sway of an incorrect theory that such an idea occurred to none of them. It was decided that the chief magistrate ought to be reëligible, and therefore should not be elected by Congress.

An immediate choice by the people, however, Suggestion of did not meet with general favour. To
an electoral
college. obviate the difficulty, Ellsworth and King suggested the device of an electoral college, in which the electors should be chosen by the state legislatures, and should hold a meeting at the federal city for the sole purpose of deciding upon a chief magistrate. It was then objected that it would be difficult to find competent men

who would be willing to undertake a long journey simply for such a purpose. The objection was felt to be a very grave one, and so the convention returned to the plan of an election by Congress, and again confronted the difficulty of the chief magistrate's intriguing to secure his reëlection. Wilson thought to do away with this difficulty by introducing the element of blind chance, as in some of the states of ancient Greece, and choosing the executive by a board of electors taken from Congress by lot; but the suggestion found little support. Dickinson thought it would be well if the people of each state were to choose its best citizen, — in modern parlance, its "favourite son;" then out of these thirteen names a chief magistrate might be chosen, either by Congress or by a special board of electors. At length, on the 26th of July, at the motion of Mason, the convention resolved that there should be a national executive, to consist of a single person, to be chosen by the national legislature for the term of seven years, and to be ineligible for a second term. He was to be styled President of the United States of America.

This decision remained until the very end of August, when the whole question was reopened by a motion of Rutledge that the two houses of Congress, in electing the president, should proceed by "joint ballot." The object of this motion was to prevent either house from exerting a negative on the choice of the other. It was carried in spite of the opposition of some of the smaller states, which might hope to exercise a greater relative influence upon the choice of presidents, if the Senate were to vote separately. At this point the fears of Gouverneur Morris, that an election by Congress would result in boundless intrigue, were revived ; and in a powerful speech he persuaded the convention to return to the device of the electoral college, which might be made equal in number and similar in composition to the two houses of Congress sitting together. It need not be required of the electors, after all, that they should make a long journey to the seat of the federal government. They might meet in their respective states, and vote by ballot for two persons, one of whom must be an inhabitant of a different state. By this provision it was hoped to diminish the chances for extreme sectional partiality. A list of these votes might be sent under seal to the presiding officer of the Senate, to be counted. Should no candidate turn out to have a majority of the votes, the Senate might choose a president from the five highest candidates on the list. The candidate having the next highest number of votes might be declared vice-president, and preserve the visible continuity of the government in case of the death of the president during his term of office. By these changes the method of electing the president, as finally decided upon, was nearly completed. But Mason, Randolph, Gerry, King, and Wilson were not satisfied with the provision that the Senate might choose the president in case of a failure of choice on the part of the electoral college : they preferred to give this power to the House of Representatives. It was thought that the Senate would be likely to prove an aristocratic body, somewhat removed from the people in its sympathies, and there was a dread of intrusting to it too many important functions. Mason thought that the sway of an aristocracy would be worse than an absolute monarchy; and if the Senate might every now and then elect the president, there would be a risk that the dignity of his office might degenerate, until he should become a mere creature of the Senate. On the other hand, the small states, in order to have an equal voice with the large ones, in such an emergency as the failure of choice by the electoral college, wished to keep the eventual choice in the hands of the Senate. Among the delegates from the small states, only Langdon and Dickinson at first supported the change, and only New Hampshire voted for it. At length Sherman proposed a compromise, which was carried. It was agreed that the eventual choice should be given to the House of Representatives, and not to the Senate, but that in exercising this function the vote in the House of Representatives should be taken by states. Thus the humours of the delegates from the small states, and of those who dreaded the accumulation of powers into the hands of an oligarchy, were alike gratified. This arrangement was finally adopted by the votes of ten states against Delaware.

But in spite of all the minute and anxious care that was taken in guarding this point, the contingency of an election being thus thrown into the hands of the national legislature was not regarded as likely often to occur. In point of fact, it has hitherto happened only twice in the century, in the elections of 1800 and of 1824. It was recognized that the work would ordinarily be done through the machinery of the electoral college, and that thus the fear of intrigue between the president and Congress, as it had originally been felt by the convention, might be set aside. To make assurance doubly sure, it was provided that " no person shall be appointed an elector who is a member of the legislature of the United States, or who holds any office of profit or trust under the United States." It then appeared that the arguments which had been alleged against the eligibility of the president for a second term had lost their force; and he was accordingly made reëligible, while his term of service was reduced from seven years to four.

The scheme had thus arrived substantially at its present shape, except that the counting of the electoral vote still remained in the hands of the Senate. On the 6th of September this provision was altered, and it was decided that " the president of the Senate shall, in the presence of the Senate

How to count the votes. and the House of Representatives, open all the certificates, and the votes shall then be counted." The object of this provision was to take the office of counting away from the Senate alone, and give it to Congress as a whole; and while doing so, to guard against the failure of an election through the disagreement of the two houses. The method of counting was not prescribed, for it was thought that it might safely be left to joint rules established by the two houses of Congress themselves, after analogies supplied by the experience of the several state legislatures.

The case of double returns, sent in by rival governments in the same state, was not contemplated by the convention ; and thus the door was left open for a danger considerably greater than many of those over which the delegates were agitated. It may safely be said, however, that not even the wildest license of interpretation can find any support for the ridiculous doctrine suggested by some persons blinded by political passion in 1877, that the business of counting the votes and deciding upon the validity of returns belongs to the president of the Senate. No such idea was for a moment entertained by the convention. Any such idea is completely negatived by their action of the 6th of September. The express purpose of the final arrangement made on that day was to admit the House of Representatives to active participation in the office of determining who should have been elected president. It was expressly declared that this work was too important to be left to the Senate alone. What, then, would the convention have said to the preposterous notion that this work might safely be left to the presiding officer of the Senate ? The convention were keenly alive to any imaginable grant of authority that might enable the Senate to grow into an oligarchy. What would they have said to the proposal to create a monocrat *ad hoc*, an official permanently endowed by virtue of his office with the function of king-maker?

In this connection it is worth our while to observe that in no respect has the actual working of the Constitution departed so far from the intentions of its framers as in the case of their provi-

sions concerning the executive.   Against a host of
possible dangers they guarded most elaborately, but the dangers and inconven-
iences against which we have actually
had to contend they did not foresee.
It will be observed that Wilson's proposal for a direct election of the president by the people found
little favour in the convention.   The schemes that
were seriously considered oscillated back and forth
between an election by the national legislature and
an election by a special college of electors.   The
electors might be chosen by a popular vote, or by
the state legislatures, or in any such wise as each
state might see fit to determine for itself.   In
point of fact, electors were chosen by the legislature in New Jersey till 1816; in Connecticut till
1820; in New York, Delaware, and Vermont, and
with one exception in Georgia, till 1824; in South
Carolina till 1868.   Massachusetts adopted various plans, and did not finally settle down to an
election by the people until 1828.   Now there
were several reasons why the Federal Convention
was afraid to trust the choice of the president directly to the people.   One was that very old objection, the fear of the machinations of demagogues,
since people were supposed to be so easily fooled.
As already observed, the democratic sentiment in
the convention was such as we should now call
weak.   Another reason shows vividly how wide the
world seemed in those days of slow coaches and
mail-bags carried on horseback.   It was feared
that people would not have sufficient data wherewith to judge of the merits of public men in states

remote from their own. The electors, as eminent men exceptionally well informed, and screened from the sophisms of demagogues, might hold little conventions and select the best possible candidates, using in every case their own unfettered judgment.

In this connection the words of Hamilton are worth quoting. In the sixty-eighth number of the " Federalist " he says : " The mode of appointment of the chief magistrate of the United States is almost the only part of the system which has escaped without severe censure, or which has received the slightest mark of approbation from its opponents. The most plausible of these who has appeared in print has even deigned to admit that the election of the president is well guarded. . . . It was desirable that the sense of the people should operate in the choice of the person to whom so important a trust was to be confided. . . . It was equally desirable that the immediate election should be made by men capable of analyzing the qualities adapted to the station, and acting under circumstances favourable to deliberation and to a judicious combination of all the reasons and inducements that were proper to govern their choice. A small number of persons, selected by their fellow-citizens from the general mass, will be most likely to possess the information and discernment requisite to so complicated an investigation. . . . It was also peculiarly desirable to afford as little opportunity as possible to tumult and disorder. This evil was not least to be dreaded in the election of a magistrate who was to have so important an agency in the administration of the government."

Such was the theory as set forth by a thinker endowed with rare ability to follow out in imagination the results of any course of political action. It is needless to say that the actual working of the scheme has been very different from what was expected. In our very first great struggle of parties, in 1800, the electors divided upon party lines, with little heed to the "complicated investigation" for which they were supposed to be chosen. Quite naturally, for the work of electing a candidate presupposes a state of mind very different from that of serene deliberation. In 1800 the electors acted simply as automata recording the victory of their party, and so it has been ever since. In our own time presidents and vice-presidents are nominated, not without elaborate intrigue, by special conventions quite unknown to the Constitution; the people cast their votes for the two or three pairs of candidates thus presented, and the electoral college simply registers the results. The system is thus fully exposed to all the dangers which our forefathers dreaded from the frequent election of a chief magistrate by the people. Owing to the great good-sense and good-nature of the American people, the system does not work so badly as might be expected. It has, indeed, worked immeasurably better than any one would have ventured to predict. It is nevertheless open to grave objections. It compels a change of administration at stated astronomical periods, whether any change of policy is called for or not; it stirs up the whole country every fourth year with a furious excitement that is often largely factitious;

Actual working of the electoral scheme.

and twice within the century, in 1801 and again in 1877, it has brought us to the verge of the most foolish and hopeless species of civil war, in view of that thoroughly monarchical kind of accident, a disputed succession.[1]

The most curious and instructive point concerning the peculiar executive devised for the United States by the Federal Convention is the fact that the delegates proceeded upon a thoroughly false theory of what they were doing. As already observed, in this part of its discussions the convention had not the clearly outlined chart of local interests to steer by. It indulged in general speculations and looked about for precedents; and there was one precedent which American statesmen then always had before their eyes, whether they were distinctly aware of it or not. In creating an executive department, the members of the convention were really trying to copy the only constitution of which they had any direct experience, and which most of them agreed in thinking the most efficient working constitution in existence, — as indeed it was. They were trying to copy the British Constitution, modifying it to suit their republican ideas: but curiously enough, what they copied in creating the office of president was not the real English executive or prime minister, but the fictitious English executive, the sovereign. And this was associated

The convention supposed itself to be copying from the British Constitution.

---

[1] Since this was written, this last and most serious danger would seem to have been removed by the acts of 1886 and 1887 regulating the presidential succession and the counting of electoral votes.

in their minds with another profound misconception, which influenced all this part of their work. They thought that to keep the legislative and executive offices distinct and separate was the very palladium of liberty; and they all took it for granted, without a moment's question, that the British Constitution did this thing. England, they thought, is governed by King, Lords, and Commons, and the supreme power is nicely divided between the three, so that neither one can get the whole of it, and that is the safeguard of English liberty. So they arranged President, Senate, and Representatives to correspond, and sedulously sought to divide supreme power between the three, so that they might operate as checks upon each other. If either one should ever succeed in acquiring the whole sovereignty, then they thought there would be an end of American liberty.

Now in the earlier part of the work of the Federal Convention, in dealing with the legislative department, the delegates were on firm ground, because they were dealing with things of which they knew something by experience; but in all this careful separation of the executive power from the legislative they went wide of the mark, because they were following a theory which did not truly describe things as they really existed. And that was because the English Constitution was, and still is, covered up with a thick husk of legal fictions which long ago ceased to have any vitality. Blackstone, the great authority of the eighteenth century, set forth this theory of the division of power between King, Lords, and Commons with clearness and force, and nobody then understood English history minutely or thoroughly enough to see its fallaciousness. Montesquieu also, the ablest and most elegant political writer of the age, with whose works most of the statesmen in the Federal Convention were familiar, gave a similar description of the English Constitution, and generalized from it as the ideal constitution for a free people. But Montesquieu and Blackstone, in their treatment of this point, had their eyes upon the legal fictions, and were blind to the real machinery which was working under them. They gave elegant expression to what the late Mr. Bagehot called the "literary theory" of the English Constitution. But the real thing differed essentially from the "literary theory" even in their day. In our own time the divergence has become so conspicuous that it would not now be possible for well-informed writers to make the mistake of Montesquieu and Blackstone. In our time it has come to be perfectly obvious that so far from the English Constitution separating the executive power from the legislative, this is precisely what it does not do. In Great Britain the supreme power is all lodged in a single body, the House of Commons. The sovereign has come to be purely a legal fiction, and the House of Lords maintains itself only by submitting to the Commons. The House of Commons is absolutely supreme, and, as we shall presently see, it really both appoints and dismisses the executive. The English executive, or chief magistrate, is ordinarily the first lord of the treasury, and is commonly

[marginal note: Influence of Montesquieu and Blackstone.]

styled the prime minister.   He is chairman of the
most important committee of the House of Commons, and his cabinet consists of the chairmen of
other committees.

To make this perfectly clear, let us see what our
machinery of government would be, if it were
really like the English.   The presence or absence
of the crowned head makes no essential difference ;
it is only a kind of ornamental cupola.   Suppose
for a moment the presidency abolished, or reduced
to the political nullity of the crown in
England ; and postpone for a moment
the consideration of the Senate.   Suppose that in our House of Representatives the committee of ways and means had two
chairmen, — an upper chairman who looks after
all sorts of business, and a lower chairman who at-
tends especially to the finances.   This upper chairman, we will say, corresponds to the first lord of
the treasury, while the lower one corresponds to
the chancellor of the exchequer.   Sometimes, when
the upper chairman is a great financier, and capable of enormous labour, he will fill both places at
once, as Mr. Gladstone was lately first lord of the
treasury and chancellor of the exchequer.   The
chairmen of the other committees on foreign, military, and naval affairs will answer to the English
secretaries of state for foreign affairs and for war,
the first lord of the admiralty, and so on.   This
group of chairmen, headed by the upper chairman
of the ways and means, will then answer to the
English cabinet, with its prime minister.   To
complete the parallel, let us suppose that after

*What our gov-
ernment would
be if it were
really like that
of Great Brit-
ain.*

a new House of Representatives is elected, it chooses this prime minister, and he appoints the other chairmen who are to make up his cabinet. Suppose, too, that he initiates all legislation, and executes all laws, and stays in office three weeks or thirty years, or as long as he can get a majority of the house to vote for his measures. If he loses his majority, he can either resign or dissolve the house, and order a new election, thus appealing directly to the people. If the new house gives him a majority, he stays in office; if it shows a majority against him, he steps down into the house, and becomes, perhaps, the leader of the opposition.

Now if this were the form of our government, it would correspond in all essential features to that of England. The likeness is liable to be obscured by the fact that in England it is the queen who is supposed to appoint the prime minister; but that is simply a part of the antiquated "literary theory" of the English Constitution. In reality the queen only acts as mistress of the ceremonies. Whatever she may wish, the prime minister must be the man who can command the best working majority in the house. This is not only tested by the first vote that is taken, but it is almost invariably known beforehand so well that if the queen offers the place to the wrong man he refuses to take it. Should he be so foolish as to take it, he is sure to be overthrown at the first test vote, and then the right man comes in. Thus in 1880 the queen's manifest preference for Lord Granville or Lord Hartington made no sort of difference. Mr.

Gladstone was as much chosen by the House of Commons as if the members had sat in their seats and balloted for him. If the crown were to be abolished to-morrow, and the house were henceforth, on the resignation of a prime minister, to elect a new one to serve as long as he could command a majority, it would not be doing essentially otherwise than it does now. The house then dismisses its minister when it rejects one of his important measures. But while thus appointed and dismissed by the house, he is in no wise its slave; for by the power of dissolution he has the right to appeal to the country, and let the general election decide the issue. The obvious advantages of this system are that it makes anything like a deadlock between the legislature and the executive impossible; and it insures a concentration of responsibility. The prime minister's bills cannot be disregarded, like the president's messages; and thus, too, the house is kept in hand, and cannot degenerate into a debating club.[1]

A system so delicate and subtle, yet so strong and efficient, as this could no more have been invented by the wisest of statesmen than a chemist could make albumen by taking its elements and mixing them together. In its practical working it is a much simpler system than ours, and still its principal features are not such as would be likely to occur to men who had not had some actual ex-

---

[1] The history of President Cleveland's tariff message of 1887, however, shows that, where a wise and courageous president calls attention to a living issue, his party, alike in Congress and in the country, is in a measure compelled to follow his lead.

perience of them. It is the peculiar outgrowth of English history. As we can now see, its chief characteristic is its not separating the executive power from the legislative. As a member of Parliament, the prime minister introduces the legislation which he is himself expected to carry into effect. Nor does the English system even keep the judiciary entirely separate, for the lord chancellor not only presides over the House of Lords, but sits in the cabinet as the prime minister's legal adviser. It is somewhat as if the chief justice of the United States were *ex officio* president of the Senate and attorney-general; though here the resemblance is somewhat superficial. Our Senate, although it does not represent landed aristocracy or the church, but the federal character of our government, has still a superficial resemblance to the House of Lords. It passes on all bills that come up from the lower house, and can originate bills on most matters, but not for raising revenue. Its function as a high court of impeachment, with the chief justice for its presiding officer, was directly copied from the House of Lords. But here the resemblance ends. The House of Lords has no such veto upon the House of Commons as our Senate has upon the House of Representatives. Between our upper and lower houses a serious deadlock is possible; but the House of Lords can only reject a bill until it sees that the House of Commons is determined to have it carried. It can only enter a protest. If it is obstinate and tries to do more, the House of Commons, through its prime minis-

In the British government, the executive department is not separated from the legislative.

ter, can create enough new peers to change the vote, — a power so formidable in its effects upon the social position of the peerage that it does not need to be used. The knowledge that it exists is enough to bring the House of Lords to terms.

These features of the English Constitution are so prominent since the reform of Parliament in 1832 as to be generally recognized. They have been gradually becoming its essential features ever Circumstances which obscured the true aspect of the case a century ago. since the Revolution of 1688. Before that time the crown had really been the executive, and there had really been a separation between the executive and legislative branches of the government, which on several occasions, and notably in the middle of the seventeenth century, had led to armed strife. What the Revolution of 1688 really decided was that henceforth in England the executive was to be the mighty arm of the legislature, and not a separate and rival power. It ended whatever of reality there was in the old system of King, Lords, and Commons, and by the time of Sir Robert Walpole the system of cabinet government had become fairly established; but men still continued to use the phrases and formulas bequeathed from former ages, so that the meaning of the changes going on under their very eyes was obscured. There was also a great historical incident, after Walpole's time, which served further to obscure the meaning of these changes, especially to Americans. From 1760 to 1784, by means of the rotten borough system of elections and the peculiar attitude of political parties, the king contrived to make his will felt in the House of Commons to such an extent that it became possible to speak of the personal government of George III. The work of the Revolution of 1688 was not really completed till the election of 1784 which made Pitt the ruler of England, and its fruits cannot be said to have been fully secured till 1832. Now as our Revolutionary War was brought on by the attempts of George III. to establish his personal government, and as it was actually he rather than Lord North who ruled England during that war, it was not strange that Americans, even of the highest education, should have failed to discover the transformation which the past century had wrought in the framework of the English government. Nay, more, during this century the king had seemed even more of a real institution to the Americans than to the British. He had seemed to them the only link which bound the different parts of the empire together. Throughout the struggles which culminated in the War of Independence, it had been the favourite American theory that while the colonial assemblies and the British Parliament were sovereign each in its own sphere, all alike owed allegiance to the king as visible head of the empire. To people who had been in the habit of setting forth and defending such a theory, it was impossible that the crown should seem so much a legal fiction as it had really come to be in England. It is very instructive to note that while the members of the Federal Convention thoroughly understood the antiquated theory of the English Constitution as set forth by Blackstone, they drew very few illustrations from the

modern working of Parliament, with which they
had not had sufficient opportunities of becoming
familiar. In particular they seemed quite uncon-
scious of the vast significance of a dissolution of
Parliament, although a dissolution had occurred
only three years before under such circumstances
as to work a revolution in British politics without
a breath of disturbance. The only sort of dissolution with which they were familiar was that in
which Dunmore or Bernard used to send the colonial assemblies home about their business when-
ever they grew too refractory. Had the significance of a dissolution, in the British sense, been
understood by the convention, the pregnant suggestion of Roger Sherman, above mentioned, could
not have failed to give a different turn to the whole
series of debates on the executive branch of the
government. Had our Constitution been framed a
few years later, this point would have had a better
chance of being understood. As it was, in trying
to modify the English system so as to adapt it to
our own uses, it was the archaic monarchical feature, and not the modern ministerial feature, upon
which we seized. The president, in our system,
irremovable by the national legislature, does not
answer to the modern prime minister, but to the
old-fashioned king, with powers for mischief curtailed by election for short terms.

The close parallelism between the office of president and that of king in the minds of the framers
of the Constitution was instructively shown in the
debates on the advisableness of restraining the
president's action by a privy council. Gerry and

Sherman urged that there was need of such a coun-
cil, in order to keep watch over the presi- The American cabinet is analogous not to the British cabinet, but to the privy council.
dent. It was suggested that the privy
council should consist of " the president
of the Senate, the speaker of the House
of Representatives, the chief justice of
the supreme court, and the principal officer in each
of five departments as they shall from time to time
be established; their duty shall be to advise him in
matters which he shall lay before them, but their
advice shall not conclude him, or affect his responsibility." The plan for such a council found favour
with Franklin, Madison, Wilson, Dickinson, and
Mason, but did not satisfy the convention. When
it was voted down Mason used strong language.
" In rejecting a council to the president," said he,
" we are about to try an experiment on which the
most despotic government has never ventured; the
Grand Seignior himself has his Divan." It was
this failure to provide a council which led the convention to give to the Senate a share in some of the
executive functions of the president, such as the
making of treaties, the appointment of ambassadors, consuls, judges of the supreme court, and other
officers of the United States whose appointment
was not otherwise provided for. As it was objected
to the office of vice-president that he seemed to have
nothing provided for him to do, he was disposed of
by making him president of the Senate. No cabinet was created by the Constitution, but since then
the heads of various executive departments, appointed by the president, have come to constitute
what is called his cabinet. Since, however, the

members of it do not belong to Congress, and can neither initiate nor guide legislation, they really constitute a privy council rather than a cabinet in the modern sense, thus furnishing another illustration of the analogy between the president and the archaic sovereign.

Concerning the structure of the federal judiciary little need be said here. It was framed with very The federal little disagreement among the delegates. judiciary. The work was chiefly done in committee by Ellsworth, Wilson, Randolph, and Rutledge, and the result did not differ essentially from the scheme laid down in the Virginia plan. It was indeed the indispensable completion of the work which was begun by the creation of a national House of Representatives. To make a federal government immediately operative upon individual citizens, it must of course be armed with federal courts to try and federal officers to execute judgment in all cases in which individual citizens were amenable to the national law. But for this system of United States courts extended throughout the states and supreme within its own sphere, the federal constitution could never have been put into practical working order. In another respect the federal judiciary was the most remarkable and original of all the creations of that wonderful convention. It was charged with the duty of interpreting, in accordance with the general principles of common law, the Federal Constitution itself. This is the most noble as it is the most distinctive feature in the government of the United States. It constitutes a difference between the American and British systems more fundamental than the separation of the executive from the legislative department. In Great Britain the unwritten constitution is administered by the omnipotent House of Commons ; whatever statute is enacted by Parliament must stand until some future Parliament may see fit to repeal it. But an act passed by both houses of Congress, and signed by the president, may still be set aside as unconstitutional by the supreme court of the United States in its judgments upon individual cases brought before it. It was thus that the practical working of our Federal Constitution during the first thirty years of the nineteenth century was swayed to so great an extent by the profound and luminous decisions of Chief Justice Marshall, that he must be assigned a foremost place among the founders of our Federal Union. This intrusting to the judiciary the whole interpretation of the fundamental instrument of government is the most peculiarly American feature of the work done by the convention, and to the stability of such a federation as ours, covering as it does the greater part of a huge continent, it was absolutely indispensable.

Thus, at length, was realized the sublime conception of a nation in which every citizen lives under two complete and well-rounded systems of laws, — the state law and the federal law, — each with its legislature, its executive, and its judiciary moving one within the other, noiselessly and without friction. It was one of the longest reaches of constructive statesmanship ever known in the world. There never was anything quite like it before, and in Europe it needs much explanation to-day even **for** educated statesmen who have never seen its workings. Yet to Americans it has become so much **a** matter of course that they, too, sometimes need to be told how much it signifies. In 1787 it was the substitution of law for violence between states that were partly sovereign. In some future still grander convention we trust the same thing will be done between states that have been wholly sovereign, whereby peace may gain and violence be diminished over other lands than this which has set the example.

Great as was the work which the Federal Convention had now accomplished, none of the members supposed it to be complete. After some discussion, it was decided that Congress might at any time, by a two thirds vote in both houses, propose amendments to the constitution, or on the application of the legislatures of two thirds of the states might call a convention for proposing amendments ; and such amendments should become part of the constitution as soon as ratified by three fourths of the states, either through their legislatures or through special conventions summoned for the purpose. The design of this elaborate arrangement was to guard against hasty or ill-considered changes in the fundamental instrument of government ; and its effectiveness has been such that an amendment has come to be impossible save as the result of intense conviction on the part of a vast majority of the whole American people.

Finally it was decided that the Federal Constitution, as now completed, should be presented to the Continental Congress, and then referred to special conventions in all the states for ratification; and that when nine states, or two thirds of the whole number, should have ratified, it should at once go into operation as between such ratifying states.

When the great document was at last drafted by Gouverneur Morris, and was all ready for the signatures, the aged Franklin produced a paper, which was read for him, as his voice was weak. Some parts of this Constitution, he said, Signing the Constitution. he did not approve, but he was astonished to find it so nearly perfect. Whatever opinion he had of its errors he would sacrifice to the public good, and he hoped that every member of the convention who still had objections would on this occasion doubt a little of his own infallibility, and for the sake of unanimity put his name to this instrument. Hamilton added his plea. A few members, he said, by refusing to sign, might do infinite mischief. No man's ideas could be more remote from the plan than his were known to be; but was it possible for a true patriot to deliberate between anarchy and convulsion, on the one side, and the chance of good to be expected from this plan, on the other? From these appeals, as well as from Washington's solemn warning at the outset, we see how distinctly it was realized that the country was on the verge of civil war. Most of the members felt so, but to some the new government seemed far too strong, and there were three who dreaded despotism even more than anarchy. Mason, Randolph, and Gerry refused to sign, though Randolph sought to qualify his refusal by explaining that he could not yet make up his mind whether to oppose or defend the Constitution, when it should be laid before the people of Virginia. He wished to reserve to himself full liberty of action in the matter. That Mason and Gerry, valuable as their services had been in the making of the Constitution, would now go home and vigorously oppose it, there was no doubt. Of the delegates who were present on the last day of the convention, all but these three signed the Constitution. In the signatures the twelve states which had taken part in the work were all represented, Hamilton signing alone for New York.

Thus after four months of anxious toil, through the whole of a scorching Philadelphia summer, after earnest but sometimes bitter discussion, in which more than once the meeting had seemed on the point of breaking up, a colossal work had at last been accomplished, the results of which were most powerfully to affect the whole future career of the human race so long as it shall dwell upon the earth. In spite of the high-wrought intensity of feeling which had been now and then displayed, grave decorum had ruled the proceedings; and now, though few were really satisfied, the approach to unanimity was remarkable. When all was over, it is said that many of the members seemed awe-struck. Washington sat with head bowed in solemn meditation. The scene was ended by a characteristic bit of homely pleasantry from Franklin. Thirty-three years ago, in the days of George II., before the first mutterings of the Revolution had been heard, and when the French dominion in

America was still untouched, before the banish-
ment of the Acadians or the rout of Braddock,
while Washington was still surveying lands in the
wilderness, while Madison was playing in the
nursery and Hamilton was not yet born, Franklin
had endeavoured to bring together the thirteen
colonies in a federal union. Of the famous Albany plan of 1754, the first complete outline of a
federal constitution for America that ever was
made, he was the principal if not the sole author.
When he signed his name to the Declaration of
Independence in this very room, his years had
rounded the full period of threescore and ten.
Eleven years more had passed, and he had been
spared to see the noble aim of his life accomplished. There was still, no doubt, a chance of
failure, but hope now reigned in the old man's
breast. On the back of the president's quaint
black armchair there was emblazoned a half-sun,
brilliant with its gilded rays. As the meeting
was breaking up and Washington arose, Franklin
pointed to the chair, and made it the text for
prophecy. "As I have been sitting here all these
weeks," said he, "I have often wondered whether
yonder sun is rising or setting. But now I know
that it is a rising sun!"

CHAPTER VII.

CROWNING THE WORK.

IT was on the 17th of September, 1787, that the Federal Convention broke up. For most of the delegates there was a long and tedious journey home before they could meet their fellow-citizens and explain what had been done at Philadelphia during this anxious summer. Not so, however, with Benjamin Franklin and the Pennsylvania delegation. At eleven o'clock on the next morning, radiant with delight at seeing one of the most cherished purposes of his life so nearly accomplished, the venerable philosopher, attended by his seven colleagues, presented to the legislature of Pennsylvania a copy of the Federal Constitution, and in a brief but pithy speech, characterized by his usual homely wisdom, begged for it their most favourable consideration. His words fell upon willing ears, for nowhere was the disgust at the prevailing anarchy greater than in Philadelphia. But still it was not quite in order for the assembly to act upon the matter until word should come from the Continental Congress. Since its ignominious flight to Princeton, four years ago, that migratory body had not honoured Philadelphia with its presence. It had once flitted as far south as Annapolis, but at length had chosen for its abiding-place the city of New York, where it was now in session. To Congress the new Constitution must be submitted before it was in order for the several states to take action upon it. On the 20th of September the draft of the Constitution was laid before Congress, accompanied by a letter from Washington. The forces of the opposition were promptly mustered. At their head was Richard Henry Lee, who eleven years ago had moved in Congress the Declaration of Independence. He was ably supported by Nathan Dane of Massachusetts, and the delegation from New York were unanimous in their determination to obstruct any movement toward a closer union of the states. Their tactics were vigorous, but the majority in Congress were against them, especially after the return of Madison from Philadelphia. Madison, aided by Edward Carrington and young Henry Lee, the famous leader of light horse, succeeded in every division in carrying the vote of Virginia in favour of the Constitution and against the obstructive measures of the elder Lee. The objection was first raised that the new Constitution would put an end to the Continental Congress, and that in recommending it to the states for consideration Congress would be virtually asking them to terminate its own existence. Was it right or proper for Congress thus to have a hand in signing its own death-warrant? But this flimsy argument was quickly overturned. Seven months before Congress had recognized the necessity for calling the convention together; whatever need for its

The new Constitution is laid before Congress and submitted forthwith to the several states for ratification.

work existed then, there was the same need now; and by refusing to take due cognizance of it Congress would simply stultify itself. The opposition then tried to clog the measure by proposing amendments, but they were outgeneralled, and after eight days' discussion it was voted that the new Constitution, together with Washington's letter, "be transmitted to the several legislatures, in order to be submitted to a convention of delegates in each state by the people thereof, in conformity to the resolves of the convention."

The submission of the Constitution to the people of the states was the signal for the first formation of political parties on a truly national issue. During the war there had indeed been Whigs and Tories, but their strife had not been like the ordinary strife of political parties; it was actual warfare. Irredeemably discredited from the outset, the Tories had been overridden and outlawed from one end of the Union to the other. They had never been able to hold up their heads as a party in opposition. Since the close of the war there had been local parties in the various states, divided on issues of hard and soft money, or the impost, or state rights, and these issues had coincided in many of the states. During the autumn of 1787 all these elements were segregated into two great political parties, whose character and views are sufficiently described by their names. Those who supported the new Constitution were henceforth known as Federalists; those who were opposed to strengthening the bond between the states were called

First American parties, Federalists and Antifederalists.

Antifederalists. It was fit that their name should have this merely negative significance, for their policy at this time was purely a policy of negation and obstruction. Care must be taken not to confound them with the Democratic-Republicans, or strict constructionists, who appear in opposition to the Federalists soon after the adoption of the Constitution. The earlier short-lived party furnished a great part of its material to the later one, but the attitude of the strict constructionists under the Constitution was very different from that of the Antifederalists. Madison, the second Republican president, was now the most energetic of Federalists; and Jefferson, soon to become the founder of the Democratic-Republican party, wrote from Paris, saying, "The Constitution is a good canvas, on which some strokes only want retouching." He found the same fault with it that was found by many of the ablest and most patriotic men in the country,—that it failed to include a bill of rights; but at the same time he declared that while he was not of the party of Federalists, he was much further from that of the Antifederalists. The Federal Convention he characterized as "an assembly of demi-gods."

The first contest over the new Constitution came in Pennsylvania. The Federalists in that state were numerous, but their opponents had one point in their favour which they did not fail to make the most of. The constitution of Pennsylvania was peculiar. Its legislature consisted of The contest in a single house, and its president was Pennsylvania. chosen by that house. Therefore, said the Antifederalists, if we approve of a federal constitution which provides for a legislature of two houses and chooses a president by the device of an electoral college, we virtually condemn the state constitution under which we live. This cry was raised with no little effect. But some of the strongest immediate causes of opposition to the new Constitution were wanting in Pennsylvania. The friends of paper money were few there, and the objections to the control of the central government over commerce were weaker than in many of the other states. The Antifederalists were strongest in the mountain districts west of the Susquehanna, where the somewhat lawless population looked askance at any plan that savoured of a stronger government and a more regular collection of revenue. In the eastern counties, and especially in Philadelphia, the Federalists could count upon a heavy majority.

The contest began in the legislature on the 28th of September, the very day on which Congress decided to submit the Constitution to the states, and before the news of the action had reached Philadelphia. The zeal of the Federalists was so intense that they could wait no longer, and they hurried the event with a high-handed vigour that was not altogether seemly. The assembly was on the eve of breaking up, and a new election was to be held on the first Tuesday of November. The Antifederalists hoped to make a stirring campaign, and secure such a majority in the new legislature as to prevent the Constitution from being laid before the people. But their game was frustrated

by George Clymer, who had sat in the Federal
Convention, and now most unexpectedly moved
that a state convention be called to consider the
proposed form of government. Great was the
wrath of the Antifederalists. Mr. Clymer was
quite out of order, they said. Congress had not
yet sent them the Constitution; and besides, no
such motion could be made without notice given
beforehand, nor could it be voted on till it had
passed three readings. Parliamentary usage was
doubtless on the side of the Antifederalists, but the
majority were clamorous, and overwhelmed them
with cries of "Question, question!" The question
was then put, and carried by 43 votes against 19,
and the house adjourned till four o'clock. Before
going to their dinners the 19 held an indignation
meeting, at which it was decided that they would
foil these outrageous proceedings by staying away.
It took 47 to make a quorum, and without these
malcontents the assembly numbered but 45. When
the house was called to order after dinner, it was
found there were but 45 members present. The
sergeant-at-arms was sent to summon the delin-
quents, but they defied him, and so it became necessary to adjourn till next morning. It was now
the turn of the Federalists to uncork the vials of
wrath. The affair was discussed in the How to make
taverns till after midnight, the 19 were a quorum.
abused without stint, and soon after breakfast,
next morning, two of them were visited by a crowd
of men, who broke into their lodgings and dragged
them off to the state house, where they were forcibly held down in their seats, growling and mut-

tering curses. This made a quorum, and a state convention was immediately appointed for the 20th of November. Before these proceedings were concluded, an express-rider brought the news from New York that Congress had submitted the Constitution to the judgment of the states.

And now there ensued such a war of pamphlets, broadsides, caricatures, squibs, and stump-speeches, as had never yet been seen in America. Cato and Aristides, Cincinnatus and Plain Truth, were out in full force. What was the matter with the old confederation? asked the Antifederalists. Had it not conducted a glorious and triumphant war? Had it not set us free from the oppression of England? That there was some trouble now in the country could not be denied, but all would be right if people would only curb their extravagance, wear homespun clothes, and obey the laws. There was government enough in the country already. This Philadelphia convention ought to be distrusted. Some of its members, such as John Dickinson and Robert Morris, had opposed the Declaration of Independence. Pretty men these, to be offering us a new government! You might be sure there was a British cloven foot in it somewhere. Their convention had sat four months with closed doors, as if they were afraid to let people know what they were about. Nobody could tell what secret conspiracies against American liberty might not have been hatched in all that time. One thing was sure: the convention had squabbled. Some members had gone home in a huff; others had refused to sign a document fraught with untold evils to the country. And now came James Wilson, making speeches in behalf of this precious Constitution, and trying to pull the wool over people's eyes and persuade them to adopt it. Who was James Wilson, any way? A Scotchman, a countryman of Lord Bute, a born aristocrat, a snob, a patrician, Jimmy, James de Caledonia. Beware of any form of government defended by such a man. And as to the other members of the convention, there was Roger Sherman, who had signed the articles of confederation, and was now trying to undo his own work. What confidence could be placed in a man who did not know his own mind any better than that? Then there were Hamilton and Madison, mere boys; and Franklin, an old dotard, a man in his second childhood. And as to Washington, he was doubtless a good soldier, but what did he know about politics? So said the more moderate of the malcontents, hesitating for the moment to speak disrespectfully of such a man; but presently their zeal got the better of them, and in a paper signed "Centinel" it was boldly declared that Washington was a born fool!

From the style and temper of these arguments one clearly sees that the Antifederalists in Pennsylvania felt from the beginning that the day was going against them. Sixteen of the men who had seceded from the assembly, headed by Robert Whitehill of Carlisle, issued a manifesto setting forth the ill-treatment they had received, and sounding an alarm against the dangers of tyranny to which the new Constitution was already exposing them. They were assisted by Richard Henry Lee, who published a series of papers entitled "Letters from the Federal Farmer," and scattered thousands of copies through the state of Pennsylvania. He did not deny that the government needed reforming, but in the proposed plan he saw the seeds of aristocracy and of centralization. The chief objections to the Constitution were that it created a national legislature in which the vote was to be by individuals, and not by states; that it granted to this body an unlimited power of taxation; that it gave too much power to the federal judiciary; that it provided for paying the salaries of members of Congress out of the federal treasury, and would thus make them independent of their own states; that it required an oath of allegiance to the federal government; and finally, that it did not include a bill of rights. These objections were very elaborately set forth by the leading Antifederalists in the state convention; but the logic and eloquence of James Wilson bore down all opposition. The Antifederalists resorted to filibustering. Five days, it is said, were used up in settling the meanings of the two words "annihilation" and "consolidation." In this way the convention was kept sitting for nearly three weeks, when news came from "the Delaware state," as it used then to be called in Pennsylvania. The concession of an equal representation in the federal Senate had removed the only ground of opposition in Delaware, and the Federalists had everything their own way there. In a convention assembled at Dover, on the 6th of December, the Constitution was ratified with-

Delaware ratifies the Constitution, Dec. 6, 1787; Pennsylvania, Dec. 12; New Jersey, Dec. 18.

out a single dissenting voice. Thus did this little state lead the way in the good work. The news was received with exultation by the Federalists at Philadelphia, and on the 12th Pennsylvania ratified the Constitution by a two thirds vote of 46 to 23. The next day all business was quite at a standstill, while the town gave itself up to processions and merry-making. The convention of New Jersey had assembled at Trenton on the 11th, and one week later, on the 18th, it ratified the Constitution unanimously.

A most auspicious beginning had thus been made. Three states, one third of the whole number required, had ratified almost at the same moment. Two of these, moreover, were small states, which at the beginning of the Federal Convention had been obstinately opposed to any fundamental change in the government. It was just here that the Federalists were now strongest. The Connecticut compromise had wrought with telling effect, not only in the convention, but upon the people of the states. When the news from Trenton was received in Pennsylvania, there was great rejoicing in the eastern counties, while beyond the Susquehanna there were threats of armed rebellion. On the day after Christmas, as the Federalists of Carlisle were about to light a bonfire on the common and fire a salute, they were driven off the field by a mob armed with bludgeons, their rickety old cannon was spiked, and an almanac for the new year, containing a copy of the Constitution, was duly cursed, and then burned. Next day the Federalists, armed with muskets, came back, and went through their ceremonies. Their opponents did not venture to molest them; but after they had dispersed, an Antifederalist demonstration was made, and effigies of James Wilson and Thomas McKean, another prominent Federalist, were dragged to the common, and there burned at the stake.

The action of Delaware and New Jersey had shown that the Antifederalists could not build any hopes upon the antagonism between large and small states. It was thought, however, that the southern states would unite in opposing the Constitution from their dread of becoming commercially subjected to New England. But the compromise on the slave-trade had broken through this opposition. On the 2d of January, 1788, the Constitution was ratified in Georgia without a word of dissent. One week later Connecticut ratified by a vote of 128 to 40, after a session of only five days. The hopes of the Antifederalists now rested upon Massachusetts, where the state convention assembled on the 9th of January, the same day on which that of Connecticut broke up. Should Massachusetts refuse to ratify, there would be no hope for the Constitution. Even should nine states adopt it without her, no one supposed a Federal Union feasible from which so great a state should be excluded. Her action, too, would have a marked effect upon other states. It could not be denied that the outlook in Massachusetts was far from encouraging. The embers of the Shays rebellion still smouldered there, and in the mountain counties of Worcester and Berkshire were heard loud

Georgia ratifies, Jan. 2, 1788; Connecticut, Jan. 9. The outlook in Massachusetts.

murmurs of discontent. Laws impairing the obligation of contracts were just what these hard-
pressed farmers desired, and by the proposed Constitution all such laws were forever prohibited.
The people of the district of Maine, which had
formed part of Massachusetts for nearly a century,
were anxious to set up an independent government
for themselves; and they feared that if they were
to enter into the new and closer Federal Union
as part of that state, they might hereafter find it
impossible to detach themselves. For this reason
half of the Maine delegates were opposed to the
Constitution. In none of the thirteen states, moreover, was there a more intense devotion to state
rights than in Massachusetts. Nowhere had local
self-government reached a higher degree of efficiency; nowhere had the town meeting flourished
with such vigour. It was especially characteristic
of men trained in the town meeting to look with
suspicion upon all delegated power, upon all authority that was to be exercised from a distance. They
believed it to be all important that people should
manage their own affairs, instead of having them
managed by other people; and so far had this
principle been carried that the towns of Massachusetts were like little semi-independent republics,
and the state was like a league of such republics,
whose representatives, sitting in the state legislature, were like delegates strictly bound by instructions rather than untrammelled members of a deliberative body. To men trained in such a school, it
would naturally seem that the new Constitution
delegated altogether too much power to a govern-

ing body which must necessarily be remote from most of its constituents. It was feared that some sort of tyranny might grow out of this, and such fears were entertained by men who were not in the slightest degree infected with Shaysism, as the political disease of the inland counties was then called. Such fears were entertained by one of the greatest citizens that Massachusetts has ever produced, the man who has been well described as preëminently "the man of the town meeting," — Samuel Adams. The limitations of this great man, as well as his powers, were those which belonged to him as chief among the men of English race who have swayed society through the medium of the ancient folk mote. At this time he was believed by many to be hostile to the new Constitution, and his influence in Massachusetts was still greater than that of any other man. Besides this, it was thought that the governor, John Hancock, was half-hearted in his support of the Constitution, and it was in everybody's mouth that Elbridge Gerry had refused to set his name to that document because he felt sure it would create a tyranny.

Such symptoms encouraged the Antifederalists in the hope that Massachusetts would reject the Constitution and ruin the plans of the " visionary young men " — as Richard Henry Lee called them — who had swayed the Federal Convention. But there were strong forces at work in the opposite direction. In Boston and all the large coast towns, even those of the Maine district, the dominant feeling was Federalist. All well-to-do people had been alarmed by the Shays insurrection, and merchants,

shipwrights, and artisans of every sort were convinced that there was no prosperity in store for
them until the federal government should have
control over commerce, and be enabled to make its
strength felt on the seas and in Europe. In these
views Samuel Adams shared so thoroughly that his
attitude toward the Constitution at this moment
was really that of a waverer rather than an opponent. Amid balancing considerations he found it
for some time hard to make up his mind.

In the convention which met on the 9th of January there sat Gorham, Strong, and King, who
had taken part in the Federal Convention. There
were also Samuel Adams and James Bowdoin ; the
revolutionary generals, Heath and Lincoln ; and
the rising statesmen, Sedgwick, Parsons, and Fisher
Ames, whose eloquence was soon to become so
famous. There were twenty-four clergymen, of
various denominations, — men of sound scholar-
ship, and several of them eminent for worldly wisdom and liberality of temper. Governor Hancock
presided, gorgeous in crimson velvet and finest
laces, while about the room sat many browned and
weatherbeaten farmers, among whom were at least
eighteen who hardly a year ago had marched over
the pine-clad mountain ridges of Petersham, under
the banner of the rebel Shays. It was a wholesome no less than a generous policy that let these
men come in and freely speak their minds. The
air was thus the sooner cleared of discontent ; the
disease was thus the more likely to heal itself. In
all there were three hundred and fifty-five delegates present, — a much larger number than took

part in any of the other state conventions. The
people of all parts of Massachusetts were very
thoroughly represented, as befitted the state which
was preëminent in the active political life of its
town meetings, and the work done here was in
some respects decisive in its effect upon the adoption of the Constitution.

The convention began by overhauling that document from beginning to end, discussing it clause
by clause with somewhat wearisome minuteness.
Some of the objections seem odd to us at this time,
with our larger experience. It was several days before the minds of the country members could be reconciled to the
election of representatives for so long a period as
two years. They had not been wont to delegate
power to anybody for so long a time, not even to
their selectmen, whom they had always under their
eyes. How much more dangerous was it likely to
prove if delegated authority were to be exercised
for so long a period at some distant federal city,
such as the Constitution contemplated! There
was a vague dread that in some indescribable way
the new Congress might contrive to make its sittings perpetual, and thus become a tyrannical oligarchy, which might tax the people without their
consent. And then as to this federal city, there
were some who did not like the idea. A district
ten miles square! Was not that a great space to
give up to the uncontrolled discretion of the federal
government, wherein it could wreak its tyrannical
will without let or hindrance? One of the delegates thought he could be reconciled to the new

Debates in the Massachusetts convention.

Constitution if this district could only be narrowed down to one mile square. And then there was the power granted to Congress to maintain a standing army, of which the president was to be *ex officio* commander-in-chief. Did not this open the door for a Cromwell? It was to be a standing army for at least two years, since this was the shortest period between elections. Why, even the British Parliament, since 1688, did not keep up a standing army for more than one year at a time, but renewed its existence annually under what was termed the Mutiny Act. But what need of a standing army at all? Would it not be sure to provoke needless disorders? Had they already forgotten the Boston Massacre, in spite of all the orations that had been delivered in the Old South Meeting-House? A militia, organized under the town-meeting system, was surely all-sufficient. Such a militia had won glorious triumphs at Lexington and Bennington; and at King's Mountain, had not an army of militia surrounded and captured an army of regulars led by one of England's most skilful officers? What more could you ask? Clearly this plan for a standing army foreboded tyranny. Upon this point Mr. Nason, from the Maine district, had his say, in tones of inimitable bombast. "Had I the voice of Jove," said he, " I would proclaim it throughout the world; and had I an arm like Jove, I would hurl from the globe those villains that would dare attempt to establish in our country a standing army!"

Next came the complaint that the Constitution did not recognize the existence of God, and provided no religious tests for candidates for federal offices. But, strange to say, this objection did not come from the clergy. It was urged by some of the country members, but the ministers in the con-

Liberal atti-
tude of the
clergy.

vention were nearly unanimous in opposing it. There had been a remarkable change of sentiment among the clergy of this state, which had begun its existence as a theocracy, in which none but church members could vote or hold office. The seeds of modern liberalism had been planted in their minds. When Amos Singletary of Sutton declared it to be scandalous that a Papist or an infidel should be as eligible to office as a Christian, — a remark which naively assumed that Roman Catholics were not Christians, — the Rev. Daniel Shute of Hingham replied that no conceivable advantage could result from a religious test. Yes, said the Rev. Philip Payson of Chelsea, " human tribunals for the consciences of men are impious encroachments upon the prerogatives of God. A religious test, as a qualification for office, would have been a great blemish." " In reason and in the Holy Scripture," said the Rev. Isaac Backus of Middleborough, " religion is ever a matter between God and the individual; the imposing of religious tests hath been the greatest engine of tyranny in the world." With this liberal stand firmly taken by the ministers, the religious objection was speedily overruled.

Then the clause which allows Congress to regulate the times, places, and manner of holding federal elections was severely criticised. It was feared that Congress would take advantage of this provision to destroy the freedom of elections. It was further objected that members of Congress, being paid their salaries from the federal treasury, would become too independent of their constituents. Federal collectors of revenue, moreover, would not be so likely to act with moderation and justice as collectors appointed by the state. Then it was very doubtful whether the people could support the expense of an elaborate federal government. They were already scarcely able to pay their town, county, and state taxes; was it to be supposed they could bear the additional burden with which federal taxation would load them? Then the compromise on the slave-trade was fiercely attacked. They did not wish to have a hand in licensing this nefarious traffic for twenty years. But it was urged, on the other hand, that by prohibiting the foreign slave-trade after 1808 the Constitution was really dealing a death-blow to slavery; and this opinion prevailed.

During the whole course of the discussion, observed the Rev. Samuel West of New Bedford, it seemed to be taken for granted that the federal government was going to be put into the hands of crafty knaves. " I wish," said he, " that the gentlemen who have started so many *possible* objections would try to show us that what they so much deprecate is *probable*. . . . Because power *may* be abused, shall we be reduced to anarchy? What hinders our state legislatures from abusing their powers? . . . May we not rationally suppose that the persons we shall choose to administer the government will be, in general, good men?" General

Thompson said he was surprised to hear such an argument from a clergyman, who was professionally bound to maintain that all men were totally depraved. For his part he believed they were so, and he could prove it from the Old Testament. "I would not trust them," echoed Abraham White of Bristol, "though every one of them should be a Moses."

The feeling of distrust was strongest among the farmers from the mountain districts. As Rufus King said, they objected, not so much to the Constitution as to the men who made it and the men who sang its praises. They hated lawyers, and were jealous of wealthy merchants. "These lawyers," said Amos Singletary, "and men of learning, and moneyed men that talk so finely and gloss over matters so smoothly, to make us poor illiterate people swallow the pill, expect to get into Congress themselves. They mean to be managers of the Constitution. They mean to get all the money into their hands, and then they will swallow up us little folk, like the great Leviathan, Mr. President; yes, just as the whale swallowed up Jonah." Here a more liberal-minded farmer, Jonathan Smith of Lanesborough, rose to reply with references to the Shays rebellion, which presently called forth cries of "Order!" from some of the members. Samuel Adams said the gentleman was quite in order, — let him go on in his own way. "I am a plain man," said Mr. Smith, "and am not

Speech of a Berkshire farmer.

used to speak in public, but I am going to show the effects of anarchy, that you may see why I wish for good government.

Last winter people took up arms, and then, if you went to speak to them, you had the musket of death presented to your breast. They would rob you of your property, threaten to burn your houses, oblige you to be on your guard night and day. Alarms spread from town to town, families were broken up; the tender mother would cry, ' Oh, my son is among them! What shall I do for my child? ' Some were taken captive; children taken out of their schools and carried away. . . . How dreadful was this! Our distress was so great that we should have been glad to snatch at anything that looked like a government. . . . Now, Mr. President, when I saw this Constitution, I found that it was a cure for these disorders. I got a copy of it, and read it over and over. . . . I did not go to any lawyer, to ask his opinion; we have no lawyer in our town, and we do well enough without. My honourable old daddy there [pointing to Mr. Singletary] won't think that I expect to be a Congressman, and swallow up the liberties of the people. I never had any post, nor do I want one. But I don't think the worse of the Constitution because lawyers, and men of learning, and moneyed men are fond of it. I am not of such a jealous make. They that are honest men themselves are not apt to suspect other people. . . . Brother farmers, let us suppose a case, now. Suppose you had a farm of 50 acres, and your title was disputed, and there was a farm of 5,000 acres joined to you that be-longed to a man of learning, and his title was involved in the same difficulty: would you not be glad to have him for your friend, rather than to stand alone in the dispute? Well, the case is the same. These lawyers, these moneyed men, these men of learning, are all embarked in the same cause with us, and we must all sink or swim together. Shall we throw the Constitution overboard because it does not please us all alike? Suppose two or three of you had been at the pains to break up a piece of rough land and sow it with wheat: would you let it lie waste because you could not agree what sort of a fence to make? Would it not be better to put up a fence that did not please every one's fancy, rather than keep disputing about it until the wild beasts came in and devoured the crop? Some gentlemen say, Don't be in a hurry; take time to consider. I say, There is a time to sow and a time to reap. We sowed our seed when we sent men to the Federal Convention, now is the time to reap the fruit of our labour; and if we do not do it now, I am afraid we shall never have another opportunity."

It may be doubted whether all the eloquence of Fisher Ames could have stated the case more forcibly than it was put by this plain farmer from the Berkshire hills. Upon Ames, with King, Parsons, Bowdoin, and Strong, fell the principal work in defending the Constitution. For the first two weeks, Samuel Adams scarcely opened his mouth, but listened with anxious care to everything that was said on either side. The convention was so evenly divided that there could be no doubt that his single voice would decide the result. Every one eagerly awaited his opinion. In the debate on the two years' term of

Attitude of Samuel Adams.

members of Congress, he had asked Caleb Strong
the reason why the Federal Convention had decided
upon so long a term; and when it was explained
as a necessary compromise between the views of so
many delegates, he replied, "I am satisfied." "Will
Mr. Adams kindly say that again?" asked one of
the members. "I am satisfied," he repeated; and
not another word was said on the subject in all
those weeks. So profound was the faith of this
intelligent and skeptical and independent people
in the sound judgment and unswerving integrity of
the Father of the Revolution! As the weeks went
by, and the issue seemed still dubious, the work-
ingmen of Boston, shipwrights and brass-founders
and other mechanics, decided to express their opinion in a way that they knew Samuel Adams would
heed. They held a meeting at the Green Dragon
tavern, passed resolutions in favour of the Constitution, and appointed a committee, with Paul
Revere at its head, to make known these resolutions to the great popular leader. When Adams
had read the paper, he asked of Paul Revere,
"How many mechanics were at the Green Dragon
when these resolutions passed?" "More, sir, than
the Green Dragon could hold." "And where were
the rest, Mr. Revere?" "In the streets, sir."
"And how many were in the streets?" "More,
sir, than there are stars in the sky."

Between Samuel Adams and Thomas Jefferson
there were several points of resemblance, the chief
of which was an intense faith in the sound common sense of the mass of the people. This faith
was one of the strongest attributes of both these

great men.   It has usually been supposed that it
was this incident of the meeting at the Green
Dragon that determined Adams's final attitude in
the state convention.   Unquestionably, such a demonstration must have had great weight with him.
But at the same time the affair was taking such a
turn as would have decided him, even without the
aid of this famous mass-meeting.   The long delay
in the decision of the Massachusetts convention
had carried the excitement to fever heat throughout the country.   Not only were people from New
Hampshire and New York and naughty Rhode
Island waiting anxiously about Boston to catch
every crumb of news they could get, but intrigues
were going on, as far south as Virginia, to influence
the result.   On the 21st of January the " Boston
Gazette " came out with a warning, headed by
enormous capitals with three exclamation-points :
" *Bribery and Corruption ! ! !*   The most diabol-
ical plan is on foot to corrupt the members of the
convention who oppose the adoption of the new
Constitution.   Large sums of money have been
brought from a neighbouring state for that purpose, contributed by the wealthy.   If so, is it not
probable there may be collections for the same
accursed purpose nearer home ? "   No adequate
investigation ever determined whether this charge
was true or not.   We may hope that it was ill-
founded ; but our general knowledge of human
nature must compel us to admit that there was
probably a grain of truth in it.   But what was undeniable was that Richard Henry Lee wrote a letter to Gerry, urging that Massachusetts should not

adopt the Constitution without insisting upon sundry amendments; and in order to consider these amendments, it was suggested that there should be another Federal Convention. At this anxious crisis, Washington suddenly threw himself into the breach with that infallible judgment of his which always saw the way to victory. "If another Federal Convention is attempted," said Washington, "its members will be more discordant, and will agree upon no general plan. The Constitution is the best that can be obtained at this time. . . . The Constitution or disunion are before us to choose from. If the Constitution is our choice, a constitutional door is open for amendments, and they may be adopted in a peaceable manner, without tumult or disorder."

Washington's fruitful suggestion.

When this advice of Washington's reached Boston, it set in motion a train of events which soon solved the difficulty, both for Massachusetts and for the other states which had not yet made up their mind. Chief among the objections to the Constitution had been the fact that it did not contain a bill of rights. It did not guarantee religious liberty, freedom of speech and of the press, or the right of the people peacefully to assemble and petition the government for a redress of grievances. It did not provide against the quartering of soldiers upon the people in time of peace. It did not provide against general search-warrants, nor did it securely prescribe the methods by which individuals should be held to answer for criminal offences. It did not even provide that nobody should be burned at the stake or stretched on the rack, for

holding peculiar opinions about the nature of God
or the origin of evil. That such objections to the
Constitution seem strange to us to-day is partly
due to the determined attitude of the men who,
amid all the troubles of the time, would not consent to any arrangement from which such safe-
guards to free thinking and free living should be
omitted. The friends of the Constitution in Boston now proposed that the convention, while adopting it, should suggest sundry amendments containing the essential provisions of a bill of rights. It
was not intended that the ratification should be
conditional. Under the circumstances, a conditional ratification might prove as disastrous as
rejection. It might lead to a second Federal Convention, in which the good work already accomplished might be undone. The ratification was to
be absolute, and the amendments were offered in
the hope that action would be taken upon them as
soon as the new government should go into operation. There could be little doubt that the suggestion would be heeded, not only from the importance
of Massachusetts in the Union, but also from the
fact that Virginia and other states would be sure
to follow her example in suggesting such amendments. This forecast proved quite correct, and it
was in this way that the first ten amendments
originated, which were acted on by Congress in
1790, and became part of the Constitution in 1791.
As soon as this plan had been matured, Hancock
proposed it to the convention; the hearty support
of Adams was immediately insured, and within a
week from that time, on the 6th of February, the

Constitution was ratified by the narrow majority of 187 votes against 168. On that same day Jefferson, in Paris, wrote to Madison: "I wish with all my soul that the nine first conventions may accept the

Massachusetts ratifies, proposing amendments, Feb. 6, 1788.

new Constitution, to secure to us the good it contains; but I equally wish that the four latest, whichever they may be, may refuse to accede to it till a declaration of rights be annexed; but no objection to the new form must produce a schism in our Union." But as soon as he heard of the action of Massachusetts, he approved it as preferable to his own idea, and he wrote home urging Virginia to follow the example.

Massachusetts was thus the sixth state to ratify the Constitution. On that day the name of the Long Lane by the meeting-house where the convention had sat was changed to Federal Street. The Boston people, said Henry Knox, had quite lost their senses with joy. The two counties of Worcester and Berkshire had given but 14 yeas against 59 nays, but the farmers went home declaring that they should cheerfully abide by the decision of the majority. Not a murmur was heard from any one.

About the time that the Massachusetts convention broke up, that of New Hampshire assembled at Exeter; but after a brief discussion it was decided to adjourn until June, in order to see how the other states would act. On the 21st of April the Maryland convention assembled at Annapolis. All the winter Patrick Henry had been busily at work, with the hope of inducing the southern states to establish a separate confederacy; but he had made little headway anywhere, and none at all in Maryland, where his influence was completely counteracted by that of Washington. Above all things, said Washington, do not let the convention adjourn till the matter is decided, for the Antifederalists are taking no end of comfort from the postponement in New Hampshire. Their glee was short-lived, however. Some of Maryland's strongest men, such as Luther Martin and Samuel Chase, were Antifederalists; but their efforts were of no avail. After a session of five days the Constitution was ratified by a vote of 63 to 11. Whatever damage New Hampshire might have done was thus more than made good. The eyes of the whole country were now turned upon the eighth state, South Carolina. Her convention was to meet at Charleston on the 12th of May, the anniversary of the day on which General Lincoln had surrendered that city to Sir Henry Clinton; but there had been a decisive preliminary struggle in the legislature in January. The most active of the Antifederalists was Rawlins Lowndes, who had opposed the Declaration of Independence. Lowndes was betrayed into silliness. "We are now," said he, "under a most excellent constitution, — a blessing from Heaven, that has stood the test of time [!!], and given us liberty and independence; yet we are impatient to pull down that fabric which we raised at the expense of our blood." This was not very convincing to the assembly, most of the members knowing full well that the fabric had not stood the test of time, but had already

Maryland ratifies, April 28.

tumbled in by reason of its vicious construction.
A more effective plea was that which referred
to the slave-trade. "What cause is there," said
Lowndes, "for jealousy of our importing negroes?
Why confine us to twenty years? Why limit us
at all? This trade can be justified on the principles of religion and humanity. They
do not like our having slaves because
they have none themselves, and there-
fore want to exclude us from this great advantage."
Cotesworth Pinckney replied: "By this settlement
we have secured an unlimited importation of negroes for twenty years. The general government
can never emancipate them, for no such authority
is granted, and it is admitted on all hands that the
general government has no powers but what are
expressly granted by the Constitution. We have
obtained a right to recover our slaves in whatever
part of the country they may take refuge, which is
a right we had not before. In short, considering
all circumstances, we have made the best terms in
our power for the security of this species of property. We would have made better if we could;
but, on the whole, I do not think them bad." Perhaps Pinckney would not have assumed exactly
this tone at Philadelphia, but at Charleston the
argument was convincing. Lowndes then sounded
the alarm that the New England states would
monopolize the carrying-trade and charge ruinous
freights, and he drew a harrowing picture of ware-
houses packed to bursting with rice and indigo
spoiling because the owners could not afford to pay
the Yankee skippers' prices for carrying their

*Debates in the South Caro-
lina legisla-
ture.*

goods to market. But Pinckney rejoined that a Yankee shipmaster in quest of cargoes would not be likely to ruin his own chances for getting them, and he called attention to the great usefulness of the eastern merchant marine as affording material for a navy, and thus contributing to the defence of the country. Finally Lowndes put in a plea for paper money, but with little success. The result of the debate set the matter so clearly before the people that a great majority of Federalists were elected to the convention. Among them were Gadsden, the Rutledges and the Pinckneys, Moultrie, and William Washington, who had become a citizen of the state from which he had helped to expel the British invader. The Antifederalists were largely represented by men from the upland counties, belonging to a population in which there was considerable likeness all along the Appalachian chain of mountains, from Pennsylvania to the southern extremity of the range. There were among them many "moonshiners," as they were called, — distillers of illicit whiskey, — and they did not relish the idea of a federal excise. At their head was Thomas Sumter, a convert to Patrick Henry's scheme for a southern confederacy. Their policy was one of delay and obstruction, but it availed them little, for on the 23d of May, after a session of eleven days, South Carolina ratified the Constitution by a vote of 149 against 73.

South Caro-
lina ratifies,
May 23.

The sound policy of the Federal Convention in adopting the odious compromise over the slave-trade was now about to bear fruit. In Virginia there

had grown up a party which favoured the establishment of a separate southern confederacy. By the
action of South Carolina all such schemes were now
nipped in the bud. Of the states south of Mason
and Dixon's line, three had now ratified the Constitution, so that any separate confederacy could
now consist only of Virginia and North
Carolina. The reason for this short-
lived separatist feeling in Virginia was
to be found in the complications which had grown
out of the attempt of Spain to close the Mississippi
River. It will be remembered that only two years
before Jay had actually recommended to Congress that the right to navigate the lower Mississippi be surrendered for twenty-five years, in
exchange for a favourable commercial treaty with
Spain. The New England states, caring nothing
for the distant Mississippi, supported this measure
in Congress; and this narrow and selfish policy
naturally created alarm in Virginia, which, in her
district of Kentucky, touched upon the great river.
Thus to the vague dread of the southern states in
general, in the event of New England's controlling
the commercial policy of the government, there was
added, in Virginia's case, a specific fear. If the
New England people were thus ready to barter
away the vital interests of a remote part of the
country, what might they not do? Would they
ever stop at anything so long as they could go on
building up their commerce? This feeling strongly
influenced Patrick Henry in his desire for a separate confederacy; and we have seen how Randolph
and Mason, in the Federal Convention, were so

Important effect upon Virginia.

disturbed at the power given to Congress to regulate commerce by a simple majority of votes that
they refused to set their names to the Constitution.
They alleged further reasons for their refusal, but
this was the chief one. They wanted a two thirds
vote to be required, in order that the south might
retain the means of protecting itself. Under
these circumstances the opposition to the Constitution was very strong, and but for the action of
South Carolina the party in favour of a separate
confederacy might have been capable of doing much
mischief. As it was, since that party had actively
intrigued both in South Carolina and Maryland,
the ratification of the Constitution by both these
states was a direct rebuff. It quite demoralized
the advocates of secession. The paper-money men,
moreover, were handicapped by the fact that two
of the most powerful Antifederalists, Mason and
Lee, were determined opponents of a paper currency, so that this subject had to be dropped or
very gingerly dealt with. The strength of the
Antifederalists, though impaired by these causes,
was still very great. The contest was waged with
all the more intensity of feeling because, since
eight states had now adopted the Constitution, the
verdict of Virginia would be decisive. The convention met at Richmond on the 2d of June, and
Edmund Pendleton was chosen president. Foremost among the Antifederalists was Patrick Henry,
whose eloquence was now as zealously
employed against the new government
as it had been in bygone days against
the usurpations of Great Britain. He was sup-

Debates in the Virginia Convention.

ported by Mason, Lee, and Grayson, as well as by
Benjamin Harrison and John Tyler, the fathers of
two future presidents ; and he could count on the
votes of most of the delegates from the midland
counties, from the south bank of the James River,
and from Kentucky. But the united talents of the
opposition had no chance of success in a conflict
with the genius and tact of Madison, who at one
moment crushed, at another conciliated, his opponent, but always won the day. To Madison, more
than any other man, the Federalist victory was due.
But he was ably seconded by Governor Randolph,
whom he began by winning over from the opposite
party, and by the favourite general and eloquent
speaker, " Light-Horse Harry." Conspicuous in
the ranks of Federalists, and unsurpassed in debate,
was a tall and gaunt young man, with beaming
countenance, eyes of piercing brilliancy, and an indescribable kingliness of bearing, who was by and
by to become chief justice of the United States, and
by his masterly and far-reaching decisions to win
a place side by side with Madison and Hamilton
among the founders of our national government.
John Marshall, second to none among all the illustrious jurists of the English race, was then, at the
age of thirty-three, the foremost lawyer in Virginia.
He had already served for several terms in the state
legislature, but his national career began in this
convention, where his arguments with
those of Madison, reinforcing each other,
bore down all opposition. The details
of the controversy were much the same
as in the states already passed in review, save

Madison and
Marshall pre-
vail and Vir-
ginia ratifies,
June 25.

in so far as coloured by the peculiar circumstances
of Virginia. After more than three weeks of debate, on the 25th of June, the question was put to
vote, and the Constitution was ratified by the narrow majority of 89 against 79. Amendments were
offered, after the example of Massachusetts, which
had already been followed by South Carolina and
the minority in Maryland; and, as in Massachusetts, the defeated Antifederalists announced their
intention to abide loyally by the result.

The discussion had lasted so long that Virginia
lost the distinction of being the ninth state to ratify
the Constitution. That honour had been reserved
New Hamp-
shire had al-
ready ratified,
June 21. for New Hampshire, whose convention
had met on the anniversary of Bunker
Hill, and after a four days' session, on
the 21st of June, had given its consent to the new
government by a vote of 57 against 46. The
couriers from Virginia and those from New Hampshire, as they spurred their horses over long miles
of dusty road, could shout to each other the joyous
news in passing. Though the ratification of New
Hampshire had secured the necessary ninth state,
yet the action of Virginia was not the less significant and decisive. Virginia was at that time, and
for a quarter of a century afterward, the most populous state in the Union, and one of the greatest in
influence. Even with the needed nine states all in
hand, it is clear that the new government could not
have gone into successful operation with the leading state, the home of Washington himself, left out
in the cold. The New Roof, as men were then
fond of calling the Federal Constitution, must

speedily have fallen in without this indispensable
prop. When it was known that Virginia had ratified, it was felt that the victory was won, and the
success of the new scheme assured. The 4th of
July, 1788, witnessed such loud rejoicings as have
perhaps never been seen before or since on American soil. In Philadelphia there was a procession
miles in length, in which every trade was represented, and wagons laden with implements of industry or emblematic devices alternated with bands
of music and gorgeous banners. There figured
the New Roof, supported by thirteen columns, and
there was to be seen the Ship of State, the good
ship Constitution, made out of the barge which
Paul Jones had taken from the shattered and
blood-stained Serapis, after his terrible fight. As
for the old scow Confederacy, Imbecility master,
it was proclaimed she had foundered at sea, and
"the sloop Anarchy, when last heard from, was
ashore on Union Rocks." All over the country
there were processions and bonfires, and in some
towns there were riots. In Providence the Federalists prepared a barbecue of oxen roasted whole,
but a mob of farmers, led by three members of the
state legislature, attempted to disperse them, and
were with some difficulty pacified. In Albany the
Antifederalists publicly burned the Constitution,
whereupon a party of Federalists brought out another copy of it, and nailed it to the top of a pole,
which they planted defiantly amid the ashes of the
fire their opponents had made. Out of these proceedings there grew a riot, in which knives were
drawn, stones were thrown, and blood was shed.

Such incidents might have served to remind one that the end had not yet come. The difficulties were not yet surmounted, and the rejoicing was in some respects premature. It was now settled that the new government was to go into operation, but how it was going to be able to get along without the adhesion of New York it was not easy to see. The struggle in New York. It is true that New York then ranked only as fifth among the states in population, but commercially and militarily she was the centre of the Union. She not only touched at once on the ocean and the lakes, but she separated New England from the rest of the country. It was rightly felt that the Union could never be cemented without this central state. So strongly were people impressed with this feeling that some went so far as to threaten violence. It was said that if New York did not come into the Union peacefully and of her own accord, she should be conquered and dragged in. That she would come in peacefully seemed at first very improbable. When the state convention assembled at Poughkeepsie, on the 17th of June, more than two thirds of its members were avowed Antifederalists. At their head was the governor, George Clinton, hard-headed and resolute, the bitterest hater of the Constitution that could be found anywhere in the thirteen states. Foremost among his supporters were Yates and Lansing, with Melanchthon Smith, a man familiar with political history, and one of the ablest debaters in the country. On the Federalist side were such eminent men as Livingston and Jay; but the herculean task of vanquishing this great hostile majority, and converting it by sheer dint of argument into a majority on the right side, fell chiefly upon the shoulders of one man. But for Alexander Hamilton the decision of New York would unquestionably have been adverse to the Constitution. Nay, more, it is very improbable that, but for him, the good work would have made such progress as it had in the other states. To get the people to adopt the Constitution, it was above all things needful that its practical working should be expounded, in language such as every one could understand, by some writer endowed in the highest degree with political intelligence and foresight. Upon their return from the Federal Convention, Yates and Lansing had done all in their power to bring its proceedings into ill-repute. Pamphlets and broadsides were scattered right and left. The Constitution was called the "triple-headed monster," and declared to be "as deep and wicked a conspiracy as ever was invented in the darkest ages against the liberties of a free people." It soon occurred to Hamilton that it would be well worth while to explain the meaning of all parts of the Constitution in a series of short, incisive essays. He communicated his plan to Madison and Jay, who joined him in the work, and the result was the "Federalist," perhaps the most famous of American books, and undoubtedly the most profound and suggestive treatise on government that has ever been written. Of the eighty-five numbers originally published in the "Independent Gazetteer," under the common signature of "Publius," Jay wrote five, Madison The "Federalist."

twenty-nine, and Hamilton fifty-one. Jay's papers
related chiefly to diplomatic points, with which his
experience abroad had fitted him to deal. The
first number was written by Hamilton in the cabin
of a sloop on the Hudson, in October, 1787 ; and
they continued to appear, sometimes as often as
three or four in a week, through the winter and
spring. Madison would have contributed a larger
share than he did had he not been called early in
March to Virginia to fight the battle of the Constitution in that state. The essays were widely
and eagerly read, and probably accomplished more
toward insuring the adoption of the Constitution
than anything else that was said or done in that
eventful year. They were hastily written, — struck
out at white heat by men full of their subject.
Doubtless the authors did not realize the grandeur
of the literary work they were doing, and among
the men of the time there were few who foresaw
the immortal fame which these essays were to earn.
It is said of one of the senators in the first Congress that he made the memorandum, "Get the
'Federalist,' if I can, without buying it. It is n't
worth it." But for all posterity the "Federalist"
must remain the most authoritative commentary
upon the Constitution that can be found ; for it is
the joint work of the principal author of that Constitution and of its most brilliant advocate.

In nothing could the flexibleness of Hamilton's
intellect, or the genuineness of his patriotism, have
been more finely shown than in the hearty zeal and
transcendent ability with which he now wrote in
defence of a plan of government so different from

what he would himself have proposed. He made Madison's thoughts his own, until he set them forth with even greater force than Madison himself could command. Yet no arguments could possibly be less chargeable with partisanship than the arguments of the "Federalist." The judgment is as dispassionate as could be shown in a philosophical treatise. The tone is one of grave and lofty eloquence, apt to move even to tears the reader who is fully alive to the stupendous issues that were involved in the discussion. Hamilton was supremely endowed with the faculty of imagining, with all the circumstantial minuteness of concrete reality, political situations different from those directly before him; and he put this rare power to noble use in tracing out the natural and legitimate working of such a Constitution as that which the Federal Convention had framed.

When it came to defending the Constitution before the hostile convention at Poughkeepsie, he had before him as arduous a task as ever fell to the lot of a parliamentary debater. It was a case where political management was out of the question. The opposition were too numerous to be silenced, or cajoled, or bargained with. They must be converted. With an eloquence scarcely equalled before or since in America until Webster's voice was heard, Hamilton argued week after week, till at last Melanchthon Smith, the foremost debater of Clinton's party, broke away, and came to the Federalist side. It was like crushing the centre of a hostile army. After this the Antifederalist forces were confused and easily routed. The de

cisive struggle was over the question whether New
York could ratify the Constitution conditionally,
reserving to herself the right to withdraw from the
Union in case the amendments upon which she
had set her heart should not be adopted. Upon
this point Hamilton reinforced himself with the
advice of Madison, who had just returned to New
York. Could a state once adopt the Constitution,
and then withdraw from the Union if not satisfied?
Madison's reply was prompt and decisive. No,
such a thing could never be done. A state which
had once ratified was in the federal bond
forever. The Constitution could not provide for nor contemplate its own overthrow. There could be no such thing
as a constitutional right of secession. When Melanchthon Smith deserted the Antifederalists on
this point, the victory was won, and on the 26th of
July New York ratified the Constitution by the
bare majority of 30 votes against 27. Rejoicings
were now renewed throughout the country. In the
city of New York there was an immense parade,
and as the emblematic federal ship was drawn
through the streets, with Hamilton's name emblazoned on her side, it was doubtless the proudest
moment of the young statesman's life.

Hamilton wins the victory, and New York ratifies, July 26.

New York, however, clogged her acceptance by
proposing, a few days afterward, that a second
Federal Convention be called for considering the
amendments suggested by the various states. The
proposal was supported by the Virginia legislature, but Massachusetts and Pennsylvania opposed
it, as having a dangerous tendency to reopen the

whole discussion and unsettle everything. The proposal fell to the ground. People were weary of the long dispute, and turned their attention to electing representatives to the first Congress. With the adhesion of New York all serious anxiety came to an end. The new government could be put in operation without waiting for North Carolina and Rhode Island to make up their minds. The North Carolina convention met on the 21st of July, and adjourned on the 1st of August without coming to any decision. The same objections were raised as in Virginia; and besides, the paper-money party was here much stronger than in the neighbouring state. In Rhode Island paper money was the chief difficulty; that state did not even take the trouble to call a convention. It was not until the 21st of November, 1789, after Washington's government had been several months in operation, that North Carolina joined the Federal Union. Rhode Island did not join till the 29th of May, 1790. If she had waited but a few months longer, Vermont, the first state not of the original thirteen, would have come in before her.

The laggard states, North Carolina and Rhode Island.

The autumn of 1788 was a season of busy but peaceful electioneering. That remarkable body, the Continental Congress, in putting an end to its troubled existence, decreed that presidential electors should be chosen on the first Wednesday of January, 1789, that the electors should meet and cast their votes for president on the first Wednesday in February, and that the Senate and House of Representatives should assemble on the first

Wednesday in March. This latter day fell, in 1789, on the 4th of the month, and accordingly, three years afterward, Congress took it for a precedent, and decreed that thereafter each new administration should begin on the 4th of March. It was further decided, after some warm debate, that until the site for the proposed federal city could be selected and built upon, the seat of the new government should be the city of New York.

In accordance with these decrees, presidential elections were held on the first Wednesday in January. The Antifederalists were still potent for mischief in New York, with the result that, just as that state had not joined in the Declaration of Independence until after it had been proclaimed to the world, and just as she refused to adopt the Federal Constitution until after more than the requisite number of states had ratified it, so now she failed to choose electors, and had nothing to do with the vote that made Washington our first president. The other ten states that had ratified the Constitution all chose electors. But things moved slowly and cumbrously at this first assembling of the new government. The House of Representatives did not succeed in getting a quorum together until the 1st of April. On the 6th, the Senate chose John Langdon for its president, and the two houses in concert counted the electoral votes. There were 69 in all, and every one of the 69 was found to be for George Washington of Virginia. For the second name on the list there was nothing like such unanimity. It was to be expected that the other name would

First presidential election, Jan. 7, 1789.

be that of a citizen of Massachusetts, as the other leading state in the Union. The two foremost citizens of Massachusetts bore the same name, and were cousins. There would have been most striking poetic justice in coupling with the name of Washington that of Samuel Adams, since these two men had been indisputably foremost in the work of achieving the independence of the United States. But for the hesitancy of Samuel Adams in indorsing the Federal Constitution, he would very likely have been our first vice-president and our second president. But the wave of federalism had now begun to sweep strongly over Massachusetts, carrying everything before it, and none but the most ardent Federalists had a chance to meet in the electoral college. Voices were raised in behalf of Samuel Adams. While we honour the American Fabius, it was said, let us not forget the American Cato. It was urged by some, with much truth, that but for his wise and cautious action in the Massachusetts convention, the good ship Constitution would have been fatally wrecked upon the reefs of Shaysism. His course had not been that of an obstructionist, like that of his old friends Henry and Lee and Gerry; but at the critical moment — one of the most critical in all that wonderful crisis — he had thrown his vast influence, with decisive effect, upon the right side. All this is plain enough to the historian of to-day. But in the political fervour of the election of 1789, the fact most clearly visible to men was that Samuel Adams had hesitated, and perhaps made things wait. These points came out most distinctly on the issue of his election to the Federal Congress, in which he was defeated by the youthful Fisher Ames, whose eloquence in the state convention had been so conspicuous and useful ; but they serve to explain thoroughly why he was not put upon the presidential list along with Washington.   His cousin, John Adams, had just returned from his mission to England, weary and disgusted with the scanty respect which he had been able to secure for a feeble league of states that could not make good its own promises.   His services during the Revolution had been of the most splendid sort : and after Washington, he was the second choice of the electoral college, receiving 34 votes, while John Jay of New York, his nearest competitor, received only 9.   John Adams was accordingly declared vice-president.

On the 14th of April Washington was informed of his election, and on the next day but one he bid adieu again to his beloved home at Mount Vernon, where he had hoped to pass the remainder of his days in that rural peace and quiet for which no one yearns like the man who is burdened with greatness and fame unsought for.   The position to which he was summoned was one of unparalleled splendour, — how splendid we can now realize much better than he, and our grandchildren will realize it better than we, — the position of first ruler of what was soon to become at once the strongest and the most peace-loving people upon the face of the earth.   As he journeyed toward New York, his thoughts must have been busy with the arduous problems of the time.   Already, doubtless, he had marked out the two great men, Jefferson and Hamilton, for his chief advisers: the one to place us in a proper attitude before the mocking nations of Europe; the other to restore our shattered credit, and enlist the moneyed interests of all the states in the success of the Federal Union. Washington's temperament was a hopeful one, as befitted a man of his strength and dash. But in his most hopeful mood he could hardly have dared to count upon such a sudden and wonderful demonstration of national strength as was about to ensue upon the heroic financial measures of Hamilton. His meditations on this journey we may well believe to have been solemn and anxious enough. But if he could gather added courage from the often-declared trust of his fellow-countrymen, there was no lack of such comfort for him. At every town through which he passed, fresh evidences of it were gathered, but at one point on the route his strong nature was especially wrought upon. At Trenton, as he crossed the bridge over the Assunpink Creek, where twelve years ago, at the darkest moment of the Revolution, he had outwitted Cornwallis in the most skilful of stratagems, and turned threatening defeat into glorious victory, — at this spot, so fraught with thrilling associations, he was met by a party of maidens dressed in white, who strewed his path with sweet spring flowers, while triumphal arches in softest green bore inscriptions declaring that he who had watched over the safety of the mothers could well be trusted to protect the daughters. On the 23d he arrived in New York, and was entertained at dinner by Governor Clin-

ton.   One week later, on the 30th, came the inauguration.   It was one of those magnificent days of
clearest sunshine that sometimes make
one feel in April as if summer had come.

Inauguration
of Washing-
ton, April 30.

At noon of that day Washington went
from his lodgings, attended by a military es-
cort, to Federal Hall, at the corner of Wall and
Nassau streets, where his statue has lately been
erected.   The city was ablaze with excitement.   A
sea of upturned eager faces surrounded the spot,
and as the hero appeared thousands of cocked hats
were waved, while ladies fluttered their white hand-
kerchiefs.   Washington came forth clad in a suit
of dark brown cloth of American make, with white
silk hose and shoes decorated with silver buckles,
while at his side hung a dress-sword.   For a moment all were hushed in deepest silence, while the
secretary of the Senate held forth the Bible upon
a velvet cushion, and Chancellor Livingston administered the oath of office.   Then, before Washington had as yet raised his head, Livingston
shouted, — and from all the vast company came
answering shouts, — " Long live George Washington, President of the United States ! "

BIBLIOGRAPHICAL NOTE

————•————

THE bibliography of the period covered in this book is most copiously and thoroughly treated in the seventh volume of Winsor's *Narrative and Critical History of America*, Boston, 1888. For the benefit of the reader who may not have ready access to that vast storehouse of information, the following brief notes may be of service.

The best account of the peace negotiations is to be found in chapter ii. of Winsor's volume just cited, written by Hon. John Jay, who had already discussed the subject quite thoroughly in his *Address before the New York Historical Society on its Seventy-Ninth Anniversary*, Nov. 27, 1883. Of the highest value are Lord Edmond Fitzmaurice's *Life of Lord Shelburne*, 3 vols., London, 1875–76, and Adolphe de Circourt, *Histoire de l'action commune de la France et de l'Amérique, etc.*, tome iii., *Documents originaux inédits*, Paris, 1876. See also Sparks, *Diplomatic Correspondence of the American Revolution*, 12 vols., Boston, 1829–30 ; Trescot's *Diplomacy of the American Revolution*, N. Y., 1852 ; Lyman's *Diplomacy of the United States*, Boston, 1826 ; Elliot's *American Diplomatic Code*, 2 vols., Washington, 1834 ; Chalmers's *Collection of Treaties*, 2 vols., London, 1790 ; Lord Stanhope's *History of England*, vol. vii., London, 1853 ; Lecky's *History of England*, vol. iv., London, 1882 ; Lord John Russell's *Memorials of Fox*, 4 vols., London, 1853–57 ; Albemarle's *Rockingham and his Contemporaries*, 2 vols., London, 1852 ; Walpole's *Last Journals*, 2 vols., London, 1859 ; Force's *American Archives*, 4th series, 6 vols., Washington, 1839–46 ; John Adams's *Works*, 10 vols., Boston, 1850–56 ; Rives's *Life of Madison*, 3 vols., Boston, 1859–68 ; Madison's *Letters and other Writings*, 4 vols., Phila., 1865 ; the lives of Franklin, by Bigelow and Parton ; the lives of Jay, by Jay, Flanders, and Whitelocke ; Morse's *John Adams*, Boston, 1885 ; *Correspondence of George III. with Lord North*, 2 vols., London, 1867 ; Wharton's *Digest of International Law*, Washington, 1887, *Appendix* to vol. iii. ; Hale's *Franklin in France*, 2 vols., Boston, 1888. The view of the treaty set forth in 1830 by Sparks, according to which Jay and Adams were quite mistaken in their suspicions of the French court, we may now regard as disposed of by the evidence presented by Circourt and Fitzmaurice. It has led many writers astray, and even with all the lights which Mr. Bancroft has had, the account in the last revision of his *History of the United States*, vol. v., N. Y., 1886, though in some respects one of the best to be found in the general histories, still leaves much to be desired.

The general condition of the United States under the articles of confederation is well sketched in the sixth volume of Bancroft's final revision, and in Curtis's *History of the Constitution*, 2 vols., N. Y., 1861. An excellent summary is given in the first volume of Schouler's *History of the United States under the Constitution*, of which vols. i.–iii. (Washington, 1882–85) have appeared. Mr. Schouler's book is suggestive and stimulating. The work most rich in details is Professor McMaster's *History of the People of the United States*, of which the first volume rather more than covers the period 1783–89. The author is especially deserving of praise for the diligence with which he has searched the newspapers and obscure pamphlets of the period. He has thus given much fresh life to the narrative, besides throwing valuable light upon the thoughts and feelings of the men who lived under the " league of friendship." I take pleasure in acknowledging my indebtedness to Professor Mc-Master for several interesting illustrative details, chiefly in my third, fourth, and seventh chapters. At the same time one is sorely puzzled at some of his omissions, as in the account of the Federal Convention, in which one finds no allusion whatever to the all-important question of the representation of slaves, or to the compromise by which New England secured to Congress full power to regulate commerce by yielding to Georgia and South Carolina in the matter of the African slave-trade. So the discussion as to the national executive is carried on till July 26th, when it was decided that the president should be chosen by Congress for a single term of seven years ; then the subject is dropped, and the reader is left to suppose that such was the final arrangement. Instances of what seems like carelessness are sufficiently numerous to make the book in some places an unsafe guide to the general reader, but in spite of such defects, which a careful revision might remedy, its value is great. Further general information as to the period of the Confederation may be found in Morse's admirable *Life of Alexander Hamilton*, 3d ed., 2 vols., Boston, 1882 ; J. C. Hamilton's *Republic of the United States*, 7 vols., Boston, 1879 ; Frothingham's *Rise of the Republic*, Boston, 1872, chapter xii. ; Von Holst's *Constitutional History*, 5 vols., Chicago, 1877–85, chapter i. ; Pitkin's *History of the United States*, 2 vols., New Haven, 1828, vol. ii. ; Marshall's *Life of Washington*, 5 vols., Phila., 1805–07 ; *Journals of Congress*, 13 vols., Phila., 1800 ; *Secret Journals of Congress*, 4 vols., Boston, 1820–21.

On the loyalists and their treatment, the able essay by Rev. G. E. Ellis, in Winsor's seventh volume, is especially rich in bibliographical references. See also Sabine's *Loyalists of the American Revolution*, 2 vols., Boston, 1864 ; Ryerson's *Loyalists of America*, 2 vols., Toronto, 1880 ; Jones's *New York during the Revolution*, 2 vols., N. Y., 1879. Although chiefly concerned with events earlier than 1780, the *Journal and Letters of Samuel Curwen*, 4th ed., Boston, 1864, and especially the *Diary and Letters of Thomas Hutchinson*, 2 vols., Boston, 1884–86, are valuable in this connection.

For the financial troubles the most convenient general survey is to be found in A. S. Bolles's *Financial History of the United States*, 1774–1789, N. Y., 1879 ; Sparks's *Life of Gouverneur Morris*, 3 vols., Boston, 1832 ; Pelatiah Webster's *Political Essays*, Phila., 1791 ; Phillips's *Colonial and Continental Paper Currency*, 2 vols., Roxbury, 1865–66 ; Varnum's *Case of Trevett* v. *Weeden*, Providence, 1787; Arnold's *History of Rhode Island*, 2 vols., N. Y., 1859–60. The best account of the Shays rebellion in G. R. Minot's *History of the Insurrections in Massachusetts*, Worcester, 1788 ; see also Barry's *History of Massachusetts*, 3 vols., Boston, 1855–57 ; Austin's *Life of Gerry*, 2 vols., Boston, 1828–29. A new and interesting account of the northwestern cessions and the Ordinance of 1787 is B. A. Hinsdale's *Old Northwest*, N. Y., 1888; see also Dunn's *Indiana*, Boston, 1888; Cutler's *Life, Journal, and Correspondence of Manasseh Cutler*, 2 vols., Cincinnati, 1887.

In the *Johns Hopkins University Studies in Historical and Political Science*, the following articles bear especially upon subjects here treated and are worthy of careful study : II., v., vi., H. C. Adams, *Taxation in the United States*, 1789–1816; III., i., H. B. Adams, *Maryland's Influence upon Land Cessions to the United States ;* III., ix., x., Davis, *American Constitutions ;* IV., v., Jameson's *Introduction to the Constitutional and Political History of the Individual States ;* IV., vii.–ix., Shoshuke Sato's *History of the Land Question in the United States.*

For the proceedings of the Federal Convention in framing the Constitution, and of the several state conventions in ratifying it, the great treasure-house of authoritative information is Elliot's *Debates in the Conventions*, 5 vols., originally published under the sanction of Congress in 1830–45; new reprint, Phila., 1888. The contents of the volumes are as follows : —

I.   Sundry preliminary papers, relating to the ante-revolutionary period, and the period of the Confederation; journal of the Federal Convention ; Yates's minutes of the proceedings ; the official letters of Martin, Yates, Lansing, Randolph, Mason, and Gerry, in explanation of their several courses; Jay's address to the people of New York ; and other illustrative papers.

II., III., IV.   Proceedings of the several state conventions; with other documents, including the Virginia and Kentucky resolutions of 1798, and data relating thereto.

V.   Madison's journal of debates in the Congress of the Confederation, Nov. 4, 1782 – June 21, 1783, and

Feb. 19 – April 25, 1787 ; Madison's journal of the Federal Convention ; letters from Madison to Washington, Jefferson, and Randolph, Sept. 1787 – Nov. 1788 ; and other papers.

The best edition of the "Federalist" is by H. C. Lodge, N. Y., 1888. See also Story's *Commentaries on the Constitution*, 4th ed., 3 vols., Boston, 1873 ; the works of Daniel Webster, 6 vols., Boston, 1851 ; Hurd's *Theory of our National Existence*, Boston, 1881. The above works expound the Constitution as not a league between sovereign states but a fundamental law ordained by the people of the United States. The opposite view is presented in *The Republic of Republics*, by P. C. Centz [Plain Common Sense, pseudonym of B. J. Sage of New Orleans], Boston, 1881 ; the works of Calhoun, 6 vols., N. Y., 1853–55 ; A. H. Stephens's *War between the States*, 2 vols., Phila., 1868 ; Jefferson Davis's *Rise and Fall of the Confederate Government*, 2 vols., N. Y., 1881.

Several volumes of the "American Statesmen" contain interesting accounts of discussions in the various conventions, as Tyler's *Patrick Henry*, Hosmer's *Samuel Adams*, Lodge's *Hamilton*, Magruder's *Marshall*, Roosevelt's *Morris*. Gay's *Madison* falls far below the general standard of this excellent and popular series. No satisfactory biography of Madison has yet been written, though the voluminous work of W. C. Rives contains much good material. For judicial interpretations of the Constitution one may consult B. R. Curtis's *Digest of Decisions*, 1790–1854 ; Flanders's *Lives of the Chief Justices*, Phila., 1858 ; Marshall's *Writings on the Federal Constitution*, ed. Perkins, Boston, 1839 ; see also Pomeroy's *Constitutional Law*, N. Y., 1868 ; Wharton's *Commentaries*, Phila., 1884 ; Von Holst's *Calhoun*, Boston, 1882; Tyler's *Letters and Times of the Tylers*, 2 vols., Richmond, 1884–85. Among critical and theoretical works, Fisher's *Trial of the Constitution*, Phila., 1862, and Lockwood's *Abolition of the Presidency*, N. Y., 1884, are variously suggestive; Woodrow Wilson's *Congressional Government*, Boston, 1885, is a work of rare ability, pointing out the divergence which has arisen between the literary theory of our government and its practical working. Walter Bagehot's *English Consti-*

tution, revised ed., Boston, 1873, had already, in a most profound and masterly fashion, exhibited the divergence between the literary theory and the actual working of the British government. Some points of weakness in the British system are touched in Albert Stickney's *True Republic*, N. Y., 1879 ; see also his *Democratic Government*, N. Y., 1885. The constitutional history of England is presented, in its earlier stages, with prodigious learning, by Dr. Stubbs, 3 vols., London, 1873–78, and in its later stages by Hallam, 2 vols., London, 1842, and Sir Erskine May, 2 vols., Boston, 1862–63 ; see also Freeman's *Growth of the English Constitution*, London, 1872 ; *Comparative Politics*, London, 1873 ; *Some Impressions of the United States*, London, 1883 ; Rudolph Gneist, *History of the English Constitution*, 2 vols., London, 1886 ; J. S. Mill, *Representative Government*, N. Y., 1862 ; Sir H. Maine, *Popular Government*, N. Y., 1886 ; S. R. Gardiner's *Introduction to the Study of English History*, London, 1881. In this connection I may refer to my own book, *American Political Ideas*, N. Y., 1885; and my articles, " Great Britain," " House of Lords," and " House of Commons," in Lalor's *Cyclopædia of Political Science*, 3 vols., Chicago, 1882–84. It is always pleasant to refer to that cyclopædia, because it contains the numerous articles on American history by Prof. Alexander Johnston. One must stop somewhere, and I will conclude by saying that I do not know where one can find anything more richly suggestive than Professor Johnston's articles.

MEMBERS OF THE FEDERAL CONVENTION.

———◆———

THE names of those who for various reasons were absent when the Constitution was signed are given in italics; the names of those who were present, but refused to sign, are given in small capitals.

New Hampshire . . . John Langdon.
       Nicholas Gilman.
Massachusetts . . . . ELBRIDGE GERRY.
       Nathaniel Gorham.
       Rufus King.
       Caleb Strong.
Connecticut . . . . . William Samuel Johnson.
       Roger Sherman.
       Oliver Ellsworth.
New York . . . . . . *Robert Yates.*
       Alexander Hamilton.
       John Lansing.
New Jersey . . . . . William Livingston.
       David Brearley.
       William Churchill Houston.
       William Paterson.
       Jonathan Dayton.
Pennsylvania . . . . Benjamin Franklin.
       Thomas Mifflin.
       Robert Morris.
       George Clymer.
       Thomas Fitzsimmons.
       Jared Ingersoll.
       James Wilson.
       Gouverneur Morris.

Delaware . . . . . . George Read.
Gunning Bedford.
John Dickinson.
Richard Bassett.
Jacob Broom.

Maryland . . . . . . James McHenry.
Daniel of St. Thomas Jenifer.
Daniel Carroll.
John Francis Mercer.
Luther Martin.

Virginia . . . . George Washington.
EDMUND RANDOLPH.
John Blair.
James Madison.
GEORGE MASON.
George Wythe.
James McClurg.

North Carolina . . . *Alexander Martin.*
William Richardson Davie.
William Blount.
Richard Dobbs Spaight.
Hugh Williamson.

South Carolina . . . . John Rutledge.
Charles Cotesworth Pinckney.
Charles Pinckney.
Pierce Butler.

Georgia . . . . William Few.
Abraham Baldwin.
William Pierce.
William Houstoun.

Of those who signed their names to the Federal Constitution, the six following were signers of the Declaration of Independence : —

Roger Sherman,
Benjamin Franklin,
Robert Morris,
George Clymer,
James Wilson,
George Read.

The ten following were appointed as delegates to the Federal Convention, but never took their seats : —

New Hampshire . . . John Pickering.
                           Benjamin West.
Massachusetts . . . . Francis Dana.
New Jersey . . . . . John Nelson.
                           Abraham Clark.
Virginia . . . . Patrick Henry (declined).
North Carolina . . . Richard Caswell (resigned).
                           Willie Jones (declined).
Georgia . . . . George Walton.
                           Nathaniel Pendleton.

No delegates were appointed by Rhode Island. In a letter addressed to " the Honourable the Chairman of the General Convention," and dated " Providence, May 11, 1787," several leading citizens of Rhode Island expressed their regret that their state should not be represented on so momentous an occasion. At the same time, says the letter, "the result of your deliberations . . . we still hope may finally be approved and adopted by this state, for which we pledge our influence and best exertions." The letter was signed by John Brown, Joseph Nightingale, Levi Hall, Philip Allen, Paul Allen, Jabez Bowen, Nicholas Brown, John Jinkes, Welcome Arnold, William Russell, Jeremiah Olney, William Barton, and Thomas Lloyd Halsey. The letter was presented to the Convention on May 28th by Gouverneur Morris, and, "being read, was ordered to lie on the table for further consideration." See Elliot's *Debates*, v. 125.

The Constitution was ratified by the thirteen states, as follows : —

      1. Delaware . . . . Dec. 6, 1787.
      2. Pennsylvania . . . . . Dec. 12, 1787.
      3. New Jersey . . . . . . Dec. 18, 1787.
      4. Georgia . . . . Jan. 2, 1788.
      5. Connecticut . . . . . . Jan. 9, 1788.
      6. Massachusetts . . . . . Feb. 6, 1788.
      7. Maryland . . . . April 28, 1788.

8. South Carolina . . . . . May 23, 1788.
9. New Hampshire . . . . June 21, 1788.
10. Virginia . . . . June 25, 1788.
11. New York . . . . July 26, 1788.
12. North Carolina . . . . . Nov. 21, 1789.
13. Rhode Island . . . . . . May 29, 1790.

PRESIDENTS OF THE CONTINENTAL CONGRESS.

1. Peyton Randolph of Virginia . . . . . . Sept. 5, 1774.
2. Henry Middleton of South Carolina . . . Oct. 22, 1774.
   Peyton Randolph . . . . May 10, 1775.
3. John Hancock of Massachusetts . . . . . May 24, 1775.
4. Henry Laurens of South Carolina . . . . Nov. 1, 1777.
5. John Jay of New York . . . . Dec. 10, 1778.
6. Samuel Huntington of Connecticut . . . Sept. 28, 1779.
7. Thomas McKean of Delaware . . . . . . July 10, 1781.
8. John Hanson of Maryland . . . . Nov. 5, 1781.
9. Elias Boudinot of New Jersey . . . . . . Nov. 4, 1782.
10. Thomas Mifflin of Pennsylvania . . . . . Nov. 3, 1783.
11. Richard Henry Lee of Virginia . . . . . Nov. 30, 1784.
12. Nathaniel Gorham of Massachusetts . . . June 6, 1786.
13. Arthur St. Clair of Pennsylvania . . . . . Feb. 2, 1787.
14. Cyrus Griffin of Virginia . . . . Jan. 22, 1788.

INDEX.

DATE DUE

69. 9 1 TOO		
OCT 1 6 '63		
OCT 1 7 '63		
OCT 1 8 '63		
OCT 2 8 '63		
UC 29'77		
GAYLORD		PRINTED IN U.S.A.